Safari

I Won't Cry Mumma

Janet Seath
with Frank Scaysbrook

BANTAM BOOKS
SYDNEY • AUCKLAND • TORONTO • NEW YORK • LONDON

SAFARI
A BANTAM BOOK

First published in Australia and New Zealand in 2004
by Bantam

National Library of Australia
Cataloguing-in-Publication Entry

Seath, Janet.
Safari.

ISBN 1 86325 444 7.

1. Kamanthi, Safari. 2. RPA (Television program). 3. Surgery, Plastic – Patients – New South Wales – Sydney – Biography. 4. Burns and scalds in children – Treatment – New South Wales – Sydney. I. Scaysbrook, Frank. II. Royal Prince Alfred Hospital (Sydney, NSW). III. Title.

362.1092

Transworld Publishers,
a division of Random House Australia Pty Ltd
20 Alfred Street, Milsons Point, NSW 2061
http://www.randomhouse.com.au

Random House New Zealand Limited
18 Poland Road, Glenfield, Auckland

Transworld Publishers,
a division of The Random House Group Ltd
61-63 Uxbridge Road, Ealing, London W5 5SA

Random House Inc
1745 Broadway, New York, New York 10036

Cover design by John Bull, The Book Design Company
Cover photographs by Vicki Leopold
Typeset by Midland Typesetters, Maryborough, Victoria
Printed and bound by Griffin Press, Netley, South Australia

10 9 8 7 6 5 4 3 2

Contents

This book is dedicated to the memory of:

Alma Scaysbrook
Ngayau Kimanzi

Prologue

In a mud hut in a remote village in Kenya a four-year-old child was being washed in a plastic bowl by his two elder sisters. The gloom inside the hut was broken by the flickering light from a kerosene candle. He was a beautiful baby, the last-born son of John and Ngayau Kimanzi and his sisters Penina and Kanini were very proud of their charge.

Penina and Kanini wrapped him in a synthetic sarong and sat him on the hard-packed earthen floor of the hut. It was the family cooking hut and the thatch on the roof and the mud-daubed walls reeked from the smell of smoke from countless hours of cooking for the family of nine.

The teenage girls were distracted by something outside and they left the hut for a few short moments. Inside the child wriggled in his wrapping as four-year-olds do. A breath of wind set the stage for a disaster.

The edge of the sarong flicked into the path of the candle's dancing flame and within seconds the tiny candle light had given birth to an inferno licking upwards along the filmy synthetic cloth. The fabric melted as it burned and the child's entire left side was alight, melting the delicate skin of his tiny body. Strangely, he didn't cry out and seconds later when his sisters returned, the shocking sight befell their eyes. They raced to fetch their mother and the three looked in horror at the child's terrible burns.

Reacting in the only way they knew, they hastily daubed him with water and mud, wrapped him in a cloth and hurried to the village health clinic half a kilometre away.

There they met the village medical officer, Silas Nthaka, and he too was shocked by the sight. But he had seen it all before; accidents involving children and fire are not uncommon in a developing country where open fires and candle lighting are the norm.

Silas acted quickly. Although hampered by extremely limited facilities and a lack of medical supplies, like many medicos in difficult circumstances he had skills and resourcefulness.

Using clean water from the clinic's dilapidated rainwater tank, Silas washed away the mud and dried the scorched flesh with the cloth in which Ngayau had wrapped the child. He then gave an anti-tetanus injection from his very limited stock of medical supplies that were stored in the clinic's gas-powered refrigerator.

There was nothing else that Silas could do by way of first aid and he advised Ngayau to take the child to a simple mission hospital 50 kilometres away in a small town called Mutomo.

From the meagre savings of subsistence farming the family scraped together the bus fare and Ngayau took her child to the hospital, desperately hoping for a miracle.

There was little the hospital in that poor country could do except attempt some rudimentary but ineffective skin grafts. After some weeks there was no improvement and the child teetered between life and death. The hospital could do no more and Ngayau knew in her heart that her youngest child would die. She wanted for him to die in the bosom of the family.

Without the money for her return bus fare, the equivalent of $1.70 Australian, Ngayau set out walking the 50-kilometre journey home in the blazing equatorial sun, her fragile charge wrapped lovingly in her arms. The journey took two days and the pair slept by the roadside at night.

Back in the family dwelling she washed him in cooled boiled water as instructed and Silas attended to the horrific burns to the left side of his body, face and arms with antibiotic powder.

Amazingly, the child, Safari Kimanzi, survived and this is his story.

Part One

Australia

Chapter 1

'Frank, I think it's us.'

These five words were to impact on our lives, far beyond whatever we could have imagined. We were committing ourselves to care for a little Kenyan boy, six and a half years old, soon to come to Australia for burns reconstructive surgery. Safari Kimanzi was to travel to Australia from his village in remote south-east Kenya, 300 kilometres from the capital, Nairobi.

In 1997 Frank Scaysbrook and I renewed our friendship from 38 years earlier. I had first become acquainted with Frank and his family through my then fiancé and husband, Andrew. Both Frank's and Andrew's families had migrated from the United Kingdom to Australia in the 1920s to start a new life in a wonderful new country. Andrew's family lived two doors away from Frank's family at Pennant Hills, then a semi-rural area on Sydney's north-western outskirts, and my mother-in-law had a long friendship with Frank's mum, Alma. They had attended the same school in the Hunter Valley coalmining town of Kurri Kurri many years ago.

My own family had always called Australia home. My father was a country lad, born in the New South Wales town of Coonamble and raised along with his five siblings in Orange in the state's Central West.

My mother, Beryl Gage, was a city woman, born in Manly, a seaside suburb on Sydney Harbour. She was one of seven children. Her mother – my grandmother, Emily Sinclair – was very close to me and I spent a lot of time with her. I loved her dearly. A softly-spoken woman, she was gentle with a lot of patience; I never heard her raise her voice. In hindsight I believe she has influenced my life in many ways.

I attribute my mothering skills to my own mother, who was a very good listener and very understanding. She loved children. I can remember her making dresses for two little girls whose parents were having financial difficulties; she was very kind.

Mum always considered herself very blessed with our family. She loved her grandchildren and great-grandchildren and they loved her. I wish she could have lived a little longer to meet Safari. She would have loved him and looked upon him as one of her own. She would have dined out on stories about his ways and antics for a long time. In her latter years she used to say to me, 'I have time now to remember and think.' She would have thought a lot about Safari and I know she would have been very pleased by the way our family embraced him.

My early life was spent on a 25-hectare farm at Peats Ridge in the Central Coast's Mangrove Mountain area. My father, Pat Gage, was a farmer. He had a jovial personality and liked to recite verses from Australia's legendary poet A.B. ('Banjo') Paterson.

A day in my childhood that really stands out as unforgettable was when a violent storm struck our area of Peats Ridge in 1947. I was at school in the little one-roomed schoolhouse where each row of chairs represented a class. As young children we were terrified by the storm's fury and our teacher tried to calm us.

That storm was to change our lives. Riding home on my bike I was amazed to see the devastation that had come to our farm. The sight that met my eyes was of the small galvanised iron farmhouse flattened to the ground, the contents strewn everywhere. My mother later told the story of how she, my sister Judy and a neighbour were having afternoon tea when the storm struck. They had to dodge the sheets of iron flying through the air as they picked their way to the shed on higher ground. I felt a sense of awe mixed with shock, fear and bewilderment that day as I surveyed the scene of destruction.

Where were we going to live? My mother soon afterwards became ill with stress and had to be hospitalised. We moved in with my grandparents at Stanmore in the inner west of Sydney for a short while before moving to Pennant Hills.

My sister Judy and Frank were in the same class in Pennant Hills Primary School so many of our childhood memories intersect, although it was not until my marriage to Andrew that I really got to know Frank and his family.

I kept intermittent contact with the Scaysbrooks over the years, and I felt privileged to be the beneficiary of much wisdom from Frank's mum Alma. In 1997 when Alma and her husband, Ted, asked me to write to Frank in Victoria it seemed the natural thing to do. He was experiencing marital difficulties and had separated from his wife who remained in Sydney while he was transferred to Geelong. I had been involved in counselling and Alma and Ted thought I might be able to help him.

I recalled that the last time I had seen Frank was in about 1959. I was travelling home from work in the city on one of the old electric trains known as the 'red rattlers'. He had dark auburn hair, big dimples and an engaging smile.

How do you write to someone you haven't seen for 38 years? Driving home from Pennant Hills I mulled over Alma and Ted's request, and regretted that I had agreed to make the contact. I felt that I was putting myself under unnecessary pressure. Did I want to take on a counselling role with him? What was I going to say? Oh damn, what was I getting myself into? Nevertheless, that night I put a letter together and posted it off.

He rang me a few evenings later while I was minding my four small grandchildren. I tried to have a sensible conversation while World War III was breaking out in the room. Frank said he was coming to Sydney the following weekend, and could he see me? For some unknown reason I felt a little nervous about our meeting after such a long time.

A knock at the door the following Saturday and there

was Frank, a teacake in one hand and a potplant in the other. That afternoon we talked and talked, remembering different people we had known over the years. We talked about our families, our marriage break-ups, the pain and the hurt we felt during those times. I could see that Frank was still suffering and struggling and needed a lot of support. He was a dedicated father to his three daughters and was always considering them, and hoping all the marital turmoil wasn't impacting on them too much. Frank always thought of everyone else before himself.

He suggested that we dine out that evening, which we did, still reminiscing.

He outlined his life over the past 38 years. Although he would have preferred a flying career in aviation, the closest he came was to join the Department of Civil Aviation. He worked as an electronics technician in the radio area, installing and maintaining radio transmitters and receivers and aircraft navigation equipment.

Seeking adventure, he spent a year at the Australian Antarctic base of Wilkes in 1968, seconded to the Weather Bureau. By the way he spoke of that remote, cold and totally alien landscape I could see that he had enjoyed the experience immensely. He said that it was the nearest thing to being on the moon; he had traversed areas where probably no human had ever set foot before.

Soon after his return to Australia he married a telephonist at the Department of Civil Aviation and in 1973 they embarked on a journey to another remote land, Saudi Arabia. This time the secondment was to an agency of the United Nations, ICAO, the International Civil Aviation

Organization. There he taught electronics to Saudi trainees. Frank and Pam's eldest daughter Helen was born there and Frank told of his amusement at the reception she received as a fair-skinned, blonde-haired baby amongst the locals at the *souk*, the marketplace. The people were astonished by her pale skin and 'white' hair.

They returned from Saudi Arabia to Sydney and over the years had two more daughters, Anne and Sarah. Eventually Frank needed a career change. He joined the CSIRO, working in electronics and computing.

In the early 1990s his marriage deteriorated and the most difficult part of Frank's life began.

Eventually, after a huge amount of soul-searching, Frank decided that the marriage could not be saved.

In 1996 a short reprieve to the stress came in the form of a one-month motorcycling adventure trip to India with his old schoolmate Cliff Coverdale. Frank's eyes lit up when he recounted the trip. 'It was as if my guardian angel had said "Frank, what you need is a bloody good holiday and I'm going to make sure you get it." '

Frank moved to Geelong when CSIRO's Wool Divisions were amalgamated but he was distressed at abandoning his daughters in Sydney. The love and support from Frank's family and friends upheld the girls through this difficult time. Eventually they moved into a unit at Strathfield. Three years later, that unit was a really welcome place to stay during our frequent trips to Sydney and hospital with Safari.

As Frank and I continued our reminiscences throughout that afternoon and evening, I also filled him in on the course of my life.

I have always considered myself fortunate to be a 'stay-at-home mum'. I enjoyed and treasure those years with my children David, Kate and Elizabeth. During this time another very special child entered my life – Glenda. Glenda came to live with my grandparents in Stanmore when she was six years old. Her father had contracted TB and couldn't look after her. Glenda is a family treasure; we love her dearly. She joined our family in 1965 when she was eleven; my eldest child David was then seven and Kate five. They can't remember a time without Glenda. Six years later my youngest child Elizabeth was born and my family was complete.

In 1977 we moved from Sydney to a 26-hectare farm on the Central Coast hinterland at Kulnura. My son David's mate Ian, fifteen, came as well and stayed until he married. Ian and David were great pals and were on the same soccer team, 'The Redbacks'. Ian's mother had died a couple of years earlier and he spent quite a lot of time with us. When we talked about moving to the country he was very interested and it seemed natural to include him. Andrew and I built a large country-style home where our family and friends were always welcome. I still have contact with my friends on 'the mountain' there and catch up each month when I go to the garden club.

My children grew up, left home and while Andrew managed his drafting business I bought and operated a ladies boutique in Gosford for several years, at the same time being involved in telephone crisis counselling at Lifeline. I was a foundation member of Lifeline Central Coast. As its name suggests, Lifeline is an organisation that through telephone counsellors offers help and an empathic ear to those who are troubled. I stayed with them for fifteen years before retiring.

Through my time with Lifeline I learnt so much about people, their feelings, their sufferings and the human condition in general.

In our discussions that day, Frank had been very open with me and in turn I spoke candidly to him about how my world fell apart on a spring day in 1989.

After being married for over 29 years I was superseded by a younger model.

I was completely devastated by this event. I was completely broken. My adult children were supportive and tried to comfort me but nothing could quell the anguish I felt inside. Life didn't seem worth living. The pain in my chest was there day and night for months. It was explained to me later that the pain represented a hug that belonged to that special person but now had nowhere to go.

They were very dark days. My dear mother would sit beside my bed with her hand on my forehead to comfort me. She later told me that often, I was sobbing in my sleep.

I would look at Mum and think, if only we could change places. If only I was older and nearer the grave.

My good friend Letitia Barrett was always there for me. On one occasion she insisted I put on a coat and made me walk briskly around the oval to stop me sinking too deeply into myself. We would laugh about this, years later. At this time she would reinforce in me, 'It doesn't matter what happens, you still have yourself.' She stopped me dead in my tracks the day she asked 'How long are you going to be a victim?' They were very strong words; they were very painful times.

People kept telling me all I needed was time – how I loathed that remark and vowed never to use it on anyone else. They were right though; time was the healer. In later years I came to appreciate that period of my life for what it had taught me. I knew that if I could come through such pain – and I know that one can die of a broken heart – I was also capable of great love.

The years that followed the break-up were extremely difficult. At first I concentrated on caring for myself physically, mentally and spiritually as best I could. The feelings of abandonment weighed heavily and left me scarred for a long time. I saw myself as a cork, bobbing up and down on a vast ocean, not knowing where I was heading. I moved house six times in four years, each time endeavouring to gain a sense of stability. But this didn't happen until eventually a property settlement was obtained and I purchased my present home.

During those years I returned to the rag trade in Gosford in the employ of a lady who quickly became a close friend, Bev Benson. The chatter in the shop and the human contact gave me a reason to go on when often life seemed so purposeless. Two other great friends were Marie Airlie and Dawn Woodhouse, who cared for me so lovingly when I couldn't care for myself.

The legacy of those dark days has made me very strong within myself. I really have no fear of facing the unknown future. I believe I survived a situation that was heart-breaking in order to be led into a new life – meeting more wonderful people, a retirement that is exciting and fulfilling – and to be a second mother to two fine boys, initially Safari and now his cousin Amin. I am indeed blessed.

As I look back I am very grateful for the insight of wonderful friends who upheld me during my dark night of the soul and who recognised that I was worth saving. My friend Mal Leask from Lifeline taught me a valuable lesson. He said, 'No-one has control over the way you choose to process your thoughts.' These wise words have come to my mind many times.

Frank and I renewed and strengthened a wonderful friendship that day; one which we still enjoy. His hair is now grey but the smile and dimples that I remembered are still there. He still has his great sense of humour and his funny sayings keep me laughing.

Eventually the time came for Frank to retire and in 1998 I invited him to share my home on the New South Wales Central Coast. We enjoy each other's company, have the same values system and our families are our first priority. I was pleased to be able to help and counsel Frank in his recovery from the depression that he found so terribly debilitating. Frank was rudderless, as I had been in my 'twilight time' and I imagined the way he felt.

Another valuable asset to our companionship is the fact that we have a lot of shared memories from our youth. He can remember my family and me when I was young and likewise I have memories of the Scaysbrooks. He can remember and relate stories about people we both knew, stories about my dad, Pat, who passed away many years ago. So in this way we have a shared past.

Over the years – and even before I renewed my friendship with Frank – I had heard the name of Cliff Coverdale many times. Cliff and his wife Lesley were to have a pivotal role in the saga of Safari yet to unfold.

Cliff and Frank had gone to school together at the inner city Enmore Boys' High School in the late 1950s. Cliff and Lesley are close to the Scaysbrook family and are to this day welcome visitors to the Scaysbrook home in Pennant Hills.

I was very keen to meet them. In some ways I felt that I already knew them. Frank had told me about certain events in their lives and the harsh difficulties they had overcome. So when they invited us down to see the hull of their boat under construction in a Caringbah boatyard, we were excited and I was pleased to meet them officially.

Cliff and Lesley had sold their large home on acreage in the northern New South Wales coastal town of Taree and were living in the concrete hull of their boat. As we alighted from the car it was as if we had stepped into another world. A world of people living and working from strange makeshift dwellings surrounded by maritime equipment, bits and pieces and just plain junk. It reminded me very much of a *Steptoe and Son* TV production set.

After receiving a warm welcome from Cliff and Lesley I was invited to climb the tall, rickety ladder to the ship's deck. Lesley quickly climbed the ladder with all the agility of a child. I was a little more wary, taking the climb slowly and determined not to look down. With subsequent visits I became quite good at going up the ladder.

Once inside the hull, I looked around with admiration at all the work this couple had done, and were still doing. They had achieved such a lot. While all this construction was under way they were also both working at full-time day jobs. They had two adult sons who lived in Sydney and a very aged fox terrier 'ship's dog', Stanley. Stanley in some ways was almost human and certainly deserved respect. I believe that Stanley is now in dog heaven.

I have great admiration for Lesley. I tried to picture myself in her position and wondered how I would have coped. The laundry seemed to be done under difficulties and a simple trip to the toilet and communal shower was fraught with pitfalls. When I embarked on a trip to the loo I needed to watch carefully as I walked. There were plenty of puddles, holes and uneven ground. Like everything in the boatyard the pathway was makeshift, consisting of planks of scrap wood. Every step was an exploratory one and not to be taken for granted. It was okay for me to do this once or twice during a visit, but on a regular basis? And in the winter months and the middle of the night? Yes, I admired Lesley. She showed endurance and I never heard her complain. Perhaps in another lifetime she had been a pioneer.

Lesley painted and rubbed the hull down and was generally jill-of-all-trades and a great help to Cliff.

We were regular visitors to 'the Hull' and on one occasion in mid-1998 Lesley mentioned that she had decided to visit

Kenya in February 1999 with her friend for a few weeks' holiday. The friend had a daughter living in a remote village 300 kilometres from the capital, Nairobi. Lesley had always wanted to see Africa and this was a great opportunity. She was looking forward to her break and it was well deserved. She had been working so hard, a holiday would be beneficial to her. We looked forward to hearing of her experiences.

Our visit to Cliff and Lesley after her return was interesting. Cliff had done a lot of work building cupboards, a writing desk and completing the galley, all to surprise Lesley and welcome her home. Bunks were finished and we were invited to stay. We spent a couple of very relaxed and happy days with them.

Lesley described her trip to Kenya and to Tsavo East National Park, 300 kilometres south-east of Nairobi. Lesley and her friend were going to an entrance of the park that was generally not open to the public. The tiny village of Kasaala adjoins that corner of the park. She said that as the jeep weaved its way along a narrow track marked only by bicycle ruts and the footprints of walkers she suddenly became aware that they had become somewhat lost. A waterhole came into sight and standing nearby were a couple of small boys obtaining water for their family. One of the boys was terribly disfigured. Lesley asked the Kenya Wildlife Service warden, did he know anything about this boy? The warden told her that the boy had been burned.

Seeing the *wazungu* (white women) the boys fled. But the sight that had met Lesley's eyes and was to remain in her mind was that of a child with his left ear burnt off; his face appeared to have melted onto a very small left shoulder;

his lower lip was attached to his chest, making it impossible for him to close his mouth and barely able to close his left eye. Later we were to learn that in the village the boy needed to lie down in order to drink. His left upper arm was fused to his chest and a web joined his upper left arm to his forearm. The fingers of his left hand were a confused tangle emerging from the back of his wrist, making it impossible for the casual observer to ascertain the various parts of his hand.

Lesley resolved that night to help. The next day she made enquiries through her friends at ADRA, the Adventist Development and Relief Agency in the next village of Ikutha. They were the daughter and son-in-law of her travelling companion. She asked them to find out the boy's name and see if his parents would be agreeable to medical help in Nairobi.

The boy's name was Safari Kimanzi. While telling us the story Lesley produced a small photo of Safari. We looked at the photo and tried to absorb all that Lesley was telling us. The picture showed a child dressed in shorts and a pink T-shirt, standing in front of a crude shed, and his eyes looking back at us seemed forlorn and pleading for help. His legs were very thin and the T-shirt was wet with dribble from his permanently open mouth. I wondered what he had been thinking as the photo was being taken. For me, I knew I just wanted to help in some way.

On our way home Frank and I discussed the child in the photo at length. We both felt compelled to help Lesley and Cliff in their efforts to fundraise for his treatment.

Almost immediately upon Lesley's return the Coverdales heard from Safari's family through ADRA. Yes, they would be very grateful for any help for their son. Cliff and Lesley set about working tirelessly to raise funds for Safari's treatment in a Nairobi hospital.

Within a year they personally raised $23 000, sufficient for plastic surgery in Nairobi. Lesley and Cliff worked with great enthusiasm, gathering unwanted bric-a-brac and selling it at the local markets. We helped them with a 'trash and treasure' night at their local Seventh-day Adventist church and they gave talks within their church community.

At one of the fundraising talks they gave, Dr David Pennington, also a Seventh-day Adventist, came forward from his congregation. After looking at the small photos of Safari that Lesley carried, he said he doubted whether the work could be performed satisfactorily in Nairobi. It was a case that he considered needed microsurgery; a technique not available there. Dr Pennington was the Head of the Department of Plastic and Reconstructive Surgery at Sydney's Royal Prince Alfred Hospital. He is a plastic surgeon with a considerable reputation in reconstructive surgery. If Lesley could bring Safari to Australia he would volunteer to do the work and he would approach Royal Prince Alfred Hospital to seek their help.

Living in a boat and working full time, Cliff and Lesley were unable to look after Safari and his 26-year-old uncle, Kilonzo, who would come as family member to sign the necessary medical release forms prior to each operation. Lesley found one family from her Seventh-day Adventist Church community willing to take Safari and Kilonzo; but only for one week after their arrival. It seemed to us that Safari would be in need of a family home-life, and the sense of security that could give, and we were not quite sure how that would be arranged. Still, Lesley was confident that someone suitable would turn up. The travellers included Safari, his uncle, and Zipporah Wanjohi, a trained nurse required by the Kenyan Government to accompany Safari. Zipporah would stay about two weeks before returning home.

Early in January 2001, ten days out from the Kenyan party's arrival, Frank and Cliff were talking on the phone. After the call I enquired as to whether a family had been found. 'No, but Lesley's confident,' came the reply.

A thought flashed into my mind and I said, 'Frank, I think it's us.' Making a quick decision seemed a very natural thing to do, requiring no discussion on our part. We rang Cliff back and said, 'We will take care of Safari.'

Having made the decision to take Safari we wanted to discuss this matter with our families. Frank's three daughters, Helen, Anne and Sarah, thought it was a great idea. My children, David, Kate, Glenda and Libby (Elizabeth), thought so too; however, all wondered if we were taking on too much. They were concerned we might overdo it. My grandchildren were very excited and kept asking, 'When will he be here?' 'How much longer will it all take?' 'How will you talk to him, Gran, if he doesn't speak English?' We would find a way, I reassured them.

Many thoughts raced through my mind as I took my afternoon walk the day before the Kenyans' arrival. I started questioning myself. What were we really letting ourselves in for? I had reared four children, I had twelve grandchildren and now at 62 I was taking on another child for twelve months. One who couldn't speak English, couldn't close his mouth to eat. Was I equal to the task? Could I meet his needs, could I be a surrogate mother, could I comfort him, and could I love him? And yet somewhere in the deepest recesses of my being I knew I had to do this. It was almost like a directive coming from somewhere. The job was mine. A feeling of trepidation and excitement pervaded my body. All these thoughts crowded into my mind and at the same time I was thinking that if under different circumstances I needed help for one of my own grandchildren, surely someone would come to their aid. We had to do it.

I was also aware that Frank and I would lose our freedom. We were accustomed to quiet meals listening to the news in peace and doing things on the spur of the moment, eating when we felt like it. All this would have to go. The house would be full of people for a year.

I stood in the doorway of my third bedroom, looking at the very feminine colour scheme: cream walls, various shades of mauve and a pink bedspread. In the past this room had become a retreat for family and friends at times when the world just seemed to be too much. It was a place to relax; to listen to soothing music, to heal and receive loving care.

It would still be that haven, but it needed a few changes to accommodate the Kenyans. We quickly dismantled the double bed and packed away the furnishings. The rest of the day we perused the local opportunity shops for two single beds and anything 'African' to make our visitors feel at home and welcomed. My daughter Kate arrived with her surplus stocks of single sheets and doonas for 'our boys'. This room soon took on a new look.

We spent the Sunday night before the Kenyans' arrival at Frank's girls' unit in Strathfield. This haven made our early morning arrivals at Royal Prince Alfred Hospital fifteen minutes away so much easier than travelling 80 kilometres from the Central Coast. It was an exciting and challenging time. I felt confident now and with Frank's comment, 'Don't worry, everything will be fine' reiterated several times, what was there to worry about? After all, I had had a lot of children come into my care over the years. I felt ready for any challenge that might come my way.

Chapter 2

Safari, Uncle Kilonzo and travelling nurse Zipporah arrived at Sydney airport early on the morning of 12 January 2001.

We offered to pick Lesley up from the boatyard and drive her to the airport with us to meet the Kenyans. She expressed nervousness as she thought about the impending television interview. She was keen for it all to go very well. She said that it was important for her Seventh-day Adventist Church that their ADRA become as well known as the Salvation Army and that the organisation was looking at the Safari story as a great publicity opportunity. I could sense she felt very responsible for a successful outcome that day. After all, what was to commence shortly was of her making.

At the airport we met Danny Milosavljevic, the *RPA* television program's executive producer. Danny's TV network, TCN 9, produced a medical reality program. Called simply *RPA*, it focuses on patients undergoing treatment and care at the Royal Prince Alfred Hospital. The show was in its seventh year and Nine were very interested in following the progress of this child from Africa.

We had determined before this day that we didn't want to be in the filming and Danny completely understood. We felt that television just wasn't our scene.

With hindsight we now laugh at our naivety. It wasn't long before we realised that a family background was essential to give context and depth to Safari's story and we agreed to be part of the program. The film crew with whom we worked was absolutely wonderful. They were very sensitive to Safari's situation and mindful of all he was going through. They were amazed at what they witnessed during his operations and his endurance through his pain. And they soon learnt – as we did – of his personality and special qualities. Soon, very naturally, a bond was forged between Safari, Danny, cameraman Chris Roles, sound recordist Tony Clunes, and Frank and me.

There was a feeling of controlled excitement at Sydney airport as we all waited to meet Safari and Uncle Kilonzo. A lot of planning had taken place to reach this moment. Lesley introduced us to Dr Pennington along with David Syme, the Executive Director of ADRA Australia, a man with whom we were to have many dealings in the future. He was there along with many ADRA and Seventh-day Adventist people.

Eventually an African lady emerged, escorted by an Emirates Airline attendant dressed in a quasi-Bedouin uniform resplendent with filmy scarf tucked partially under her maroon beret. Holding Zipporah's hand was a diminutive African boy dressed in baggy trousers, a white T-shirt and new shoes. His clothes looked too big for his small frame. Following and completing the entourage was a young man who had to be Safari's Uncle Kilonzo, pushing a trolley piled high with luggage.

The little boy's eyes widened as he walked forward. We became aware that the normal crowd of airport arrivals and visitors began to part to allow the Kenyan group to move forward. They were preceded in a strange way by cameraman Chris walking backwards, his huge camera on his shoulder, accompanied by the strange image of Tony the sound recordist wearing earmuffs and carrying a furry object on the end of a long stick. To a little bush boy from Kenya the sight must have been surreal. Producer Danny clutched his notes and looked on keenly. Later in the year Safari would refer to him as 'Danny with the book'. The ever-present notebook was Danny's signature.

Shortly afterwards, Lesley, Dr Pennington and David Syme were introduced to the Kenyans and escorted to a seat in a garden outside the terminal where the interview of their arrival took place. I observed many onlookers. People were murmuring and in hushed tones whispering, 'He must be going to be on TV.' The air seemed filled with excitement – or was the excitement just within me, I wondered.

After the greetings and interview, people drifted away and we two walked up to Safari, Zipporah and Kilonzo. Through Zipporah, I said, 'I'm going to be your Australian Mumma and Frank is going to be your Australian Pappa.' This dear little boy looked up at us, smiled and put his hand in mine. Instantly all my qualms dissipated. I was reassured that with this little boy who was about to walk into our lives forever we would be all right. We walked to the car. I felt amazed at the trust he had immediately placed in me. Kilonzo and Frank chatted; Kilonzo asked Frank where he worked. Frank felt strange admitting to the fact that he was retired – a luxury he was sure would never be enjoyed by poor villagers from Kenya.

Safari, Kilonzo and Zipporah were all excited to see the city with its tall buildings towering above a huge harbour. Safari quickly identified the sounds that trucks make with their air brakes, as we were to see in the evening at home as he imitated the sound with a toy truck.

We were treated to the beautiful experience of rediscovering the world through the eyes of a child as we drove around the Eastern Suburbs and Watsons Bay. Areas so familiar to us but very strange to this wide-eyed boy. Frank drove around Rushcutters Bay and we all walked to the water's edge across a beautiful park with Moreton Bay fig trees. Safari had never seen boats before and was soon asking his uncle many questions, like, 'Why do some boatshave tall sticks with strange shapes attached?' He was referring to sailing boats. The idea that a boat could be pushed by the wind was a completely new concept to him. Later at South Head he wondered at the vast expanse of blue water reaching as far as the eye could see. Frank tried to explain the completely foreign idea that if one went far enough out there, Africa and Kenya's Mombasa port would be reached. Later on when Safari's English developed he would say with a twinkle in his eye, 'You're trickin' me, Pappa.'

Uncle Kilonzo, however, seemed worried and withdrawn. He told us that he'd thought he would be in Australia for three months. At the airport in the interview he learnt that he would be here for twelve months. This came as a shock, no-one had told him. He was very disconcerted. He had left his wife Mary and his two little girls, Janet and Lucy, at home. Twelve months was too long for him to be away.

On the way north to Gosford a glance towards the back seat revealed three Kenyans sound asleep. It seemed the long trip to Australia and all the excitement had caught up with them.

Our arrival home seemed very quiet compared to the noise and bustle of Sydney. The leafy bush setting near a mountain is where we call home and it seemed to have a calming effect on us all. It was so good to be back, and to breathe the fresh air. As Kilonzo got out of the car he looked around and asked Frank, 'What crops do you grow here?' Frank had to sheepishly admit, 'We only grow flowers.'

Now that we were home from the airport, our new family had lots of questions to ask us. Safari went from room to room, looking all around and taking in his new surroundings. Frank suggested that we all look at a video he had taken of the arrival at the airport. Safari surveyed the scenes on the video with amazement and a look of pleasure showed on his face.

Without any prompting, Safari sat next to me on the lounge, sidled up a little closer, put his head on my shoulder and his arm around my neck. In this instant an understanding passed between us and I knew that we were going to be okay. All would be well and words were not needed.

I have since been told that this display of affection was unusual behaviour for a 'bush boy'. It seems to me that village children are intrinsically aware of the continual love and acceptance of their kin; there is no need for physical confirmation. Maybe at some level he needed to make this same connection with me, his Australian Mumma, and he became demonstrative in this way. For me, I felt as if I had known Safari before. He didn't seem new to me; even though there was much to be learnt about him, I felt that on a deeper level we had already made a connection.

A knock at the door announced our neighbour Jeannie, arms full of T-shirts and shorts for Safari. These were very welcome. Safari's distended mouth caused him to dribble incessantly, so many T-shirts were needed in a day. Many wonderful neighbours came to the house that afternoon with clothes and offers to help in any way they could.

That first night at home is indelibly printed on our minds. Images of Safari taking his first shower. The water cascading over his fragile body. He couldn't contain his laughter at the water splashing over him. His laughter was infectious. Plenty of running warm water; a simple thing we take for granted here. I remember noticing his distended tummy, a telltale sign of chronic malnutrition. I had no way of understanding his life or suffering in the village of Kasaala.

A source of amusement that first night was the electric

lights. From Safari's quizzical expression we could see his mind at work. 'How come you can touch that thing on the wall and make a light in the middle of the room come off and on?' He was incredulous. These are very special memories for us. Here was a child who in spite of his afflictions was full of the joy of life. He would double over in laughter. We were to learn Safari has a great sense of humour.

Little did we know that our lives would be changed forever. We were about to embark on a journey without an ending, and discover a love for a little Kenyan boy whose personality and charisma is as dynamic as his courage and bravery. A little boy who raises stoicism to new heights in an unusually mature way.

Safari's spirit, courage and charisma was to change not only our lives in a way we could never have visualised, but also the lives of many Australians who came into his orbit through the TV program *RPA*. This was reality TV at its best, showing expertly and with great sensitivity the many facets of a unique child in his journey to wellness.

Chapter 3

The City of Gosford is located on the New South Wales Central Coast some 70 kilometres north of Sydney. A beautiful coastal area, it has for many years been a popular holiday destination for the people of metropolitan Sydney. It attracted retirees and later developed its own identity and businesses. We live in a suburb of Gosford, called Narara. It is on the northern railway line and tucks in under an escarpment 7 kilometres from the ocean. The land is of a hilly, elevated character and many houses, including mine, are split-level and have pleasant views of gullies and bush-land. This was the setting for my home, 'Pinetop' – Safari's Australian home.

The local community is predominantly of European extract but as is becoming more the case in Australia there is a multicultural element emerging. We hadn't really noticed before, but now our focus had changed we began to see Africans in the district. There were Somalis and Sudanese immigrant refugees from the turmoil in parts of Africa. Up until now we knew nothing of their lives.

The need to become familiar with Africa and African people was initially spurred by our concern over catering for the food preferences of our new family members. This led us to friendships with many people we otherwise would not have met and has enriched our lives.

Some days before Safari and his companions arrived in Australia, pondering this question of 'what food do they eat?' in Gosford's Imperial Shopping Centre, Frank spotted two African women dressed in the traditional headscarf of Muslim women. Sensitive to the fact that they might be embarrassed if approached by a man, Frank went looking for me to ask me to introduce myself. A step ahead, I had already met and introduced myself to them in the Medicare office.

The ladies were from Somalia, which joins Kenya's north-eastern border. They knew exactly what villagers in Kenya liked to eat – *ugali*, a maize meal made from grinding the dried kernels of white corn or maize. It is the main crop and staple for poor subsistence farmers and is eaten all over East Africa. People there say that a meal is not complete without ugali. The Somali ladies explained that it is cooked in a saucepan with a little water and quickly thickens and sets into very thick starch porridge, much like polenta. It is then turned out onto a plate and cut into cubes ready to be dipped into a chilli and vegetable sauce and eaten. And yes, it was available in ethnic grocery stores in Sydney. Otherwise, the ladies explained, meat cooked any way would be very acceptable.

As it turned out, Zipporah had thought ahead and brought from Nairobi a few packets of the best brand of ugali as emergency rations to ward off homesickness. These were consumed within a few weeks, but in any case we needn't have worried about food. As long as plenty of meat was provided, our three visitors were happy. Kilonzo bragged that meat was in abundance in the village but we didn't believe him. Later when we knew him better the real story of an ever-present shortage of all food, let alone meat, emerged. Zipporah recounted a funny story from the flight over. At mealtime Safari was presented with a dish of salad vegetables. He retorted to Zipporah, 'What's this, raw food! Only good for the goats left back home!'

I was preparing a cold chicken for lunch a couple of days after the Kenyans' arrival. After stripping what I thought was the totality of the meat I was about to discard the remains of bone, skin and gristle. Safari, who had been watching my actions intently, very quickly motioned to me that if I was thinking of discarding them I should do so in his direction. When I gave them to him his eyes shone with delight. Within five minutes there was nothing left but a tiny pile of polished bones. We learnt very soon of Safari's voracious appetite and encouraged him to eat his fill as his swollen belly that first night in the shower had told me that he was malnourished and needed all our help if he were to be ready for the surgical ordeal in ten days' time.

In the days that followed, Safari eagerly settled in. He was always cooperative and keen to please, and I guess I was the same. Although his vocabulary only consisted of the universal 'Mumma' and 'thank you very much', a nicety we could imagine his family drilling into him, he was very responsive to meeting members of the family. He would gesticulate, nod and shake his head until he was understood. With children words were not necessary; the gestures of play were sufficient.

Safari's first full day in Australia was Saturday and he was up really early to survey his surrounds, much like a child on Christmas morning.

My daughter Kate, her husband, John, and their three daughters – Kellie, Jessica and Ellen – arrived and immediately took to Safari and he to them. Kate and John owned a surf clothing shop at the nearby suburb of Kincumber and Kate some weeks later showered him with the latest statements from the world of youth fashion. She enjoyed fitting him out and indulging him; he was to become the son she never had.

Also a treasured friend of mine, Jenny Murray, came to visit. Jenny and I go back many years. We have supported each other in good and troubled times. Jenny has long been part of our families and now she was becoming part of our African family.

On that Saturday in January 2001 she suggested, 'How about I take Safari and Kilonzo to the Koala Park in West Pennant Hills tomorrow so they can see some Australian wildlife?' What a great idea: the boys had been very keen to see those strange Australian animals called kangaroos ever since they arrived.

On Sunday Jenny came to take Kilonzo and Safari to visit the Koala Park. Recalling this trip now, Frank tells me that in growing up, he had passed the park thousands of times but had never been inside. Here were a couple of complete strangers to Australia from a faraway village in Africa on their way to the park on day three of their trip. 'It's strange how we ignore things that are right on our doorstep,' he said.

Jenny and Kilonzo chatted as she drove along the freeway to Sydney. Kilonzo was probably quite amazed seeing a woman in the role of driver, so unlike the role of women in Kasaala.

They all had a wonderful time at the park, Jenny told us later. As they walked around Jenny was aware of Safari's self-consciousness, either pulling the collar of his shirt up towards his eyes or the long sleeve down over his mangled left hand. His eyes were constantly scanning his environment; the people as well as the animals. He was reluctant at first to touch the koalas and kangaroos but after seeing other children patting them he hesitatingly did the same. It seemed he had a healthy respect for animals, especially unknown ones.

Kilonzo was likewise very tentative about these strange creatures. He commented to Jenny that the kangaroos had paws very much like human hands. Much later when talking to Kilonzo about kangaroo meat being a delicacy amongst some Australians he said that because the kangaroos' paws looked like hands he could never eat kangaroo meat. We gained the impression that his revulsion came from the human resemblance he had commented on.

Lunchtime came and Jenny produced a cut lunch of sandwiches. However, the Kenyans weren't impressed. After eating the meat filling, they left the bread. They did, however, enjoy their chocolate biscuits on the way out. As they got in Jenny's car Safari ended the excursion with his characteristic, 'Thank you very much.'

In the week that followed, Safari continued to impress us with his helpfulness and eagerness to settle in. He soon acquainted himself with the Garside family next door. It was through the Garside children, Louis and Georgia, that he learnt about 'sleep overs'. Next door to the Garsides live Jeannie and her two sons, Chad and Todd, who also very quickly became great buddies of Safari.

Directly opposite our house live Stuart and Kate Rabe and their grown-up son and daughter Justin and Samara. These people were to become important in Safari's life and he in theirs. Safari developed a great love and respect for Stuart, who he saw as a father figure.

Chapter 4

Some tests and a consultation with Dr Pennington were necessary before Safari's first operation. On Monday, three days after the Kenyans' arrival, we all travelled back down the freeway to Sydney and Dr Pennington's rooms in Macquarie Street. As we drove, Zipporah chatted about herself and her background.

We were very grateful to have Zipporah's support during those early days. About the same age as Kilonzo, she was a fascinating, dynamic woman. She was engaged to Fred Kumah, then ADRA Kenya's Country Director in Nairobi. At that time Zipporah also worked for ADRA Kenya and was responsible for the administration of US rehabilitation aid to the Kenyans injured in the US Embassy bomb blast in Nairobi in 1998.

We were quite early for our 9 am appointment so after parking the car in the Opera House carpark we strolled across to Macquarie Street via the beautiful Botanical Gardens. There was a slight breeze caressing us on that summery morning as we walked, the lush grass soft under our feet. Suddenly Frank's mobile phone rang and an African male voice asked for Zipporah. It was Freddy, Zipporah's boyfriend calling from Angola. What a surprise! Someone in deepest Africa was calling us in the very English and colonial Botanical Gardens. Handing the phone to Zipporah, Frank mused at what Captain James Cook would have thought, had he been able to see into the future from the spot where his barque lay at anchor over 200 years ago. The world has changed immeasurably, bringing people together in an astonishing way.

As the time for our appointment drew near we took a break for coffee and toast underneath the Segafredo umbrella of a footpath café next to the 1940s brick AMA House where Dr Pennington had his rooms.

Early-morning pedestrians hurrying to work brushed by, some glimpsing the little boy with the disfigured face. We ordered coffee, a large plate of raisin toast and a milkshake for Safari. Our African charges took in the city vista and we relaxed in the fresh morning air.

The refreshments arrived and Zipporah and Safari tucked in. Kilonzo, however, took a few moments, seemingly quietly reflecting before joining them. I noticed this very subtle act of thanksgiving – no-one else did – and at once recognised that Kilonzo had a deeper side. Following this insight, a few weeks later I suggested that should he want to go to church, I could arrange it with a friend of mine. Kilonzo was very happy to take up my suggestion.

Morning tea over, we took the lift in AMA House to Dr Pennington's level. There Lesley, Danny's film crew and

Dr Pennington's anaesthetist Dr Chris Borton met us in the crowded waiting room. We introduced ourselves to Dr Borton and retold the events of the last few days. He was an erudite middle-aged man with a pleasant, relaxed and humane manner, sporting a grey-tinged beard.

Dr Borton explained, 'David and I work together quite a lot of the time and I'm very pleased to be helping with Safari's operations.' Both men throughout the year gave graciously of their time and great skill to help this small child.

The door to the inner office opened, Dr Pennington emerged and shook hands all round. The consultation went ahead with the film crew from Channel Nine recording the event for inclusion in that year's series of *RPA* to go to air eight months hence. For the camera, Lesley described how she had first seen Safari in the Kenyan bush.

The lighter side of Safari's personality shone through his scarred exterior when he giggled with ticklishness as Dr Pennington lifted him by his bare torso onto the examination table. Chris Roles' camera work showed something that children everywhere do. Safari was swinging his feet to and fro as he sat in a chair too high for his short legs – legs in baggy long pants, feet in new check brown socks and new black Bata shoes all the way from Nairobi.

We listened carefully to what Dr Pennington proposed for the first operation the following Monday morning. In what he described as a challenging operation they were going to release Safari's distended lower lip and neck from his chest. They would then fill the enormous gap of raw flesh with large patches from his groin. Slowly the magnitude of the surgery was impacting on us. This was an incredibly big operation in anyone's terms. We could only speculate how sore and painful the surgery would be. Safari was only six years old in a foreign country with strange white faces peering down on him. Nothing familiar, only Uncle Kilonzo and Zipporah. So much for a small boy to cope with.

As we left Dr Pennington's rooms and waited in the small lobby for the lift, Safari said through Zipporah, 'I know the doctors are going to cut me but I won't cry.' Emotions welled up inside me and I found it hard to retain my composure. I kept thinking of the pain and soreness that lay ahead, taking some solace in the thought that in Safari's case, ignorance was bliss.

We discussed all this later with Kilonzo and Zipporah when Safari had gone to bed. We felt confident he would be able to endure the pain in order for his face to look like those of other children. We didn't know then of Safari's inner strength or his strong will; we were yet to discover the courage and inspiration of a small child in extreme and extraordinary circumstances.

Following the examination, X-rays and blood tests needed to be done at the RPA Medical Centre in Camperdown. The first operation was now less than a week away, so there was no time to be lost; it was straight off to the medical centre.

Curiously, although we were sure that Safari didn't know what an X-ray was, he knew to stand still while they were being taken. Taking X-rays of his damaged left hand posed a challenge for the staff. Because of the very limited movement in Safari's left arm due to the webbing, it was necessary to stand him on a pile of phone books in order to be able to position his hand to photograph the correct angles. We were relieved to hear the radiologist say that in spite of Safari's contorted neck and hand, the X-rays revealed that the bones had suffered no real distortion. One bone in the left wrist, which should have been the same length as its neighbour, was a little shorter. Overall it was good news.

After the tests we went to the Hospital Admissions Desk and checked our little man in for the following Monday. He was to be first cab off the rank at 8 am.

Going through all these procedures methodically I'm sure I gave an outward impression of calmness. I felt very differently on the inside, where the same turmoil I had experienced while waiting for the lift in Macquarie Street was churning around.

All our medical work done, we bought a bag of bread rolls and some bananas and drove down Parramatta Road to a leafy park in Five Dock and enjoyed our first lunch and play in the park. Safari was very happy on the swings, tentative at first and then pleased when I pushed him higher in the air. He was fun to watch as he ran from the swings to the slippery dip. Everyone was relaxed, Kilonzo seemed happy and resigned to his twelve-month stay, Zipporah had spoken to her man that morning and we were glad that things were progressing smoothly.

On the way home we dropped in to Frank's family home in Pennant Hills. Ted, in his nineties, and Alma, in her late eighties, were always pleased to see us. They were especially pleased to meet Safari, Kilonzo and Zipporah that day. The family, too, was very concerned for Safari and what lay ahead.

Alma's wheelchair seemed to fascinate Safari; it was quite likely the first time he had seen one. He studied the big bicycle-like wheels for a while but wasn't able to express his thoughts.

Back home, before the operation day our local newspaper had heard that a little boy with bad burn scars was living in the area and had come all the way from Africa for surgery. We made contact with Julie Hartigan, a journalist from the *Central Coast Express Advocate*. Julie suggested she write a story accompanied by a photo of Safari. Thus Safari won his first heart on the Central Coast. Julie has since followed Safari's every move and has brought heartwarming stories of his progress to her readers.

Pinetop had another visitor prior to operation day – ADRA's executive director for Australia, David Syme. We were very interested to learn what we could of Africa and David's twenty years there, four in Kenya, qualified him as a useful source of knowledge. The Adventist Development and Relief Agency is a non-government organisation (NGO) based in Washington DC and the third-largest recipient of US Government aid money in the world. David is a middle-aged, suave, urbane Englishman, at ease in the corridors of power.

David came bearing cameras to record the first parts of Safari's journey. He was keen to photograph Safari in his new setting and he had all the latest 'state of the art' equipment and a course in video production under his belt. His plan was to take photos and videos back to Safari's family in Kasaala, which we thought an excellent idea. Safari always cooperated at these times; however, he became very nervous when asked to pose in front of a hydrangea bush in the front garden. David picked up the problem instantly from his intimate knowledge of Africa and assured Safari that there were no snakes in the garden. It was our first inkling of the serious threat that snakes posed to Safari and other rural Kenyans.

One last task remained. Safari needed pyjamas for hospital, which meant a trip to Erina Fair Shopping Mall. I was feeling a little nervous about taking him into such a crowded complex, thinking he might be overawed by it all. However, it just had to be done.

Safari walked between us holding our hands tightly while Kilonzo, who by this time Frank had nicknamed 'Big K', and Zipporah brought up the rear. We felt very protective towards our boy. Children openly stared, most adults looked away but a couple of people inquired quite openly, 'What happened to him?' We told what we knew.

Zipporah changed some money at Thomas Cook and we continued to Target department store for a pair of blue and red check shortie PJ's. Pyjamas were a new idea for Safari as in the village, Kilonzo explained, everyone slept in their clothes. Family finances did not reach to special nightwear.

Apart from looking after Safari's sartorial and dietary needs, the days before the first operation were spent getting to know Kilonzo and Zipporah.

Kilonzo was 26 when he arrived. A shy, retiring man but a man who curiously has a good understanding of world politics and who speaks a number of European languages including German, Italian, English of course and a smattering of French. Plus, as many Africans do, Kilonzo speaks a number of African languages. Kilonzo and Safari belong to the Kamba tribal group and their mother tongue is Kikamba. He amazed us with his knowledge of world events and politics and was an avid viewer of SBS news and news from Africa on the Internet. He had accompanied Safari because he was the family member who had the best grasp of English to understand the nature of the consent he was giving the doctors to perform the operations. For the most part, Kilonzo remained quiet and reserved. He did, however, enjoy a beer or two or more and this relaxed him. At such times he became quite open, happy and talkative.

Kilonzo and Zipporah were keen in these early days to meet as many of our family members as possible. Frank's brother Howard lives with his wife Dianne and family on the Central Coast at Umina. It was still the Christmas holiday season and so one day in that early 'getting to know you' period, Safari, Kilonzo and Howard went fishing at Patonga, a picturesque village tucked away on the northern shore of Broken Bay. From Patonga you can look across the bay to Lion Island and the northern beach suburbs of Sydney.

Kilonzo was curious, looking at people throwing back what he saw as perfectly edible but somewhat small fish. Howard explained that we throw back juvenile fish so that the fish stocks won't be diminished. Kilonzo had had very little aquatic experience but quickly realised the reasons for this conservation.

On the old timber wharf from which they were fishing Safari noticed a five-cent piece wedged in between the weathered grain of the wharf timbers. Determined to get it out, he spent a good three-quarters of an hour prising at the coin with a screwdriver. Doggedly he persevered until he proudly extracted the coin, which he announced was *mbesa*, Kikamba for money. It seemed that he appreciated the value of money, even down to this trivial five-cent piece.

Chapter 5

Royal Prince Alfred Hospital is a large public hospital located in the busy inner-city Sydney suburb of Camperdown and attached to Sydney University as a teaching hospital. RPA was established in 1882 and has an enviable worldwide reputation for medical research and nursing excellence. The grand foyer reflects its Edwardian past, with elegantly carved Sydney sandstone and stained-glass windows reminiscent of a period when craftsmanship was proudly displayed. Eminent early doctors and administrators are remembered in marble busts along the wide entrance corridor. The floor is tessellated ceramic tiles in step with the hospital's past. Large prints of old black and white photos along the walls depict a history of nursing, and display boxes show surgical instruments from an earlier era.

The period architecture of the hospital's street front soon gives way to a modern-day hospital with all the facilities of a world-class institution. Here medical practice and research advance the frontiers and medical miracles occur daily. Safari's transformation was one such miracle.

The Alfred Café occupies a place along the entrance corridor; a place where we were to spend many hours waiting for the call to tell us that the day's operation was over and that we should come downstairs to the recovery ward to see Safari. Safari endured seven major and seven minor operations in ten months. With the exception of the first operation where Zipporah was to ease him onto the operating table, I was privileged to be with him while the anaesthetic took effect.

On Monday 22 January 2001, only ten days after his arrival, Safari's first operation took place. At 8 am in Theatre 4 in the John Lowenthal Theatre Block, Safari commenced the journey to restore his body. This was to be his time and his theatre for the rest of the year.

Safari had been admitted the previous afternoon to the children's ward. We arranged for Zipporah to be accommodated at the University College rooms across the road. Zipporah's nursing background and her ability to converse with Safari were to be relied upon by the doctors and nurses in what was to be a major operation – one to challenge the skills of the surgical team headed by Dr David Pennington and assisted by Drs John Kippen and Luke Stradwick, the hospital's plastic surgery registrars. Dr Chris Borton managed Safari's anaesthetics.

Safari had no idea what was in store for him as he was wheeled along the tunnel below the street that links the children's ward to the main hospital complex. We didn't go to the hospital that day as Zipporah's presence was more important and we thought that Safari would be semi-conscious until at least Tuesday. But at home as the appointed hour approached we silently wished him well and wondered how it was all going to work out. Later in August when *RPA* went to air, we saw that he had been giggling as he was wheeled to his fate.

During the day we phoned the ward. He was still in theatre, we were told. Such a long operation we thought worrying. Then came the news late in the day that he was out of theatre and in a stable condition. Lesley phoned that evening to tell us that all had gone well that day but that it had been a huge operation, nine and a half hours in duration. It had involved releasing his chin and neck from his chest where it had become attached. In the fusion of his neck to his chest his mouth had been drawn fully open and he was unable to close his mouth and barely able to close his left eye. These were all contractures of the tissue as a result of the burns.

The operating table was covered with a water-warmed blanket; the intravenous fluids were carefully heated as were the anaesthetic gases; the unexposed parts of his body were wrapped in cotton wool. All these precautions were to avoid loss of body heat and a condition of surgical hypothermia. In a child this could be a serious problem and could cause circulatory collapse and even cardiac arrest.

Present in the operating theatre for the first time with Safari were the Channel Nine film crew: Danny, Chris and Tony. They were to see the nature of the very complicated procedures first-hand from a lay point of view.

The incisions to release Safari's neck revealed evidence

of the ash from the fire embedded in the tissue. In later hand operations the ash served as a guide as to the best path for the scalpel.

Once Safari's neck was released a huge area of raw flesh needed to be filled. This was done by taking a large piece of tissue complete with a vein and artery (known as a 'free flap') from his right groin and under the microscope attaching the vein and artery to a vein and artery in his neck. The blood vessels were tiny, one artery measuring less than 1 millimetre in diameter. Another large skin graft was taken from Safari's left groin to fill the space unable to be covered by the free flap.

Other work was done to address the problem of his lower eyelid and lower lip being severely stretched and needing surgical adjustment.

The work was a credit to the surgical skills of Dr Pennington and his team who by the operation's end must have been very tired. At 5.30 in the evening Safari was wheeled into recovery and into the Plastics Ward E10 South. It had been a very long day and he was a very sick boy.

During Safari's first operation it was decided that Kilonzo should share his room to reassure Safari and to interpret for him when necessary. We also thought Kilonzo's nearness would help Safari's confidence and take away feelings of abandonment. Safari, however, much to our amazement adapted very quickly to his new surroundings. The nursing staff were just wonderful all the time.

We felt also that Kilonzo would want to keep a watchful eye on his charge. The family in Kasaala had placed a huge responsibility on Kilonzo and he was very aware of this.

This became apparent during the following week. There were times when Kilonzo would just say as he looked at Safari, 'So much pain.'

We arrived on Tuesday afternoon to a confronting sight. Safari was plumbed up with drips and drains. A large piece of yellow sponge seemed to be holding his neck straight – a neck that looked almost like it had been removed and reattached. His lower lip looked enormously bloated and excruciatingly painful. His face was covered in Vaseline and he was whimpering through the veil of morphine. And he was hungry. Kilonzo was worried that he couldn't eat but we reassured him that the staff would look after that aspect. Even though the doctors were concerned about his malnutrition, in the ten days at home before the operation we had not been able to correct this.

I will never forget the way Safari looked. His little body in that big hospital bed. His face so swollen; his lip huge. I looked at him and wondered if he would ever look normal. I was aware my legs had suddenly become weak. I wanted to cry. I desperately wanted to hold him in my arms and comfort him.

People were chatting, the noise seemed an intrusion. He lay softly crying. I felt so helpless. There was so little I could do. I just hurt for his suffering.

On the way home in the car Frank and I discussed how the sight that day affected us. Frank said that the extremely swollen lip affected him most. 'That must have been hugely painful,' he said. He also said that hidden to us were his donor sites on his groin and the sponge hid the surgery to his neck. Not being able to see these areas made them less of a focus for concerned onlookers, even though the pain from those sites was severe. 'You know, Jan, it's our face that identifies who we are and that is why seeing it assaulted in another person is so very confronting.' I thought about this silently for a long time.

Safari was heavily sedated for days after the operation and the care extended to him by the RPA staff was wonderful. A special nurse was provided around the clock for one whole week. Absolutely nothing was left to chance. He couldn't have received better treatment anywhere in the world. The nursing staff took him under their wing and gave him a lot of love, which we believe sustained him through those weeks when everything was so painful and unfamiliar to him. The nurses also admired his courage. When we spoke to him, he replied with just a barely audible whimper. Those days were very difficult for him to endure, and for us to stand by helplessly. For most of his operations Safari was cut in more than one place and this time he was virtually ringbarked around the groin.

By Thursday Safari needed to sit up and cough and I thought he needed a cuddle. The nurses were hesitant; this was new territory for them as well as for the doctors. I suggested that if four nurses each took a corner of his lower sheet and if I sat on a large reclining hospital chair they could lower him onto my lap. This they did and I gently massaged between his shoulder blades, which was about the only place that was safe to touch. He sat there for about an hour and then I carefully lowered him back into bed. The moving was excruciating but a few minutes after returning to bed he said through Zipporah, 'Tell Mumma thank you very much.' We were touched that this little child could, through all the pain and suffering that he was experiencing, have the humility to utter those words. It was a further insight into the special qualities Safari possesses.

Just before Safari left hospital Danny wanted to film his reaction to seeing his new face in a mirror for the first time. Danny was really keen to capture this moment for the television audience. He offered Safari a round mirror he had brought from home for the occasion. Safari was thrilled by what he saw, intrigued by the stitches under his lip and by sign language indicated that he had a beard like Pappa's. He smiled broadly and put his thumb up in that characteristic way to show that he was so very happy with the new look. Words were not needed by this little boy from the backblocks of Kenya to show the world that he was on his way.

Once Safari's condition had stabilised and the doctors were happy that the skin grafts had taken, Kilonzo came home with us and Zipporah went back to Nairobi. As she was about to leave Safari, she chatted with him in Swahili. Safari was not at all fretful of being left, although he gave Zipporah detailed directions about which forks in the track she should take when she went to visit the family with a progress report on his condition. Was it that in Safari's world women needed to be given instruction and guidance? And, of course, he had messages for his brothers, his mum and dad and his sisters. Zipporah left twenty days after her arrival.

At home we sat around with Kilonzo and explored his background. He was the youngest son and his parents lived next door to Safari's home. He explained that as the youngest son it was his responsibility to look after his aged parents. Kilonzo had three brothers: John, Safari's father; Rashid; and Michael but he had no sisters. Rashid was married but unfortunately he and his wife Ruth were unable to have children. Michael was unmarried and had little interest in village life, preferring to live off the land as a bushman in the forest.

Kilonzo said that his wife Mary had recently moved with their two girls, Janet, aged seven, and Lucy, five, to Nairobi in search of work during his absence. Mary had a job as a security guard at the gate of a coffee plantation in Nairobi and lived in a small cottage on the plantation.

He described his own background. He grew up in Kasaala but like the children of most poor subsistence farmers had left school after primary school to help his parents. At various times he had worked as a labourer in a local gem mine and as a trinket salesman on the beaches of Mombasa and the streets of Nairobi, just barely eking out a living. In the course of selling trinkets to the European tourists he had developed his skill with languages.

We described our backgrounds, our families and our view of life. Many pleasant hours were spent in those early days 'getting to know you' both ways. Kilonzo was a proud man, never self-deprecating or dwelling on the circumstances of a poor African villager. But he was keen to make what he could of this extended stay in Australia in order to advance himself on his return. He said quite often, 'A man must work' and saw work as defining who he was. We could see also that it was not feasible to expect him to just 'hang around' waiting for the next time that he would be required to give permission for another surgical procedure.

Very soon all the grass was cut and the weeding done at home and all the suitable odd jobs had been taken care of. The local football club had taken him under their wing but he needed the feelings of self-worth that come with work. He was 26 and energetic. We understood and felt sorry for him.

Our friends Yulande and John Bull came to the rescue in February and suggested that Kilonzo give them a hand in their garden. They lived on very pretty acreage in nearby Ourimbah in a truly rural setting. The surrounding area was green with broad pastures and whilst Yulande and John were not farmers they had a nice garden. Kilonzo met and clicked with the Bulls and they asked if he would be happy to work for them in getting the garden in shape. Kilonzo jumped at this opportunity to show his worth and quickly set to and renovated the garden. They were all very happy but Kilonzo needed more work.

Soon Kilonzo was introduced to the farming world of Mangrove Mountain just 20 kilometres inland and our problem of keeping an energetic young man's boredom at bay was solved when he took up work on a farm.

Kilonzo now saw real purpose in his stay in Australia. He would be able to take home a nest egg which, used wisely, could remove him and his family from the cycle of poverty.

Within three weeks of that first operation Safari was at home kicking a soccer ball. After the morphine was stopped Safari was up and about. Convalescence is simply not in his vocabulary. We thought we would have him reclining on a banana lounge at home, entertaining him with colouring-in books and bringing him invalid foods. Not our boy. That mobility was to be the pattern after all his surgeries.

It was on Valentine's Day that Safari first went to school. He was so happy. Even though at that stage he spoke virtually no English the delight was present in his manner and enthusiasm as I dressed him. He stood proudly and surveyed his image. As we watched him in the mirror I wondered what was going through his mind. Was his repaired face and going to school a dream come true? In the mirror he appeared to be caressing his clothes. Was he simply recognising they were new, or was there, as it seemed to me, a deeper sense of what the clothes represented, the symbol of education? He simply murmured a satisfied, 'Mmm.'

I reflected on the occasions when I had sent each of my four children off to school for the first time. Now, many years later and in my sixties I was being mother to another dear child and experiencing again the anxiety of that first day's experience of school. However, Safari was different; he wanted to go to school – he was keen for the experience.

Since Safari came into our lives we have learnt so much about African children's enthusiasm for schooling. In contrast to many of our own children they see it as a privilege as they learn from a very early age that education is the key to escaping poverty. On reflection, Safari's keenness was probably in large part due to this attitude. Safari's mother, Ngayau, was herself illiterate. Her signature was her thumbprint but clearly she recognised very strongly the value of education.

Frank drove Safari to the school at nearby Erina. The children were in the playground just finishing their playlunch. He approached a group of kindergarten-aged children and, crouching down to their height, introduced Safari.

He spoke to me later about the experience. The honesty in the eyes of small children is always something to behold. What lay before him was a complete spectrum of perceptions of this little scarred African boy, reflected in the eyes of innocence. 'In this moment I saw in the eyes of the children honesty, candour, the lack of censorship,' he said, and I could imagine the scene. We adults employ mechanisms with our body language and facial expressions to hide from others our true feelings and opinions. Not so with children.

Frank said, 'The position each child took in the group seemed to mirror exactly the look in their eyes as they stared at this extraordinary-looking boy. Far away to the right were the obviously frightened, their brows furrowed with disbelief; then the whole gamut of emotions until close up a couple of unfrightened, curious five-year-olds.' Safari stood his ground and didn't attempt to hide behind Frank, although he was probably curious and frightened by the attention of these similar-sized but different-looking contemporaries. 'At the head of the queue immediately in front of us stood a little girl whose welcoming ambience indicated she had nothing but acceptance and empathy. Indeed, her expression was like that of a long-lost friend. Her name was Isabella Stratford.'

Frank encouraged the less fearful to shake Safari's hand and then said, 'Isabella, would you like to take Safari's hand and show him to the classroom?' Isabella touchingly reached out her hand to this little dark hand and, taking it in hers, led Safari to the classroom. Frank said that he felt then and still feels now that he had been privileged to see this moment of true unconditional love and acceptance of one human being towards another.

By March, Safari and Kilonzo had settled into our way of life very well. Kilonzo had found his interest in farming on the mountain and Safari had recovered well from his major surgery in January and was enjoying the Australian way of life.

He loved the TV, which was a great source of amusement for him. Even though he couldn't understand the dialogue, he enjoyed the children's programs and would regularly break into peals of laughter. There was strangely no sign of homesickness. He had complete faith in us and somehow understood that we had his best interests at heart. We came to realise he really lived in the moment, wherever he was; he was an intrinsically happy boy. Later in the year when I asked him if he wanted to go home, he said he would like to go back just to see his family and come back to Australia. He really loved our country and all we had here.

After two months in Australia his English was taking off amazingly. His affection for our neighbours Kate and Stuart Rabe across the road was becoming evident.

Safari hung around Stuart as he worked about the house. Always asking questions, questions and more questions. Stuart was very pleased to provide the answers. He was digging deep holes for the posts of a retaining wall when Safari sidled up. 'What you doin' Stuart?' he enquired. Then, pointing to the deep holes, he said quizzically, 'Toilet?' He was referring to the pit toilets back home, which they resembled.

Stuart laughed and said, 'No, Safari, they are holes for the posts of a wall I'm building.'

It was about lunchtime and Kate was on the verandah barbecuing some sausages. Safari, who had probably smelt the cooking aroma from across the road, had conveniently arrived to inspect Stuart's work. Would he like to stay for lunch? Well, naturally.

As Stuart cleaned up for lunch and sat down on the deck, Safari mischievously walked over to a terracotta duck, lifted it up with his good right arm and said, 'Stuart, we cook chicken?' Safari entertained and was entertained for the rest of the afternoon before Stuart carefully saw him across the road home.

Our birthdays were coming up. Mine was on 11 March and Frank's two days later. It was turning out to be a rather frantic year and we felt we needed a break before Safari's next surgery on 19 March, where it was planned to release the web in his elbow and untangle the fingers on his left hand.

My daughter Kate suggested that she and her family take care of Safari and Kilonzo while we took some time out. Safari and Kilonzo were always happy to be with Kate, John and the girls. They loved the company, the youth and the music. There was always more happening at their place than with Mumma and Pappa.

So Mumma and Pappa decided to take up Kate's kind offer. We spent a wonderful week at the Cecil Guesthouse at Katoomba in the Blue Mountains to the west of Sydney, relaxing and recharging our batteries, and making some new friends who, coincidentally, were to play their own part in Safari's story in due course.

When we returned to Gosford, revitalised after our week's break, we dropped over to Kate's to pick up our charges. Kate recounted some funny experiences that had occurred during our absence. The first night, Safari with a houseful of teenage girls was quite coy and anxious about being seen in the shower by the girls. 'Quick, Kate, girls coming,' he said, pointing to the open bathroom door. The next day, however, with not a thought about modesty, he flung his clothes off and was skinny-dipping in the pool as if he never knew that clothes existed.

The bathroom seemed to have a fascination for him. A day or two later Kate noticed he was spending an inordinate amount of time there. When she pushed at the door she was met by, 'Go away, Kate!'

'What are you doing, Safari?' she enquired quizzically. One look revealed him with one leg up on the bath and a shaver in his hand.

'I'm shaving my legs.' He was imitating what he had seen the teenage girls doing. And his toenails were painted red.

Well and truly refreshed by our short time away, we prepared for another operation. Scheduled was a procedure to untangle his fingers from the mess that the fire's after-effects had cruelly inflicted. It was the operation that Safari was keenly looking forward to – I guess because his gammy hand was always there in front of him and although he had found ways to do things single-handed, a useable left hand was his fervent wish. The hand operation had great importance for Safari, even though he was well aware of the pain that would follow. I had a real sense that with his hand 'fixed' as he would say, there was hope of his life being normal. He would talk about the things he would do: 'Do up the belt on my pants with two hands', 'Eat with a knife and fork' and 'Catch a ball'. All these things had great significance for him. It was so important for him to have the two hands working.

In that operation to untangle Safari's hand, skin needed to be taken from another part of his body to cover the entire back of his hand. The preferred donor site was somewhere where his hand could be buried for some weeks to allow the skin to take.

In April, a week or so before the hand operation was scheduled we went to Dr Pennington's rooms so that he could explore suitable sites. Initially the upper thigh looked like it might be a good place; however, Safari was unable to reach down this far. As Safari lay on the examination couch we watched his face as Dr Pennington explained that because of his webbed elbow he had insufficient extension of his left arm, so after the operation his hand would be positioned inside his abdomen for a period, rather than his thigh. Dr Pennington would cut a pocket for the hand to slide inside and five little slits for his fingers to re-emerge. Rather than be horrified by this talk of putting his hand inside his tummy Safari asked questions including, 'Will I hop like a kangaroo?'

Frank commented that he was amazed Safari had taken the whole explanation of such a bizarre procedure completely in his stride, almost as if he had a prior knowledge of what he was submitting himself to.

In order to prepare for this event, where for a few weeks he would have an immobilised left arm, I started thinking about what special clothes he would need. Elasticised pyjamas caused a problem at the waist, the area near the surgical pocket. The solution was long ankle-length kaftan-style T-shirts that could slip over his body, allowing the left arm to rest unrestricted. Safari chose his favourite colours and I set about making four such T-shirts for his stay in hospital.

Kilonzo had made friends with the local footy boys and was happy with his work and the world. Frank brought him back from the mountain on Friday afternoon, a couple of days before the hand operation. On Sunday he could come down to the hospital with us and sign the necessary consent forms. Along the way from the mountain discussion turned to the subject of the family and how they saw Kilonzo's role in Australia. Frank said to Kilonzo that his brother John must be very grateful to Kilonzo for leaving Kenya and his family to accompany his son. Kilonzo's reply was surprising but an insight into life in a developing country. Kilonzo said that, no, his brother would see that Kilonzo had an obligation to him because Kilonzo in coming to Australia had the opportunity to work and make money to bring back home. It was a logic that was different to our way of thinking, yet completely understandable in context.

On Saturday night Kilonzo was invited by his footy mates to go to a party – one where, we learnt later, there was lots to drink and a tabletop stripper. We weren't concerned as we realised that socialising with fellows his own age would be good for him and he knew we had to leave Sunday afternoon to drive down to Sydney to admit Safari for surgery the next morning.

However, when Sunday morning arrived we discovered that Kilonzo hadn't come home. The morning wore on and still no Kilonzo. We became concerned and by mid-afternoon the hospital was ringing, asking about when we planned to arrive. Not wanting to indicate that we had lost Kilonzo, I said nonchalantly, 'Oh, we'll be leaving pretty soon now.' But where was Big K? We were very annoyed with him. The hospital phoned us several times more and I was unhappy about having to fob them off. Many hours had elapsed. Had there been an accident? Was he lost? Where could he possibly be? Anxiety was building in both of us. He had to be present to sign the medical papers next morning. We felt the hospital's generosity in treating Safari was so wonderful that it seemed very ungrateful not to have him there by the appointed time.

Stuart across the road rang one of the footy boys but he wasn't with them. However, he said tangentially that we might find him at one of the local pubs. 'And where would be a good place to start?' asked Stuart. 'Try the Settler's Arms in Gosford,' came the reply.

Frank drove to 'the Arms' and struck the jackpot. Kilonzo was sitting by himself at a high bar stool. Completely relaxed, blissfully unaware of all the fuss and as drunk as a lord. He was very happy to see Frank, who declined a drink and let it be known to Big K that he was out of line. 'You can get drunk any other time but not the days we have to go to hospital,' he reprimanded.

Kilonzo obligingly came home, and was berated all the way. At home he collapsed on the lounge. Fifteen minutes later Frank nudged him. We had to leave. Such was Kilonzo's slumber that for a few seconds Frank thought he was dead. He was totally and absolutely paralytic. We poured him into the car and in the back seat he slumped over using Safari as a headrest.

We felt we couldn't let him be seen in his drunken state, so we unloaded him at Frank's girls' unit in Strathfield and continued down Parramatta Road to the hospital. Half a mile down the road a voice came from the rear seat, 'Uncle very drunk. Oh, very bad.'

At the hospital we explained to the staff that Uncle Kilonzo would be available the next morning, without spilling the beans on the state he was in. Not wanting to attract further questions, we exited stage left and beat a path back to Strathfield. Kilonzo had not budged an inch on the lounge where we had left him so we closed the door on him until the next morning.

As was to be our routine we got up in the half-dark at 5.30 in the morning. I did what I could with my make-up through bleary eyes. We ate a brief breakfast while Kilonzo sheepishly stood in the background. Into the car we joined the parade of early-morning drivers on that dodgem track called Parramatta Road.

At RPA we met the film crew in the foyer, unbelievably

bright-eyed and bushy-tailed. In a quiet corner of the Alfred Café we submitted to Tony Clunes as he politely hid his radio microphones on us. Then up to Safari's ward where he usually pretended to be asleep. We were never quite sure if this was his way of ignoring his fate that day or if he was just a sleepy head. We would play the game 'wake up Safari' to break his slumber. Awake, he would ask me, holding his open hand over his mouth and nose, 'Mask, mask, Mumma?' 'Yes, Safari' I would resignedly reply. And then, folding his arms across his chest, 'Mumma, cuddle,' his eyes searching mine. It was a difficult time for both Safari and me, however we were always truthful with him.

A nurse had bought him a pair of elastic-sided brown boots and that morning they were still on his feet, he just didn't want to remove them. Much to the amusement of the film crew we decided to leave them on until just outside the theatre. The wardsman came, tossed a sheet over Safari, boots and all, and wheeled him off. As we entered the theatre anteroom I said as I lifted the sheet, 'Dr Pennington, we have a problem. Safari refuses to take his new boots off.' He laughed and said, 'Oh, don't worry, we're not working down there today.'

As we did for all operations, after seeing Safari safely into theatre, we went to the Alfred Café and waited.

Frank again took Kilonzo to task for getting lost on the weekend and being irresponsible. He was contrite and quieter than usual.

While we sat there he pulled from his shirt pocket a letter for us to read. He had received it from his wife Mary in Nairobi on the previous Friday.

The handwriting was lovely – almost like old copperplate – and the language sweet. She referred throughout the letter to Kilonzo as 'My beloved husband'. A small photo of Mary and daughters Janet and Lucy was enclosed to remind Kilonzo and to introduce the family to us. Frank and I saw that Kilonzo had a wonderful family; an attractive and articulate wife and two lovely daughters. Our anger evaporated and we listened as he proudly described his family.

Mary's family is not from Kasaala but from the town of Kibwezi, 60 kilometres to the south. Kibwezi, while not at all large, is a stop on the Mombasa to Nairobi railway line and has the structure of a town, with a bank, petrol station and railhead. Possibly because it is that little bit bigger than a village like Kasaala it offers educational opportunities, the result of which we were seeing in Mary's writing. Kilonzo told us that at the time he and Mary married his family were somewhat concerned that she wasn't a local girl.

Mary was obviously a resourceful person, looking after her two girls while working as a security guard at the coffee plantation in Nairobi. We enjoyed talking with Kilonzo about Mary and the girls and Kilonzo was very proud of his daughters and wife. The girls, he said, were doing very well at school and he was very pleased. We got the strong feeling that Kilonzo's fervent wish was for his girls to achieve in life through a good education. No doubt education held the key to prosperity.

Frank's phone rang. It was Danny to say that Safari was in recovery, although the operation had not gone as planned. We caught the lift down to the theatre complex and to the recovery ward, where we were met by the bizarre and rather amusing sight of a pair of boots emerging from underneath the white hospital sheets. For a moment we were oblivious to his usual post-operative suffering. Safari looked like an old cowboy who had gone down fighting with his boots on.

The operation to release Safari's webbed left elbow had been more complicated than anticipated; in all Safari's exploratory procedures the doctors never quite knew what to expect. This time so much work was needed on the elbow that the hand was left for another day. It was to be a disappointment for Safari. In recovery and from under the veil of morphine he looked at his bandaged left hand, holding a drip in place and slowly whispered, 'Hand fixed?'

'No,' we had to tell him gently, 'it will be done another day.' He uttered not a word but sadly turned his head. It was a difficult time for him and heart-wrenching for us to see his disappointment.

Safari needed a second stage of surgery to complete the elbow release because in that first operation to straighten his elbow a graft of skin still attached to his stomach bridged across from his flank to his elbow joint to supply it with blood. Effectively his arm would be joined to his flank for several weeks to allow the graft to take. Although uncomfortable, he recovered quickly and once more was eager to get on with life.

Jessica, my granddaughter recognised this and felt that he needed a little fun in his life. She was a student at Kincumber High School and approached her principal to ask if the students could organise an evening of fun, a disco for Safari. He thought it a great idea so Jessica and her schoolfriends went away and put together a fantastic night for the star of the Coast, complete with music, a DJ and disco lights.

At this time Safari was in hospital having his elbow-to-flank bridging graft released. He was tiring of hospital. The smell of the hospital was onerous. He definitely needed a break. Dr Pennington saw that he would benefit from some fun and thought that provided he was careful with his arm he should be able to go to the disco. Danny from Channel Nine thought it was a great idea, too. He was eager to show his *RPA* audience the lighter side of his star and how much he had been taken to heart by the people of the Central Coast.

It was a balmy autumn evening just prior to Easter and the sports auditorium was packed with teenagers. We arrived with Safari dressed in very fashionable long shorts and trendy T-shirt courtesy of Kate's surf shop. The kids got right down to some serious disco dancing with Chris and Tony capturing the action from the floor, Chris's camera light adding some drama to the scene. Danny with his ever-present notebook in the crook of his arm looked on approvingly. You could see his mind working – 'This is great television!' Which it certainly was.

The time came for presentations and it was a case of 'Safari, come on down!' or rather *up* on stage where under the full glare of the auditorium lights he was confronted by a sea of teenage faces. A sea of waving, smiling faces, all calling, 'Safari – Safari – Safari!' A little but not too much overawed, he stepped forward and Sandra Cook, the school captain, assisted by two other students, Mark Smith and Marilyn Keller, presented him with a cellophane-wrapped chocolate Easter bunny and then announced that they had raised $1000 to help Safari's future.

On the way home from this magical evening, Frank asked Safari, through Kilonzo, what his thoughts were when he looked down on the sea of faces calling his name. The reply was simple and modest: 'I think I'm getting well known.'

Frank was driving Kilonzo to Mangrove Mountain one day. Kilonzo seemed to enjoy these times alone with Frank to talk 'men's talk'.

Kilonzo spoke about what life in the village was like and Frank was always keen to learn every detail of this place, so far away and so different an existence to our own. It was a hard life, Kilonzo said. They were very dependent on the weather and the rains. Illness was frequent and the health clinic very basic and the village medical officer was frustrated by the lack of even simple facilities. The subject turned to snakes and the attendant danger in commonplace activities, like going to the toilet at night. Frank said, 'Don't the people have torches?'

'Not very many, they are too expensive,' Kilonzo replied. Frank told me of this dangerous situation and we resolved to ask the people of the Central Coast if they could help with solar-powered lights. Our friend Julie Hartigan at the *Central Coast Express Advocate* jumped to the task and helped publicise the need to 'Light up Safari's village.' The generosity of the public was wonderful and it meant we were able to provide some solar-powered lighting – not quite enough to literally light up the whole village, but a help.

Another day Kilonzo spoke of family sizes in Kenya. The harsh realities of life meant that infant mortality was always a dreaded shadow over poor families. Malaria, for instance, was a frequent killer of the young. Parents found security in their old age when they were able to be looked after by their children. Rural families needed children to help them work their farms. These reasons and probably others led parents to have many children. However, large families increased the burdens of life, including the cost of education. As a result many children left school after only four years of primary education. With education not free, few families in Kasaala could afford to send their children on to secondary school. Kilonzo said that in Kasaala while there were 800-odd children in the primary school, the parents of only seven students could afford to send their children on to Kasaala secondary school.

As Frank picked his way along the badly corrugated mountain road Kilonzo remarked, 'Frank, you would be good driving in Kenya, many of the roads are like this.' Then he fell silent for some minutes. Then, 'You know, Frank, there is something I must tell you. When I first arrived I said to Mumma and you that Safari has four brothers and sisters. Well, he has six.'

Frank was taken aback by the change in numbers and said, 'Well, why did you say he had four?'

'Because I thought that if I said too many you would think badly of us, everyone thinks that Africans are interested too much in sex.'

Frank said, 'I'm surprised, Kilonzo, that you would think that because Mumma and I have never thought that. You know I have four brothers. But I'm glad you told me.'

That led to the subject of contraception and Kilonzo showed that he was a progressive man not entirely bound by the thinking of others and open to persuasion regarding Western methods of birth control. And not just for women but for men as well. He saw that to have too many children could be a burden – not only financially but bodily for a woman. They discussed the various methods of birth control, the pros and cons and the financial burden of the contraceptive pill. When Frank told him of men Kilonzo knew who had had vasectomies and were no less men as a result, he was very interested.

Frank and I spoke with Kilonzo a little later. We said that he should wait till he returned to Kenya and talk the idea over with Mary. I said that the operation is far safer and simpler for a man. Either way, if they wanted to go down that road we would pay for the operation in Kenya.

Since that time we haven't been approached to take the matter further but the offer still stands. Kilonzo's sister-in-law Ruth, his brother Rashid's wife, has had some fertility treatment that we have been happy to provide. But to no avail. As yet they are still childless.

When they arrived home Frank came inside and said with a smile on his face, 'Kilonzo has something to tell you, Jan.' Kilonzo bringing up the rear was smirking and had his hand over his mouth.

'Oh no, no, Mumma,' he protested and refused to say more, walking up the stairs to his room.

'Come on Kilonzo, tell Mumma what you just told me,' Frank cajoled. Then Frank told me that in Safari's family there were seven children rather than the five that we had been led to believe. We laughed and spoke with Kilonzo about the children. He realised that we were not judgmental people and I think it helped him open up about other things that he otherwise may have expected white people to take a dim view over.

Kilonzo's admission about the extra children also solved a puzzle for us. Safari had for some time been talking about brothers and sisters and the total came to six, not four. Maybe Kilonzo realised that the cat would be soon out of the bag so he might as well come clean.

Chapter 6

In this period between operations, Safari enjoyed the quiet times at home and the opportunities to get out and about, both locally and further afield.

My daughter Kate and husband John often took Safari to Terrigal for Sunday breakfast. Terrigal is a beach on the Central Coast popular with surfers and holidaymakers. It has a holiday atmosphere and its row of magnificent Norfolk Island pine trees along the beachfront likens it to Sydney's famous Manly Beach.

Kate tells the story of a visit where one of the waitresses overheard Safari say he would like some more bacon. She appeared a few minutes later with a bowl piled high with bacon. Safari, not yet seven just looked at her, smiled and said, 'Oh, thanks schweetie.' We have made a prediction: pretty girls could be his downfall in the future.

A very good friend – Patou Plummer, a Buddhist – asked me if I would address the Soka Gakkai Buddhist Conference at their centre in Homebush Bay adjacent to the Olympic

Stadium. The conference was to be held on Mother's Day and they would like me to speak on the subject of 'How my spirituality influenced my counselling work'.

So on Mother's Day we all set off to Sydney for our first encounter with this group. We were warmly welcomed. The theme of the conference was 'Winning in Life', which seemed most appropriate considering that we were witnessing daily the phenomenon of Safari winning in his own life.

I gave my talk, which was very well received. However, the real centre of interest and attention was our little charge and his story. People recognised quickly that he was somehow different, beyond his years. The audience was multicultural and their interest in Safari's story confirmed that there was something transcultural in his appeal. There were European, Indian, Japanese and Thai Australians and my friend Patou is herself French. The list goes on. From a diversity of backgrounds they were unified by the Buddhist philosophy and we were impressed by the commonality of their humanness.

At the luncheon that followed, the multicultural flavour and hospitality continued with an array of delicious dishes. The convenor, in thanking me for my words, made the comment that all the people involved in Safari's rehabilitation were practising the Buddhist tenet of loving kindness and compassion. Their warmth towards us and especially to Safari was uplifting.

Not long after this, we took our first trip to show Safari the Australian countryside.

Euston is a small New South Wales country town with a population of about 500 on the Murray River. It is in a grape-growing region and the river forms the border between New South Wales and Victoria, irrigating vast areas of farmland as it meanders from its source in the Snowy Mountains. My youngest daughter Elizabeth and family had moved to Euston in 1999 when her husband, Roger, a policeman, had been transferred. I was looking forward to catching up with them and to spending time with their children – my grandchildren – Steven, nine; Hannah, six; and Emma, three.

Safari was interested in meeting all my children who were now 'big'. He knew Frank's girls and his brothers as they all lived in Sydney but he was very curious about the distant family. He was very keen to meet my son David and his three children but unfortunately this never happened. David lived in Rockhampton in Northern Queensland, 1600 kilometres away and we just couldn't fit this visit in, with the heavy hospital schedule. Safari would ask me questions about 'your boy – Mumma'. At times I'm sure he wondered whether David really existed.

Visits to Euston were more do-able. Safari was particularly looking forward to meeting nine-year-old Steven, a change from being surrounded by so many granddaughters; not that Safari had an aversion to girls – quite the opposite! So when we decided to make the trip south he was excited to be setting out on a new adventure.

We packed the car the day before and left early in the morning so as to avoid the kangaroos hopping out in front of the car as night closed in on us at trip's end. Safari was an excellent passenger and never asked the usual child's question of, 'When are we going to be there?'

It was dark when we arrived at Euston and after lots of hugs and kisses we settled down to catch up on news. At this time my two granddaughters stood quietly to one side, carefully eyeing Safari, this little boy who had become so popular, while Steven and Safari kicked a soccer ball as if they were old mates. That night Libby served a beautiful baked dinner with a leg of lamb. Food was very important to Safari and as the year progressed we learnt about the hungry season in the village; the period before the rainy season when all the stored grain from the previous harvest is almost exhausted. Should the rains be late, a severe food crisis results. In these times the people resort to a hardy green leafed plant called *sukuma wiki*, known in the West as collard greens, which helps them through. In Swahili it means 'to push the week'.

We weren't surprised when Safari asked if he could have the abandoned bone to clean up. He tackled it with relish and gusto, eating all the meat and gristle – every piece, until there was nothing but a polished bone remaining. Watching Safari clean up the bone so voraciously brought silence to the table. The wide-eyed children took in the image of his little brown face dominated by such a huge bone. He was oblivious to how he looked; he was totally absorbed in the pleasure of his moment with the bone, and nothing else mattered. Safari had told me that in the hungry times, 'Kenya Mumma, she tell me drink water, drink water, but I eat sand.' I guess sand is better than nothing in the tummy, although I have been told that the practice is risky as diseases can be caught in this way.

The sequel to this story is that some months later we planned a return visit to Euston. However, six-year-old Hannah was not keen at all for us to come. When quizzed, it turned out that the family dog Bella had recently had pups and Hannah was sure that if Safari came he would eat the pups!

The Euston community welcomed Safari with open arms, organising social days for fundraising, inviting Libby and me to a memorable school P & C cocktail party, and offering support to my family in so many ways. I felt very grateful that these wonderful country people had embraced us all so warmly.

Euston Public School is a small school typical of those found in country towns. Set on generous land with broad playing fields and rows of apricot trees, the airconditioned classrooms underscored the fact that at the height of summer this was a hot place to live.

The principal, Mr Paul Clark, suggested that Safari might like to join and meet the children at lunchtime in the playground. Safari enjoyed this visit and fitted in to the schoolyard game of kick-ball with a very natural ease. His skill at kicking the ball was soon recognised and it didn't matter to the other boys that his left arm was contorted and only partially 'repaired'.

The trips to and from Euston showed to Safari the vastness of the country and he was very interested in the variations from the flat monotony of the Hay Plain to the undulations of the land around Gundagai. He was of course interested in the wildlife and was wide-eyed at the sight of kangaroos and emus as we crossed the Hay Plain. Frequently I would look in the rear-vision mirror and Safari would be quietly surveying the passing scenery, taking it all in as yet another lesson in his Australian 'Safari'.

On our journey home from Euston we called in to see old friends of Frank's, Charlotte and Ron Stahl, who have a property of over 600 hectares at Canyonleigh in the Southern Highlands 100 kilometres south of Sydney. The house is about 2 kilometres in from the road, set amongst the Australian bush in a wildlife sanctuary. Safari was enthralled by the sight of so many kangaroos in the one area. Up until then he had only seen the occasional one as we were driving, or the odd unfortunate roadkill victim. The kangaroos grazed in large groups of 30 or possibly 40 and were quite unperturbed by us as we drove by, lazily hopping to one side to let us pass. The way they hopped intrigued Safari.

Ron and Charlotte greeted us warmly. A hot cup of tea was soon on the table and we caught up with each other's news.

Frank grew up with Charlotte's first husband, Russell Forth, a memorable character who tragically died in an ultralight aircraft crash in 1983. Russell, Cliff Coverdale and Frank had all been schoolfriends together at high school. Cliff and Frank went to Enmore Boys' High while Russell went to Homebush Boys' High and the three met and generally played the wag on the 'red rattler' electric train ride home to Epping and Pennant Hills. They shared a great interest in motorcycles and motorcycle racing and all three of them were, in their own ways, adventurous types.

Charlotte and Russell moved to Canyonleigh in true pioneer style and set about making a farm from virtually nothing. Charlotte has the hardworking grit of the Scots and over a number of years while they were living in the original farmhouse, she made with her own hands the large open-plan stone house they now live in.

That night when Safari was eventually tucked into bed he was all smiles and kept murmuring, 'Oh nice, mmm, warm, Mumma.' This was his first experience of an electric blanket. The next day when we returned home and I was putting Safari to bed, he kept fumbling and looking for the electric blanket switch. He was crestfallen and disappointed when told I didn't have an electric blanket. 'Oh, Mumma, no good!' he exclaimed. So that started the special treatment of our heating a cotton blanket in the clothes dryer and calling out, 'Have you cleaned your teeth and are you ready?' One of us would run upstairs, wrap the blanket around him and tuck him into bed. 'Very good, Mumma, sweet dreams,' he would sigh.

Autumn had arrived and Safari and Kilonzo really felt the change in the season. They asked for warmer clothing and blankets and they watched the trees change colour and eventually drop their leaves. Safari and I would collect different leaves and gaze at their beauty and colour. It was a nice free relaxing time to just *be*.

During the week when his pals were at school we were to see him at play alone and observe his behaviour in his own company. A child of contradictions. That same gregarious, outgoing, 'life of the party' character was very comfortable in his own company; inventive, imaginative and resourceful, he spent many hours at play. One prized toy was a 25-year-old rusty three-wheeler bike with a metal carry box under the seat. Frank's girls had played on it as children. He was fascinated with it and even now, two and a half years later, when I spoke to him on the phone at school in Nairobi recently, his first question was, 'Hey, Mumma, have you still got my bike?'

'Yes, Safari,' I replied.

'Oh, very good, Mumma.'

As he played on that bike one day we stood watching unobserved through the screen front door. Up and down the bricked path, around the front concrete drive, in and back, making those engine sounds that all children seem to make. Making air brake sounds as he did with a toy truck on that first day, he was in boy heaven.

Complicated backing manoeuvres completed that phase of play. Next, into the garage and out with some empty cardboard boxes and some string to make a road train. A little later, into the house for some scissors and sticky tape to cut some card into mudflaps complete with zigzag serrations at the bottom. Then, having hitched it all together, he would pedal the ensemble to the front apron and circle the concrete pad time and time again. Safari was having a ball, playing for hours on end, completely innovative, completely confident and able to manage, even with that useless left hand; never asking for or needing help.

During these playmate-free times, Kerry Garside next door showed Safari how to make helicopters from cardboard and sticky tape. Safari was enthused and, as Frank said later, soon the house looked like a scene from *Apocalypse Now*.

We also took advantage of the break to catch up on some household garden chores, which had gradually become neglected. Safari showed an eagerness to help in many ways; carrying the shopping in from the car and helping with weeding. Possessing only one functional hand wasn't a deterrent.

Observing Pappa cooking seemed quite acceptable to Kilonzo and Safari. In Australia it was obviously the norm but not so in Kenya where cooking, cleaning, washing and housework in general was definitely work for women. Evidently men not working in the fields farming would spend their time 'relaxing' and gossiping. I think Pappa in the kitchen impressed Kilonzo as he told me just prior to his return home that he was going to do the cooking and give Mary a break.

One day I suggested to Safari that he might like to set the table in the evening, and that could be his job. He liked doing this, and would very carefully place the knives and forks in their correct positions. He took this task very seriously.

Frank was in the habit of calling Safari 'The Kenyan Kid' in a jovial way. It was, 'Come on, kid, let's do this or that.' On one particular occasion I said to Safari as he completed his table-setting task, 'Safari, go and call Pappa for dinner.' Safari replied, 'Mumma, I'll go and get the kid.'

Kilonzo soon learnt how to operate the washing machine. After he had unceremoniously dumped his clothes in the laundry, I said, 'Kilonzo, in this house we all do a bit. Now this is how you use the washing machine.' Kilonzo was wonderful with the washing machine. 'Its so easy, Mumma,' he would say. Yes, I thought, a lot easier than scrubbing with Blue Omo beside a waterhole.

Sitting around at home one evening we were all enjoying a quiet drink. Kilonzo spoke of what he might do with his new money when he got home. Kilonzo was in a real quandary. He said he would like to open a small grocery store with a house attached in Nairobi. Nairobi would be good, he said, as there were many customers and the schools for Lucy and Janet were better in the capital. But as the youngest son he had an obligation to live next to his father and mother and look after his ageing parents in the village.

Frank suggested that he open a grocery store in the village. That was the problem. 'Yes, I would like that but I cannot make a profit from my own people,' Kilonzo explained. Frank could partly see his point but said that if he was fair in his prices, how could it be bad? 'No, someone will put a curse on my shop and no-one will come,' Kilonzo explained. Ready to be surprised by things outside our orbit we listened quietly as he continued. 'And maybe I'll be bitten by a snake, Mumma,' he blurted out. This shook me to the bone. I have an unusual revulsion to reptiles; even the sight of small lizards around the house sends shivers up and down my spine.

When Frank encouraged him to push aside such fears, Kilonzo said, 'It wouldn't happen to you, Pappa, because you don't believe.'

I have always thought that there are things in this world that we rather no-nonsense Westerners don't understand; our arrogance blinds our thinking to mysticism and related matters. Here was Kilonzo – and quite likely most of his village – who embraced a duality of belief. A duality that was inclusive. He saw no contradiction in retaining the belief system of that metaphysical world of traditional African spirituality while embracing 'foreign' Western Christianity. Somehow I understood and shared his duality.

We in the West tend to be dismissive of the belief systems of many indigenous peoples of the world. Quite a bit of blame can be placed at the feet of some well-intentioned and other not so well-intentioned missionaries and colonial administrations. Blinded by their belief that their way is exclusively 'right' and 'superior', they never seek to understand the other person's, as they see it, 'primitive' beliefs. And, in an allied area, we believe there is a world of difference between guidance and paternalism.

Attempts throughout history at cultural domination have left a sorry trail of grief and deprivation across the world. Australia is no exception and the history of European interaction with Indigenous Australians is too often a story of destruction and dispossession.

Frank and I let it be known to Kilonzo that he could express his views of traditional African culture and belief as well as his Christian values to us and he would find an interested and non-dismissive ear.

At the end of May it was time for Safari to resume the ritual of the Sunday afternoon drive to Camperdown for hospital admission and yet another Monday operation.

Monday morning found us dodging the 6 am city-bound traffic in the wintery pre-dawn, in order to be on time for our meeting with Danny, Chris and Tony in the mostly deserted Alfred Café that did duty as a TV make-up room. We knew the trio very well by now. Regardless of the hour or the circumstances they were always good-humoured and ready to joke, always explaining their plans carefully. There was no tension between them – they were a very good team. Their year's worth of footage of Safari was to be condensed to just over two hours of television, yet within that time constraint they were able to convey in a very sensitive and skilful way the essence of Safari. We know this by the letters, cards and emails we have received from around the world. Through the team's skills, millions of people have been touched, many indelibly.

Wired for sound we all went up to the Plastics Ward E10 South and to Safari sitting on his bed in a blue, oversized, open-backed seersucker hospital gown. Frank and I explained to him what was going to happen that day. It was the day of days – the operation where his hand was to be fixed. Or rather the first step in a series of operations to restore function to his hand.

Dr Chris Borton came in. He was concerned at the terror his anaesthetic mask was imposing on his 'little mate' and planned a new oral pre-med that day. I told Safari that Chris was going to give him something to relax him and make him sleepy. He responded with, 'I know, like a lolly-pop.' He was referring to the medication's sweet taste.

Seven-thirty came and a wardsman wheeled Safari, sitting bolt upright on his huge bed, out of the ward along the corridor and into the lift down to the theatre complex.

There we were waiting with Safari in the area locally referred to as 'the airlock' in the heart of the John Lowenthal Theatre Block. The *RPA* film crew had also entered the airlock to don the sterile gowns that all the inhabitants of the inner sanctum wear. In the airlock reception area, patients were assembled to have their details double-checked before being wheeled off on their trolleys to their allocated theatres. Every patient was surely nervous as they awaited their fate. Then suddenly Safari sitting there on his trolley started singing gently, 'Twinkle, twinkle, little star' He had been taught this song, along with other rhymes and songs, by Maggie Smith, a nurse on Ward E10 South to whom Safari had given the nickname, 'Twinkles'. I saw an older woman amongst the waiting patients smile a mother's smile, then the others smiled gently and we could see that he had with that simple unknowing act settled down half a dozen nervous people.

Safari's turn came, we gowned up and followed him to Theatre 4's anteroom. He was still in a singing mood and the theatre staff were treated to a repeat performance of Maggie's song, this time also to a future TV audience as Chris captured the moment with his huge camera and Tony with his boom microphone. Danny stood to one side smiling, his notes clutched in the crook of his arm.

Safari was still holding his own. But when those double

doors of the theatre proper opened for his date with destiny, he stiffened and his hand, warm and starting to sweat with anxiety, clutched mine. In the theatre I took him in my arms and lifted him off the hospital trolley and his body stiffened with panic. The staff wheeled the trolley out of the equipment-crowded theatre and I stood there beside the operating table, the tiny stainless steel platform that was not much wider than an ironing board, a terrified Safari in my arms. A chair was brought in for me to sit on and Chris prepared his equipment. My mind went back to a previous operation and the cry from under the mask, 'Mumma, Mumma, please help me,' as I left the room. My heart had pounded then as it did now. I cuddled him and comforted him as best I could until his small body went limp and the terror stopped. As was the case many times before and after, a nurse helped me, shaken, from the theatre.

We walked back to the Alfred Café with Kilonzo. Cups of coffee and raisin toast all round restored us. This was the sixth time to theatre, each one traumatic. Kilonzo was concerned about all the operations and as the family member and the person authorising all this pain it weighed on him. He said that before he came he had little idea of what would be involved and although he had complete faith in the doctors and the hospital it all worried him. Frank assured him that everything would be all right, not just that day but every day. Frank said that, strangely, on no occasion waiting there for Danny to call did he ever have the slightest concern that there would be any danger to Safari's life. Kilonzo, however, remained concerned.

That day we brought a tape recorder so that Kilonzo

could make a message tape to send to Mary in Nairobi. The café was noisy so we went out to the car and Kilonzo made his tape. Mary didn't have access to a telephone and there certainly weren't any phones in Kasaala; he had a lot to say and a tape was the most personal approach. Halfway through his message the rain started and we laughed as we waited for the tattoo pounding on the roof to stop.

Kilonzo spoke to Mary in Swahili and we didn't ask him what he said. We knew it would be personal. He then made another tape to send to the family in the village along with a clipping from our local paper. Julie Hartigan had written an article telling her readers of Safari's progress and accompanied it with a nice photo of Safari playing on the slippery dip in a local park. With Mumma and Pappa looking on approvingly, of course. Kilonzo knew that a friend of Mary's would have a tape player and someone in the village would surely loan the family one.

After speaking to Mary and the family, albeit in an unusual and one-sided fashion, Kilonzo felt more peaceful and the concern he had expressed earlier dissipated.

Frank's mobile rang. It was Danny summoning us to the recovery ward. The operation to untangle Safari's left hand had gone well.

Down in recovery Safari's hand, now embedded in his tummy, was covered and not visible. Frank spoke first to reassure him. 'Look, Safari, Mumma's here,' he said. As Frank uttered the word 'Mumma', Safari, still semiconscious, jerked his head in recognition. I wondered if in that split second a part of him thought his mother in Kenya was with him. He was quiet, sedated with the morphine, which was being administered by the infusion pump. He was much more comfortable than he had been on previous occasions where the postoperative morphine had not yet taken effect. The oxygen mask was in place for a few minutes until he realised its presence and demanded it be removed. His condition stabilised, we accompanied him to the ward upstairs and to the once again loving and welcoming nurses.

Dr John Kippen, the hospital plastic surgery registrar, dropped by to check on Safari and tell us the details of the morning's operation. John is a warm, compassionate South African and the first medico in his farming family. His family must be proud to have their son well on his way to becoming an eminent surgeon. His mentor Dr Pennington is an excellent role model. John had been present and part of the medical team at every one of Safari's operations.

He explained – or as Frank remarked later, gave an excellent tutorial – about the hand and the morning's operation. The ash from the fire was still trapped in Safari's scars and was useful in guiding the surgeons along the correct path for the scalpel to open up Safari's hand. The tendons of the fingers, which John explained were the ropes which the muscles use to create movement, were in Safari's case quite shortened. This shortening was the result of years of immobility. Indeed, the finger muscles were wasted through disuse and a lot of painful physiotherapy would be needed to stretch the tendons, strengthen the muscles and restore function to his hand.

In order to keep the fingers straight while the skin from the tummy graft became the back of his new hand, they had drilled stiff wires though the length of Safari's finger bones. As John explained how these 'K' wires were inserted I shuddered at the thought of his little fingers being drilled for wires. I knew that a lot of pain was in store for this boy who fervently wanted a new hand.

John then spoke of his experiences in rural Africa. He said that as a young man he had travelled and walked all over Africa and had experienced first-hand the plight of poor rural Africans. 'They are such vulnerable people,' he said. He empathised with the plight of the African poor. He is a kind-hearted surgeon, full of humanity.

We left Safari to rest. He would need all the resources he could muster for the difficult road ahead.

The next day we arrived and Rachael Casemento, one of Safari's loving nurses, told us that he was in a lot of pain with his hand. Too much pain to be able to wear my special T-shirts yet. He was eating well but temporarily immobile. She lifted the sheets and we saw the bizarre sight of Safari's wrist disappearing into his tummy and the ends of five little fingers popping out further along. The skin of his tummy was the new back of his hand. Poking out of the skin were several stiff wires that looked so painful and out of place in a human body. Dr Pennington came by on his rounds, inspected his work and was pleased with the outcome. Physiotherapy would start in a few weeks, just as soon as the graft had taken and the hand released.

Our visit to Safari that day complete, we decided that since we were in Sydney we might drop in to the exhibition halls at Darling Harbour to catch up on a Body, Mind and Spirit Festival. We didn't know at the time but our decision was to have an enormously beneficial outcome when we were to go to Kenya to take Safari and Kilonzo home.

The festival consists of myriad stalls and counters of companies and people promoting their wares. One stall caught our attention. It was called 'Safari Tea from Kenya' and as Kenya and Safari fans we were drawn to the stand as if by a magnet. There we met a man who introduced himself as Raju Shah. Raju was a Kenyan of Indian descent. He had grown up in Kenya but had recently emigrated with his family to Australia. Raju was in the tea import business and his brand of tea was Safari Tea.

We said that his tea bore the same name as a little boy from Kenya we were looking after. He spoke to us of the plight of poor rural people in Kenya. Raju was very friendly and insisted that we take several packets of his tea. On each packet were his contact details; he lived at West Pennant Hills. This struck us as a coincidence as, of course, it was the next-door suburb to Pennant Hills where Frank and I had grown up.

After wandering around the festival for a few hours we left and made our way home to Gosford, completely unaware that our chance meeting with Raju Shah was to supply the answer to a need that we had not as yet even contemplated.

Two days later Safari was recovering but still bed-bound. He was well enough, however, to give nurse Rachael a kiss as she dropped by to check on him and give us an update.

Safari stayed in hospital for six weeks. The nurses were wonderful and took him to see the movie *The Lion King* several times at the local theatre at Broadway. He went dressed in style in his kaftan T-shirts to see his favourite film.

Once home again, Safari quickly started to recuperate. Knowing operations were still to come left him with a little tension. Fortunately he was always able to live 'in the moment' and, for a short while, future operations were forgotten.

With his hand at last free it was time for Safari to set out on a rigorous program of physiotherapy. We were to take him to the Hand Clinic three times a week where therapists Rebecca Crowley and Vanessa Grant tirelessly worked to restore movement and use to a hand that had been immobile for three years. We didn't know initially but very soon learnt what an extremely painful process this was.

My daughter Kate took Safari for those early sessions and would pack him a little lunch. Travelling down the F3 Freeway he soon memorised the names of the bridges and landmarks. Going down he would be chatty, talking about his brothers and sisters and asking endless questions, at the same time devouring his meal. Kate used to enjoy this time with Safari, especially because she knew the trip home would be so different. She tried to make the trip down a fun time.

Once at the clinic he would try to be brave but eventually the excruciating pain would take over and tears would stream down his face. At this point Kate too would start to feel sick just watching his suffering. Once out of the clinic she would often need to give him a Panadol and he would sleep all the way home from exhaustion. On one occasion, walking into the clinic and enjoying some jokes with him, Kate said, 'I don't think we'll go in there today.' To which Safari replied, 'No, Kate, we have to go – come on.' Painful as it was, he was determined to have a good hand.

It was easy to see Safari was catching on to our Western ways. One evening after a session at the Hand Clinic he awoke from his slumber just as we were approaching Gosford. Refreshed, he yawned and said nonchalantly, 'Pappa, let's eat out tonight?'

Interspersed with operations, these trips to the Hand Clinic were to continue right up until two days before Safari went home.

Chapter 7

It was a Friday afternoon in June and Safari was having a minor procedure done on his hand when I received the phone call from Frank's father telling me that his 89-year-old wife Alma had been admitted to Hornsby Hospital. Frank that day had worked and organised the street stall at Gosford, which we were holding to help raise money for Safari, his family and village. I quickly phoned Frank to tell him to meet me at Hornsby Hospital where we could both see his mum.

We were aware that Alma was becoming very frail; we could see her life slowly ebbing away. She needed total care, which Ted and the family had given unstintingly. When I received that phone call from Ted I was not surprised.

When the doctors at Hornsby Hospital advised that Alma's time with us would probably be only a week, I suggested to Ted and to Frank and his brothers that she come to my home. Alma was peaceful with this arrangement, as were the family. There I could care for her and we could all, as a family, surround her in that short remaining time with the love she freely gave to all of us. Ted and Alma were able to spend important hours together. Those few days were very precious to us as the family gathered around her.

Alma's love and thoughtfulness touched many lives over the years. Her understanding and kindness reached out to people in a very special way. She was a small woman with soft light-brown wavy hair. I could listen endlessly to her speak in her soft lilting Welsh accent. She loved babies and small children; in fact Alma loved everyone. People would come to her with their problems and would go away knowing they had been understood and not judged. Her gentle manner had a way of reaching inside the person and touching that part which felt the pain.

Alma and Ted had five sons: Richard, Frank, Brian, Howard and Peter. Their first child had been a girl, Gwyneth, who was killed in an accident at fifteen months. Alma had spoken to me at length about this tragic period in her life. She talked about 'the emptiness in my arms', and the helplessness she felt at the time. When I met Safari's mother Ngayau and looked into her face I connected these two beautiful people with the anguish and heartbreak they had each felt over their children, the private grief they carried in the inner corridors of their lives.

Alma had taken a great interest in Safari, always wanting to know the latest information on his progress. Safari responded to her in a beautiful reverent way, the way he responded to all the elderly he met. In the week before her death when we were rushing between RPA and Hornsby hospitals Alma said, 'Don't neglect the little fellow for me.' A very typical response from Alma. In turn, Safari was very tender and gentle with her, showing care that seemed beyond the age of a seven-year-old child. He seemed to be in tune with her frailty.

A few days later Alma died in the small hours of the morning.

In the days that followed we felt very much for Ted's acute sorrow and loss and reflected on our own memories and experiences. Frank felt that my knowing and sharing of his mother's life over so many years had been a great comfort to him and the family.

The reality of life meant that we were soon back in the routine of Safari's treatment. Alma certainly would have wanted this.

An appointment was made for Safari to have his teeth checked by the hospital's dentist Dr Luise Martin. So on a Tuesday we embarked on yet another trip from Gosford to the hospital and its dental clinic in the centre of Sydney, normally a one and a half-hour trip. However, on this particular day there was an accident on the freeway and we spent three hours getting there. Safari was as always a good passenger, and we thought we would reward him with a cool drink before proceeding to see Dr Martin. Frank suggested an orange drink. Safari, however, had other ideas. He wanted a bright red drink that would have left his teeth a pink colour. Even after we explained that his teeth would be inappropriately coloured for Dr Martin he was resolute – he wanted that red drink and that was that. We were in a bind so we drank the orange juice just to show him that it was the orange juice or nothing. Safari stood determinedly on the footpath, his arms crossed defiantly across his chest. Nothing by way of cajoling would budge him.

During the trip down we had phoned Dr Martin to let her know we were running late but were not about to let this little performer be a source of further delay. Frank scooped Safari up. Safari's arms and legs flayed in all directions and he cried out with gusto. I was concerned that passers-by might think we were abducting this little African boy – his appearance bore no resemblance to us at all. Fortunately whilst we attracted lots of glances no-one challenged us as we walked into the foyer of the Queen Elizabeth II Building. The last straw came when waiting for the lift and still restrained by Frank; Safari grabbed the handrail with his very strong right hand and wouldn't let it go. We were astonished – could this be our little Safari? It couldn't be. Frank gave him a firm smack on the bottom but to absolutely no avail. His level of defiance remained, or if anything increased. So as the lift door opened Frank scooped him up once more and we went up to the dental clinic and into Dr Martin's rooms and her surprised presence.

Surrounded by the authority that pervades a medical clinic we thought Safari would capitulate and become cooperative. But no, our boy was unusual in many ways and that day's performance was certainly no exception.

Dr Martin was very patient and suggested we make an appointment for another day. After three hours' travelling to get to this appointment and the prospect of the return journey plus our plans for a Safari-free week at Katoomba the next week we declined Dr Martin's invitation. I guess we were just not in the mood for compromise.

Dr Martin was successful after some persuading, which included a promise of a sit in her 'special chair' to get Safari's cooperation. The whole drama was not the result of a fear of the dentist. He had no idea of what a dentist was or did. It was simply a test of wills and an example of his exceptional resolve. A resolve which at other times and places had been such a positive feature of his make-up.

The Monday, Wednesday and Friday physiotherapy routine allowed lay days in between, days when Safari could go shopping and relax at Kate's. Of course, Safari always added his own unique perspective on these occasions.

When Safari was at Kate's he tagged along wherever she and the girls went. Quite regularly this meant the vast expanse of Erina Fair Shopping Mall with windows and fashion to lure. Passing by the fashion windows Kate glanced at the large poster in a Just Jeans shop of a handsome tanned youth stripped from the waist up proclaiming himself. Safari caught Kate's casual interest, nudged her arm, winked and startled her with, 'You wish, Kate,' a twinkle in his eye. He was a six-year-old going on not 17 but more like 27.

In the same cheeky vein, some time later at home, Kate was thumbing through a copy of *Cosmopolitan* magazine with Safari leaning over the arm of the lounge scanning the pages with her. When the page opened to a Calvin Klein underwear ad and a shiny black African man clad only in skimpy briefs, he pointed, 'Kilonzo, Kilonzo,' and with a giggle, 'You wish, Kate.' We have concluded that in the village there are few secrets.

Safari was happy to do chores like the others. It was winter and one such chore involved fetching wood for the fire. This was done with great enthusiasm. After which came the plea, 'Pocket money, Kate, yes?'

On Safari's passport his birthday is listed as 20 August 1994 although since getting to know the circumstances of Kasaala better we think that it's probably his approximate date of birth. Still, as fate would have it, his seventh birthday fell on a Monday and an operation day for Safari.

The previous Saturday, 18 August, looked an appropriate day for a birthday party and Kate and John's house at Kincumber the ideal venue. They were very happy to host the party and Danny certainly wanted to cover the joyous occasion for *RPA* which was going to air later in the month. When we spoke to Danny and his team, Chris Roles said that he wanted to go not just as a cameraman but also to join in the celebrations but unfortunately he had other commitments for that day. They had all three become like family. Kilonzo's twenty-seventh birthday was on 17 August so we settled on a combined party on 4 August.

Danny arranged for a clown, and some children's music CDs from Nine's music library to entertain the kids. My friends and Kate organised the food and drinks and bunting. We arranged a huge birthday cake; Safari's first ever birthday party. Kilonzo told us that the family finances of most people in Kasaala don't reach to celebrating birthdays in the way we do in Australia.

Kate's girls Kellie, Jessica and Ellen decorated the house and the cake. We invited the children from Safari's school at Erina. He had made firm friends there, even though he had only been to school for a few days in total. Other guests too numerous to list came along on that warm Saturday, not spring officially but spring was in the air.

Safari was showered with gifts. The clown arrived and Safari was scared; he had never seen a clown before, certainly not a real-life one. It was the clown's enormous boots I think that frightened him most and he just wouldn't go anywhere near him.

The kids played as kids everywhere play. Sarah Hurley, Safari's nurse and friend from the children's ward came and with Danny's music and her infectious enthusiasm led all the kids in several rounds of 'do the hokey-pokey'.

Cliff and Lesley Coverdale came to the party too, and Lesley had the honour of making an entrance with the birthday cake illuminated by sparklers, while Danny and the crew recorded the joy of this day for their TV audience.

On the Thursday following the birthday party the first episode for the year of the *RPA* program went to air. We all sat down, eager to revisit the arrival of our Kenyan family at Sydney airport. Prior to this, Danny warned us that the surgical scenes would become very graphic in subsequent weeks and that he wouldn't let a six-year-old of his watch. We discussed this with Safari but he insisted that he wanted to see it all, everything. As it turned out, it was beneficial for him to see that the dreaded mask was only in place until he went to sleep. He watched all the procedures intently, which led to a greater understanding of his pain.

Television was soon to show us its power. *RPA* displayed to the general public Safari's courage and personality, and the impact he was to have was unprecedented. After the program had been to air for a few weeks, we were frequently approached by people in the street who commented on the courage and personality of our little boy, many expressing how he had struck a chord with some part of their own lives.

By the end of the week after the party we were preparing for Safari's next visit to hospital. We were aware the coming operation was a big one with yet another skin graft. This operation too was going to be very painful.

During the year Dr Chris Borton did his best to ease Safari's pain and anxiety. To help distract him in the theatre annex the day of Safari's seventh birthday and his tenth operation Chris brought in a Lego dinosaur that his family had bought for Safari to assemble and so be distracted. We arrived a little late in the theatre annex. Safari looked up and with his brow wrinkled up in that cute Safari way he queried, 'Where you been?' He was engaged in a little diversion therapy. Safari was there perched on his trolley bed trying to assemble the dinosaur. Even Chris was having difficulty with it so Pappa had to step in and show them how it was done. 'I think I'll stick to anaesthetics,' Chris said resignedly.

A few minutes later Dr Pennington emerged from inside the theatre to get the show on the road. Into theatre number 4 went Safari and the dinosaur plus us. Frank said, 'Before anything else takes place we must sing Happy Birthday to

Safari!' Surely the theatre walls had never resonated before with that song. This little celebration completed, one of the medical staff let Safari see himself in the viewfinder of his video camera. Safari broke out in a rendition of 'Coco Coco Jambo' before his image. Although he was feeling nervous, his great sense of humour showed through.

Now came the tricky part and our real reason for being in that daunting room: easing Safari into oblivion. It went surprisingly smoothly that time. Chris suggested that I cuddle Safari in a chair next to the operating table that he hated so. Then with the dreaded facepiece removed from its hose the anaesthetic gas wafted gently over his face. I turned my head to one side lest I be overcome. In a few short seconds his little body was limp.

Three and a half hours later Safari emerged in recovery a very sad and sorry sight. The procedure had been very successful and a graft swung around from under his shoulder blade had corrected the scar tissue that webbed his upper arm to his chest. Skin had also been taken from his buttock. After a period when the recovery nurses established that his condition had stabilised we all went up in the lift to Ward E10 South and to the loving care of the ward staff. This time he was unable to lie down with comfort. I decided to stay overnight in the room with him. He was just too weak to press the nurse call button and he needed the comfort of knowing that I was nearby.

I sat with him all day after that morning's operation. The nurses were concerned for him to pass urine; he had also had a blood transfusion. Around midnight he wanted to go to the toilet and as usual stubbornly refused to use the bottle. I called the nurses and they helped Safari to shuffle, drip trailing behind him, to his toilet. Glancing back at the bed I could see the sheets extensively bloodstained. A nurse quickly remade the bed.

Standing in front of the toilet bowl Safari looked quite small and thin, his waist tiny. As I looked at him I thought, that body has taken such a pounding. His voice interrupted my thoughts. 'Mumma, whatya lookin' at?' I fumbled for words and said, 'Oh, you've grown so big since you've come to Australia.' The toll of many operations was telling. As I looked at his back as he stood in front of the toilet I could see the blood oozing from his shoulder dressings. It was clear that the pressure of his body lying on the bed was causing so much discomfort for him and I could understand his whimpering. From my point of view, it all looked too painful and too much. But in just a few days he would be feeling so much better and it would be all worthwhile.

Chris Borton had a real soft spot for Safari. One of the nurses in recovery told us that at the end of his pharmacy request for that day Chris had penned the words, 'for my little mate'. This latest surgery seemed to take a lot out of Safari; he was struggling to keep some of his earlier resilience.

Yet he was soon home and playing as if nothing had happened. On one occasion he had been playing with the kids in the street all day on a skateboard, dragging it one-handed up the steep driveway at Kerry and Jeff's next door then taking turns at careering down the slope sitting on it. Luckily Safari never discovered that a more exhilarating ride and an adrenalin rush could be had by standing up and possibly breaking a bone or two.

Dozens of rides later at the end of a fun-filled day came bathtime. I usually showered Safari although Kilonzo was a very good help in that way as well; he and Safari would quite often have a shower together.

As I undressed him for the shower I was shocked by the look of his buttocks. Skin had been shaved from his buttocks to repair other areas of his small frame as the doctors searched everywhere for donor sites. Sitting down on that skateboard all day had worn away the partially healed site and his buttocks were red raw just like a piece of meat. 'Oh,' I gasped, 'Safari, that must hurt?'

He simply replied, 'Yep,' and said no more, continuing with his good hand to rinse his hair and face. He had absolutely no interest in capturing the sympathy vote which, if he had realised it, was there to be well and truly had. I would have gone to the ends of the earth to relieve his suffering; all he had to do was ask. I am sure he was not putting on a macho tough-guy mannerism, he simply is more interested in the joy of life than the pain of the moment. He's just naturally a resilient little guy.

By the end of August after *RPA* had been to air for three weeks we had a phone call from a lady who introduced herself as Maxi Bell and said that she and her husband Richard and son Sam lived between Oberon and Goulburn in the New South Wales Southern Highlands. Safari's courage and personality had touched them. Maxi said that she recognised that all the medical procedures must be having their toll on both Safari and ourselves. Could she offer us all a farm holiday at their 2000-hectare sheep station, Paling Yards, near Taralga, 200 kilometres to the south-west of Sydney? Richard and Maxi run 20 000 head of fine Merino sheep on the lush hills above the Abercrombie River.

During the year a number of people offered us holidays or short breaks at their places. We thought these were wonderful gestures on their part and we would have loved to accept these invitations; however, time was at a premium.

Because we could see a timely break coming up we were able to accept Maxi's offer and incorporate a visit to the farm with another trip to Euston. Our new friends had admired the inner strength of Safari, his courage and his inimitable personality. They had watched every episode of the TV program and felt they wanted to do 'something' for him.

These two wonderful hardworking people have big hearts and made us so welcome. Their home is large and rambling, surrounded by a beautiful rose garden, shady trees and other old-fashioned plants set against a background of rolling green hills with Merino sheep grazing contentedly. We thought that the experience of a sheep station would be very interesting for Safari, giving him a view of Australian rural life; so different from the rural life he had experienced in Kenya. Maxi and Richard's son Sam was a handsome young man in his mid-twenties and had the patience to answer the myriad questions Safari asked. He developed an instant bond with Sam, who had a farm motorbike and horse and sulky. Sam loved pillioning Safari and the dog on the motorbike around the paddocks. Spurred by Safari's enthusiasm he saddled up the quiet old horse George and the two of them trotted around the driveway. Safari wore his newly acquired leather Akubra hat complete with 'Crocodile Dundee'-style crocodile teeth on the band, a gift from Maxi. In the yard Sam had a pet joey kangaroo named Ollie that he had rescued from its mother's pouch after she had been killed on the road. Safari loved feeding Ollie with an infant's bottle of milk. He was totally fascinated and absorbed with that joey.

In the shearing shed he watched, fascinated, as the sheep were being shorn, his big brown eyes growing larger. 'Very good, Mumma,' he mused. He was interested in all that he saw and I have no doubt that in the future he would love to spend more time there. It was a magical place for a young boy.

When we first arrived Maxi showed us to a little cottage where we were to stay. Safari's bed was beautifully made up with a white pillowcase embroidered with his name in bright colours. When we left for Africa this was carefully packed in his bag.

At lunch Maxi's friend Kitty joined us. Lunch was fresh bread rolls, salad and fresh fruit in a setting looking over the undulating countryside. Bread rolls never tasted better. Kitty and her patchwork quilting friends had worked hard and raised $1000 for the 'Safari Appeal', and presented to me that day a very special yellow bag filled with goodies. I carried it all the way to Kenya with my bits and pieces inside.

Around the dining room table that evening we were unwinding with a couple of gin and tonics, entertained by Safari's tales from back home. How many of the tales were true we will never know but he has the makings of a great after-dinner entertainer – and he knows it! We laughed over Safari's stories many times, especially when he accompanied them with actions. Most information from Safari started with, 'You know—.' The tale he told that night was no different. 'You know, my Kenya Mumma, she makes beer. Can't make beer, if police come big trouble. One day police come. We get the beer and run run run hide it in the bushes and come out.' Safari's head was held high, eyes to the ceiling, and he whistled as he walked around the room to imitate the family's nonchalant actions. Continuing after noticing that he had our complete attention, he said, 'And you know, my Mum she gets the money, digs a hole in the dirt under the bed, puts down some paper, puts the money in and covers it over with dirt.' Having successfully coaxed us all into laughter there was no stopping him for the rest of the evening. Reflecting now, we think there is a theatrical streak in our Saf. Oh, what a character, one just had to love this child.

After our lively evening around the dinner table listening to Safari's yarns we fell exhausted into our beds. We realised that the tensions from the previous months were beginning to leave us and we were starting to feel very relaxed. Or was it the gin and the floorshow? The countryside around the homestead was very conducive to stress-free days and Sam was such a good friend to Safari that we felt able to ease off our duties for a while. The real pain of the previous months had been endured by Safari but we couldn't help feeling stressed by all that he was going through.

The friendship between Maxi and Safari very quickly turned into genuine love. Her concern for him never wanes and she frequently rings and wants the latest news on 'her boy'. I'm quite certain that if he needed her she would be on the next plane to Kenya.

We were very grateful for Maxi and Richard's thoughtfulness. Our visit had a wonderful calming effect on us, and we left feeling renewed in body, mind and spirit.

On the road again we continued south to Euston and Libby's family.

The trip was punctuated by several comfort stops. For morning tea we stopped at the Hume Highway McDonald's takeaway at Yass. By this time, *RPA* had been on for several weeks and Safari was recognised almost everywhere we went. We talked at length to him and explained how interested people had been to watch his surgery each week and how because of his courage they felt they wanted to speak to him. He also came to understand that because he was on the show so much, people felt they knew him. His understanding of these explanations and aspects of his surgery constantly amazed us, as did his acceptance of people's attention. At these times he would just nod his head, acknowledging he understood.

Photographs were another issue. He really disliked photos, or 'potos' as he called them, being taken. This we are sure was not because of any feelings of disfigurement but requests were so frequent he simply became tired of having to pose for photos. It became necessary for us all to have a talk about this and he agreed to only four people taking his photo. They were 'Pappa', Danny from Nine, Julie Hartigan's photographer from the *Central Coast Express Advocate* and my daughter Kate.

At Yass a woman approached us and asked whether she could take Safari's photo. We suggested that she ask Safari. She replied that she had done this and that he had said 'no'. We explained that we had an agreement and that we had to stick with it. Safari later reluctantly agreed to a 'poto'.

As we sat there in the fast-food restaurant, which in some ways represented Western prosperity and affluence, we discussed his return home just three months away and the hungry season or seasons he would have to endure in the future. I thought about the abundance of food we have here, what we discard, and felt I could never enjoy a meal again knowing at that time he could be hungry. Frank agreed. Somewhere in the back of my mind I knew that we had to do something about this situation; what that would be was not yet clear.

Our arrival at Euston sparked a warm reception as usual from the family. They were all keen to be brought up to date on Safari's progress and he was keen to play with the kids.

During the evening Frank and I organised a game with the children playing with playdough, making funny shapes and the like. The children, including Safari, loved the simple game of rolling out the dough and using their imagination to make shapes and take turns in trying to guess what the shapes represented. There was, however, another unspoken agenda. We felt that playing this way would give his hand some much-needed physiotherapy. We would alternate hands: sometimes their right hands would be on their heads, other times behind their backs and sometimes they could use both hands and so on. The innocence of youth meant that they fell for the ruse and never caught on to the real motive. I know that if I told Safari now what the real purpose of the playdough game was he would grin and say, 'Ah Mumma, you're trickin' me.'

Suddenly the lights went out, a blackout. Now Safari was right in his element; it was just like home with candles and stories about evenings in the village where candlelight is the norm.

Later with the kids asleep, Frank and I talked about our experiences with Safari so far that year and how the whole Safari episode had been for us so totally unexpected, exciting, heartbreaking but most of all rewarding. Just watching this little fellow go ahead in leaps and bounds was so gratifying. But it was a year that had also engulfed us in a way we could not have in our wildest dreams anticipated. In those few 'mad' moments we had taken up the baton by volunteering to look after this Kenyan duo, absolutely ignorant of where it would take us and certainly not expecting such an unusual child. A little like giving birth, I thought, you never know what you're getting but at least with the opportunity to mould the infant. No moulding here, just a ready-made extraordinary child. We agreed that we felt like observers witnessing a beautiful unfolding story, a story that we knew was far from over and a story in which we knew we were to play an ongoing role.

The next day all the kids were up bright and early. Safari

insisted that they all play soccer in the yard. Frank watched and told me, 'You know, Safari has got really good foot control of that soccer ball.'

We could imagine him at home in Kasaala alone, all the other children at school. Amusing himself kicking a ball made from sheets of scrap paper wound one upon the other to make a ball. Then endlessly kicking, kicking all day long, unconsciously honing his skills. He was an intrinsically active, intrinsically happy child and certainly would not have been hanging around his mother's legs bewailing his fate. We were later told his mother each day would reinforce and encourage him to 'be happy'. We can understand that, unable to do anything about his physical condition, this encouragement and her love and care was as much as she could offer him.

Once again at Euston we experienced first-hand the legendary Australian country hospitality as people from all over the district attended a luncheon to support the Safari Appeal. The table was overloaded with goodies that friends and neighbours had supplied; cakes and slices, cream puffs, seemingly endless quantities of food. Safari had as always a wonderful time, playing with the kids on a homemade billy cart. At one point even Mumma allowed herself to be pushed around the yard by the kids.

Safari relished the opportunity to go boating at Euston and especially enjoyed a turn at the helm of the outboard which he promptly revved up to full throttle. We mused later how he would explain this particular adventure to his friends and family back home. On that first day in the park at Rushcutters Bay he had queried Kilonzo about the sailing boats, the concept of which was so strange he had no word for them in his village language.

On a subsequent boating excursion at Euston, during the docking manoeuvre the mooring line slipped and the boat, with Safari in it, was unexpectedly cast adrift. What followed was an image we will never forget. Alone in the aluminium runabout complete with yellow life jacket and bandaged left arm, Safari was laughing his head off as the current started drawing the boat toward midstream and in the direction of Adelaide. Our friend and boat-owner Ray thought quickly and dived in to reach the boat in a couple of strokes. Safari's hilarity progressed to a higher level as he shouted to Ray, 'You left your glasses on, Ray!'

These visits to Euston, although short, were important to me. I always enjoyed seeing the grandchildren, who were growing rapidly. Lying on the trampoline with them we would play a game of who could sight the evening's first star. After the children went to bed Libby – and Roger, if he wasn't on duty in the police station next door – would chat with us and catch up on the latest news.

All too soon it was time to start the journey home.

At West Wyalong we stopped to have lunch with Mim Staniforth, Maxi's mother. We had met earlier at our wonderfully relaxing farm stay at Taralga, and Mim had insisted we stop for lunch with her on the way back from Euston.

In the totality of the Safari story we continue to have the great pleasure of meeting a large number of very interesting and warm-hearted people. People whom, if it were not for our involvement with Safari, we would never have met.

Mim was such a person. She was well known in West Wyalong and had a women's boutique, so our visit entailed her closing her shop for a while to entertain us.

The table was beautifully set. Mim was making sure Safari had a choice of various cold meats and even cooked him a delicious lamb chop. He sat at the end of the table eating, carefully dabbing his mouth with a serviette. My mind went to how eating might be undertaken in his village and I marvelled at how he coped with any situation. Frank thought he was 'socially and culturally ambidextrous'.

Mim had a lovely inviting home surrounded by a beautiful garden with a swimming pool. Safari quickly spotted the swings and said, encouraging her to join him in play, 'Come on Mim, push!' Eventually they were both swinging high into the air. What a great sight! Mim in her sixties, her curly grey hair blowing in the breeze laughing and a seven-year-old beside her calling, 'Go faster, Mim, faster!' Here was another person into whose heart Safari had crept.

A lovely lunch and play over we reluctantly said goodbye to Mim and headed off home many hundreds of kilometres away.

Chapter 8

The visits to the Hand Clinic for sessions of physiotherapy seemed endless. Therapists Vanessa and Rebecca were making progress with mobilising Safari's left hand and the surgeons were making surgical adjustments to help restore function.

The television images of this little boy, week after week, battling along on his journey to normality struck a chord with many viewers. Through the skill of the *RPA* TV team they saw what we were continually witnessing: this child's desire and determination to be like everyone else drove him forward. He was anxious to reach the next level of treatment, anxious to see the results of the surgeons' work, submitting himself to pain and suffering in order to achieve a goal. Such maturity from such a small child to think this way we thought was most unusual and impressed us greatly.

Safari received well over 1000 letters and cards from well-wishers all over Australia and New Zealand and later, when the TV series was shown in the UK, Argentina and Africa, cards and emails from there.

Betty McCleary, an old friend from my Lifeline days, helped out in many ways. She sewed for our street stalls and was innovative with her fundraising ideas, involving many of her friends and family. In these ways we have been able to raise money for the Safari Appeal.

Seeing us snowed under with a growing amount of correspondence from Safari's well-wishers, Betty took on the task of answering it. However, what started out as personal letters of thanks had to revert through sheer volume of mail to a pro-forma letter of thanks. We have kept all of the letters for Safari to read when he is older, when he will more fully appreciate the depth and breadth of feeling within Australia for him.

Many people allude in their letters to problems they have in their own lives and thank Safari for being an inspiration to them and helping them overcome adversity. One poignant note reads:

Dear Brave Little Safari,

I watched you last night on the RPA TV Show, I was so touched by you, you truly are the bravest little boy I've ever seen.

You may not fully understand now what an inspiration you are to me. I really think you have about 100 angels watching over you. You have the most beautiful heart. I'm praying for you and I believe you really are a gift given to this world to show others the value of true beauty and love, which shines from you.

You have the courage of a lion, so thank you beautiful Boy, for being such an inspiration and encouragement to me, I will never forget you.

Touched forever,

SARN.

One day we all went to Manly on the ferry. At that stage Safari had never been on a boat before and was enthralled with the experience. He was even invited by the captain into the wheelhouse. At Manly we walked around the Corso and along the streets, which seem to always have a holiday feel. While we were on the wharf for lunch a woman came up to us and said that she and her family watched Safari on *RPA* every week. She said that her daughter aged 23 had cystic fibrosis and that seeing Safari's courage, tenacity and joy for life had strengthened her daughter and had very importantly taught her to live in the moment. Safari certainly lives in the moment and lives each moment fully.

I'm reminded of the wise words, 'Yesterday is history, tomorrow is a mystery, today is a gift; that is why it is called the present.' Frank says that although he accepts the wisdom of these words he struggles to practise them. However, he frequently remembers Safari's advice: 'Calm down, Pappa.' It seems Safari's formula for life is 'the joy of life far exceeds the pain of the moment'.

We were told how a victim of the Bali bombing, badly burned, drew strength from focusing on Safari's courage and strength as they went through their ordeal. We will talk to Safari about these things when he is older and has the maturity to fully recognise his impact on other people's lives.

Maggie Smith, the nurse who taught Safari the song 'Twinkle, Twinkle, Little Star' says the following about him:

> *Meeting Safari for the first time is a shock. Even nursing where you see shocking things doesn't prepare you for such severe burns scars.*
>
> *My first encounter with Safari was after his first operation. He was a little Kenyan boy in a big hospital bed; hooked up to different pumps and drains and covered in bandages.*
>
> *As a nurse of adults the thought of looking after a child was initially daunting, especially a child who spoke little English, had been through a major operation and needed a lot of care. The shock of seeing Safari and the fear of nursing him wore off the day after the operation and he was awake enough to smile.*
>
> *Safari has a smile and a sparkle in his eyes, that defy all that he has been through. Even when language was a problem he could have a joke with staff. He has the most contagious giggle ever.*
>
> *On his first trip to hospital I spent time looking after his dressings, teaching him some songs and watching him adapt to his surroundings.*
>
> *That's what you learn about this kid. He is very smart and very adaptable. In the months I've known Safari his use of English and his adaptation to Western culture has been amazing. There is a depth, a brightness in his eyes that far*

exceeds his years. Maybe from all he's been through his life.

For all the songs, bits of English, and Australian sayings that we may have taught Safari, he has taught us so much more. Kenyan words and songs, how to dance like a maniac with only one arm free and most importantly what a love of life is all about.

I don't know what has been more fascinating – watching the physical transformation through surgery or the social change as he gets very used to Australia, with its electricity, computers, schools, big hospitals and more bananas than one little Kenyan fellow can ever eat.

An hour with Safari will leave anyone with a smile and a story to tell. Like the time Safari went for a walk with a nurse. He saw an electrical transformer box and asked what it was. The language barrier was too much of a problem, so he squatted down, quickly cleared a patch of dirt, gave the nurse a stick and asked her to show him – Kenyan village style map drawing out the front of RPA.

His first time in hospital when he discovered the light switches and what they're for, then proceeded to run around and turn them all on and off. Momentarily turning the ward into a disco until we could catch him.

Or for me the time he borrowed my Walkman and the batteries ran out. Safari decided to fix it for me. I've yet to find all the pieces!

That's not to say Safari is always a little angel. Nursing Safari can at times take a lot of patience, like when he's decided to be uncooperative, or just getting up to cheeky six-year-old antics when the ward is busy. It can take a lot of time, talking and a bit of bribery to get him to toe the line.

There are times he can be more stubborn or set in his ways than many 80-year-olds. But if it wasn't for that stubbornness or sheer determination he may not have been here today. He certainly wouldn't be the boy we love. After knowing Safari for only a short while you forget about his scars and all his operations. You just see a beautiful, strong, smart kid. It's a surprise when you're out walking with him and people ask in a hushed tone, 'What happened to him?'

Safari has given me some of my most treasured moments as a nurse. Seeing the look on his face, after his first operation, when he turned his neck for the first time. To see that sheer amazement and joy. Being in the middle of a busy, tiring day and having a cheeky-faced kid come up and ask you if you want a hug, or just the times when you share a joke and get him laughing. You realise most of the people around are laughing too, just from hearing him.

I have had the opportunity to be part of something wonderful; something that will hopefully make some lives a whole lot better. It will be a sad day when Safari goes home. We will miss him.

I can only imagine the joy his mother will feel when she sees him again and all the changes that have happened. What she will never have a chance to see is how much her son has affected and changed the lives of the people he's met here.

Just as recently as March 2004 we were revisiting Katoomba to get away and write this book. In a chemist's shop in the main street of Katoomba as I approached the counter, the assistant looked quizzically at me and said,

'You're Safari's mother, aren't you?'

'Yes,' I replied, not too surprised. I must have one of those faces people remember. Intrigued by what had impressed her, I asked, 'What was it about Safari that for you was memorable?'

She replied, 'I watched every episode of Safari on *RPA* and his presence in the room seemed to make the room light up.'

During the year that Safari was with us Frank continued occasionally to help the Gosford Hospital as a voluntary bus driver, taking nursing home residents on lunch outings around the coastal picnic spots and clubs for which the Central Coast is well known.

Woy Woy Nursing Home cares for people with dementia and Frank often drove the residents – some capable of walking, some in wheelchairs – to the local club for lunch.

Safari happened to be at home when Frank was driving one day so he tagged along in the specially modified Toyota Coaster minibus that was equipped with lifting gear and able to carry wheelchairs. Safari was as pleased as punch to be up front with Frank and 'king of the road' in this 'big bus that Pappa was driving'.

At the nursing home the elderly ladies instantly took a shine to him and Frank could see their maternal instincts bursting forth beyond the veil of memory loss that is dementia. It was obvious that maternal feelings are deep in the psyche of women. In fact, when Frank returned several weeks later without Safari one particularly maternal woman remembered him and asked where he was.

On that first visit they headed off to Woy Woy Bowling Club for lunch. Getting a dozen oldies off and on the bus takes a little time. And Safari helped the nurse and Frank. As the residents were lowered to the ground with the bus's hydraulic lift, Safari watched Frank and then asked if he could help. He had great fun.

With the people safely in their wheelchairs on the ground he immediately started pushing them into the club; no mean feat for a small child with only one functioning hand. He was determined and the image that Frank recalls is of a small contorted stump of a hand pushing against the end of a wheelchair handle, unable to grasp it but determined to be useful in some way.

In the club Safari entertained them all with his African hip-wriggling – another unforgettable sight.

One day Frank was driving residents from Woy Woy Nursing Home to a picnic at the Woy Woy waterfront where pelicans come to be hand-fed.

At the picnic area his mobile phone rang and above the blustering wind and squawking birds he was very surprised to hear a voice at the other end say, 'My name is Steven Loyatum and I am the Kenyan High Commissioner to Australia in Canberra.' After they exchanged pleasantries he said, 'I believe you are looking after a little Kenyan boy called Safari Kimanzi.'

'Yes,' Frank replied, 'that is true.'

His Excellency went on, 'I believe I have the young man's member of parliament with me in my office. He is in

Australia and he would like to meet Safari and yourselves.' Still rather dumbfound and having difficulty hearing over the wind squalls, Frank made an appointment for the Hon. Samuel Kiminza, Safari's MP, to come to dinner with our recent friend Alfred Mutua the next Friday.

That evening we discovered how the High Commissioner had learnt of us. Alfred Mutua and his wife Josephine are Kenyans and during 2001 lived in Sydney where Alfred, a journalist, worked for SBS TV and Josephine was studying pharmacy. Alfred and Josephine came into our orbit, or rather Safari's orbit, in the same way that a whole circle of Africans and Kenyans did; they just appeared and we have benefited so much from the friendships.

After the surprise call from Canberra Alfred rang that evening to say that Samuel Kiminza was in Australia as part of an advance party for the Commonwealth Heads of Government Meeting in Queensland. Alfred had frequent contact with Mr Loyatum and had mentioned Safari and us to him.

The following Friday we welcomed our guests. We had a very pleasant evening with a traditional Australian roast leg of lamb. Kilonzo was very pleased to talk to someone from home. Samuel was a delightful man in his early forties who lives with his wife and two sons in Nairobi. He had been born and bred in Kasaala and during the evening Kilonzo and Samuel concluded that they were related in a distant way. Samuel spoke about his life and said that he had been given the opportunity to have an education and a chance in life through the generosity of a Canadian couple. Our journalist friend Alfred was also pleased to meet Samuel and to talk about the affairs of Kenyan politics. Samuel was very impressed with Safari and proud, we are sure, of this little ambassador from his own village that he met for the first time half a world away from home.

We immediately warmed to Samuel Kiminza and in turn he was very appreciative of the help given by Australians to his constituent. As he left, Samuel embraced Frank and addressed him as 'brother'.

We believe that we were meant to meet Samuel Kiminza. We have kept in touch and have a firm friendship. With a change of government in 2002, Samuel is no longer in politics but operates a freight forwarding business in Nairobi. However, he remains a prominent member of the community and as such has been able to speak on our behalf and to help us greatly in our dealings with Kenyan government authorities.

Around this time we had a phone call one day from a woman with a South African accent who introduced herself as Sherrie Cohen. Sherrie told us that she had a great affinity with Africans, especially the dispossessed. She explained that she worked at North Sydney for the large computer company Cisco Systems and the staff had been enthralled by Safari and wanted to make a web page for people globally to learn of Safari's story. Sherrie's suggestion came as a complete surprise – we had been so busy with the day-to-day events that we hadn't thought about utilising technology in this way.

A week or so later Frank and Safari went down to Cisco's North Sydney office and met the staff members keen on the website project. They discussed how the website might look and what it might contain. Frank's enthusiasm grew as he saw the potential for spreading Safari's wonderful story. Then we rang our friend Clare Collins, another of our many, many friends that Safari has brought us. She is the communications manager at RPA's corporate fundraising arm, The RPA Foundation. Clare, a dynamic lady and a very good friend to boot, asked if she could help with the site's content and liaise with Cisco. Frank had already suggested that the site contain a section publicising the wonderful contribution RPA Hospital was making to Safari's future through their unbounded medical generosity.

The team went ahead and in early December the site, safariappeal.com, was launched. However, through lack of time the site has been somewhat neglected. We are correcting this.

Safari started to ask me questions about how I would manage things when we were in Kasaala. We were planning to spend some months in the village when the time came for Safari to return. One day Frank and I were chatting with him about life in the village and the matter of washing the clothes came up as he helped me load the washing machine. 'Mumma, when we are in the village, how you wash your clothes, no washing machine?'

I thought and replied, 'Well, I suppose I'll have to do the washing the way your Kenya Mumma does, by the stream.' Safari broke out into infectious laughter; he was so amused by the idea of me washing alongside his mother, I guess – crouched down, scrubbing away.

His comment was a reminder that he knew the end of

his time in Australia was approaching. In another conversation in those last days in Australia I asked Safari what he would like to do with his life. In his usual sing-song way of speaking he replied, 'You know,' – everything started that way with Safari – 'it would be good if I could visit Kasaala, see Kenya Mumma and Pappa, my sisters, my brothers, come back to Australia, go to school, visit my family again. Over and over.'

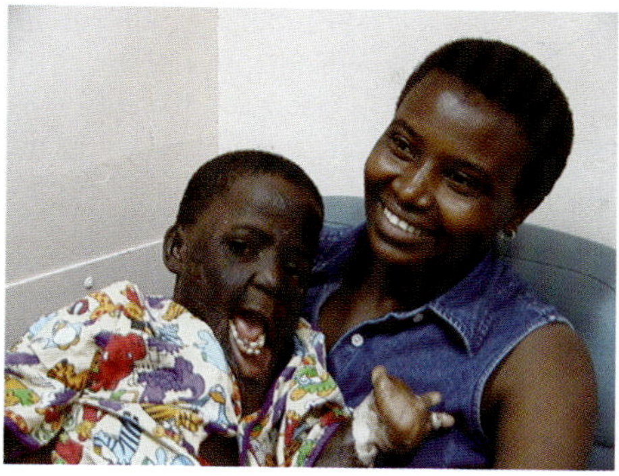

Zipporah Wanjohi with Safari a few days after their arrival in Australia. Zipporah's nursing training proved invaluable in those early days leading up to and following Safari's first operation.
Photo: Danny Milosavljevic

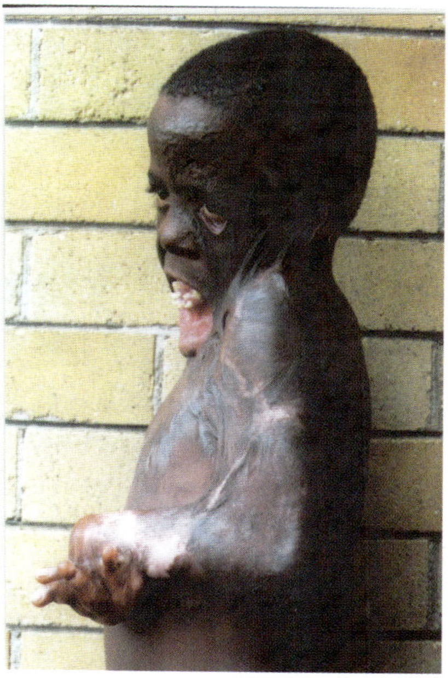

Safari, the day before his first operation.

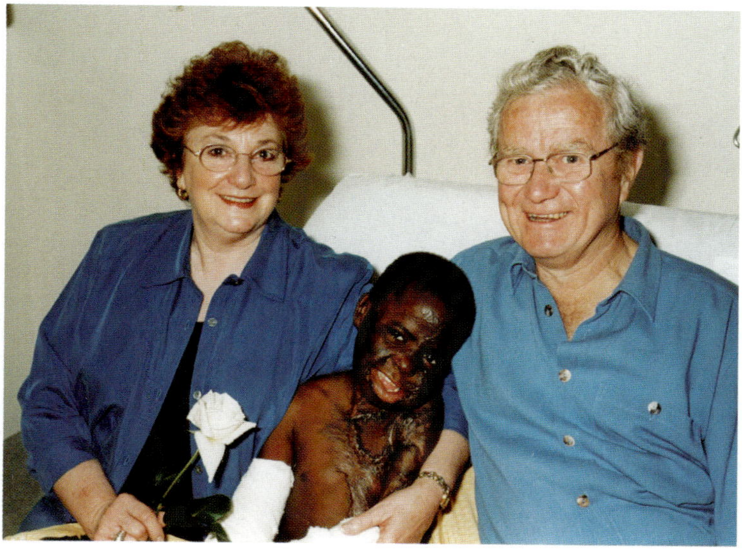

'Mumma' and 'Pappa' with Safari at RPA Hospital towards the end of his series of transforming operations.
Photo: Ray Barber

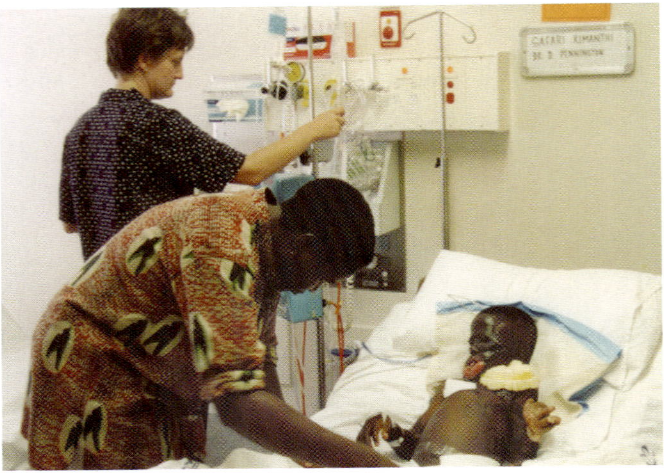

Zipporah comforting Safari after his first operation to release his chin and neck from his chest – nine hours of surgery.

Safari showing a remarkable recovery just eight days after his first operation.

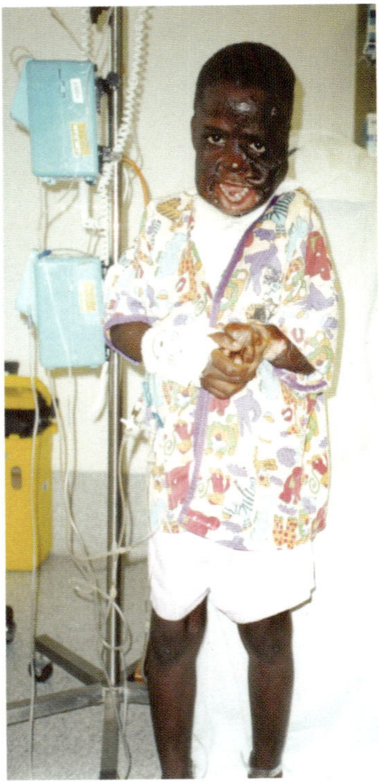

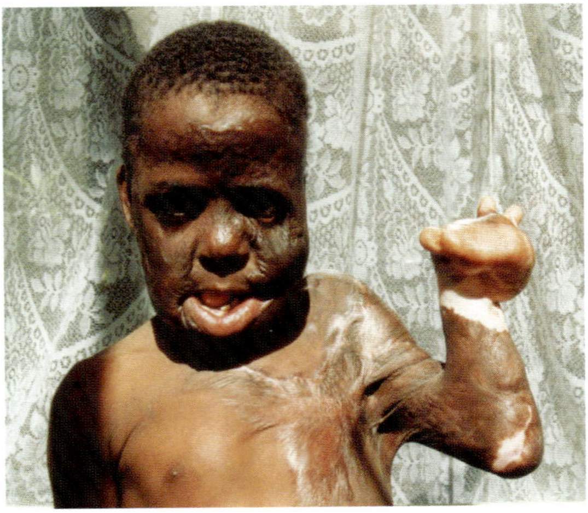

Safari's left arm and hand before surgery showing the extensive scar tissue restricting his movement and rendering his hand useless.

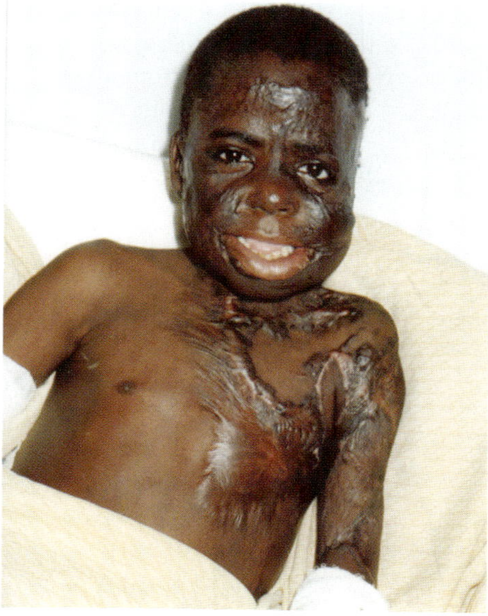

After the elbow operation, and an operation to release the contracture of his left shoulder and armpit, Safari was able to almost fully extend his arm.
Photo: Ray Barber

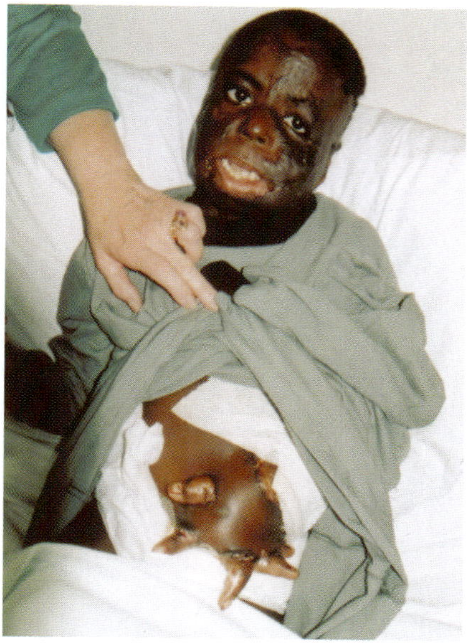

Safari with his left hand temporarily 'buried' under the skin of his stomach after the contractures of his wrist and fingers had been successfully released. A series of operations later released his hand from his stomach and arranged his fingers to be as close as possible to a normal hand.

The dedicated nursing team at RPA Hospital gave Safari a farewell party in December 2001. Nine Network's *RPA* Executive Producer, Danny Milosavljevic (far right), and cameraman, Chris Roles (second from right), joined in the celebrations.

Janet's daughter Kate formed a strong bond with Safari during his visit, becoming an important part of his extended Australian family.

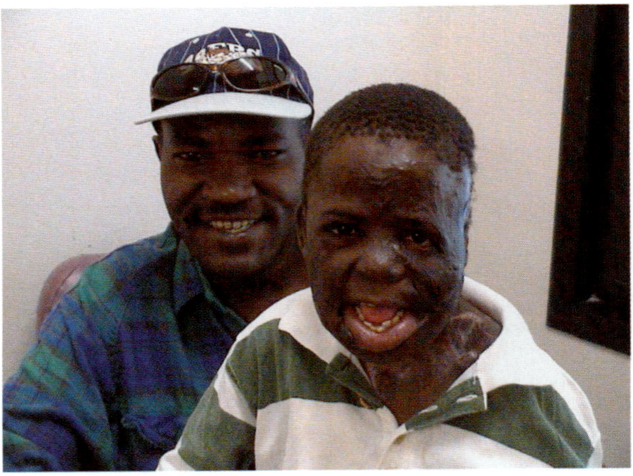

Safari with his 26-year-old uncle, Kilonzo, who came to Australia as the family member to sign the necessary medical release forms prior to each operation.
Photo: Danny Milosavljevic

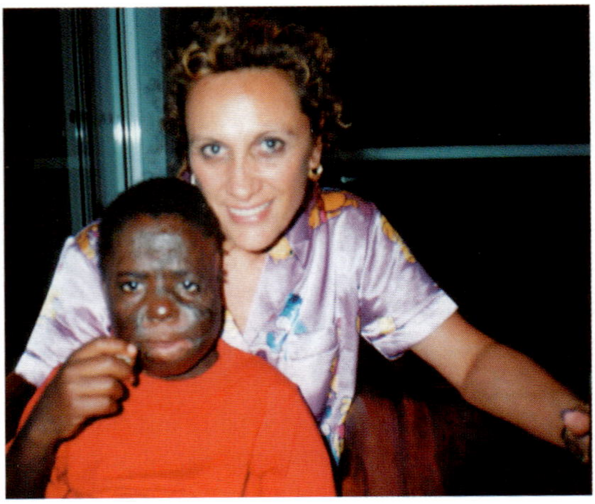

Safari with Janet and Frank's neighbour, Kate Rabe. Safari spent many evenings with Kate and her husband, Stuart, enjoying the barbecues, dancing and pop music. Stuart and Kate love Safari dearly.
Photo: Stuart Rabe

Safari with his mate Sam Bell during a farm holiday at the Bell's 5000-acre sheep station, Paling Yards, near Taralga, 200km south-west of Sydney.

Safari on safari in Kenya and wearing a T-shirt made for the Central Coast's Federation Day celebrations. Safari received much love and support from Janet and Frank's local community during his stay in Australia.
Photo: Jenny Murray

A quilt exhibition at Terrigal Uniting Church in 2003 – just one example of the many events in aid of Safari and his village.

A village warm welcome – the day Safari returned to Kasaala, Kenya. *Photo: Jenny Murray*

John's first sight of his son after the operations, December 2001. *Photo: Kate Sim*

Safari back in the arms of his mother, Ngayau.

Morning tea under the shade of a tree near Safari's home. Rear (left to right): Frank, Janet, Jenny, Kate, Richard, Chris (standing). Front (left to right): Ngayau, Mary, Tony.

Safari plays assistant to Tony Clunes, soundman for the Nine Network's *RPA* program which sent the crew to Kenya to film Safari's return to his village.

Safari all smiles with his mum and dad two months after returning home.

The family cooking hut. It was in this type of hut that Safari's tragic accident occurred. The original hut no longer exists.

The family farm or 'shamba' from the air showing the new house built by Safari's father. The two small round huts house the chickens. The large round hut gives privacy to Safari's elder sisters Penina and Kanini, and the present cooking hut is at the top left.
Photo: Danny Milosavljevic

Safari and his cousin, Amin, in class at Sathya Sai School in Uthiru, a rural suburb 10 km out of Nairobi, in February 2004.
Photo: Daniel Otieno

Chapter 9

In October my daughter Kate asked if she could take Safari along with her three daughters to Sussex Inlet on the south coast of New South Wales for a weekend. Everyone was excited over this adventure, particularly as we were all aware that time with Safari was now drawing to a close. With this in mind, the order of the weekend was to be fun, fun, fun with his extended family for Safari to remember.

At 6.30 on the Saturday evening in an emotional phone call Kate told us Safari had collided with a small girl and broken his left arm, the arm that had been immobilised by the burns three years earlier. Could we please contact Dr Pennington? This we did and he said to take him to RPA Casualty. We met her at the hospital and found Safari exhausted from pain. Kate's friend had driven them to the hospital while she comforted Safari, his arm resting on a pillow.

The scene at the hospital was distressing. Safari was distraught after enduring the pain over several hours' drive from Sussex Inlet. Kate was crying and felt responsible for what had happened. Her daughters were upset and helpless. We didn't realise it at the time, but Safari had osteoporosis in that arm due to inactivity and poor diet. Whilst he had steeled himself for the program of operations and the attendant pain, all this was so unexpected. As we sat beside his bed on Sunday morning we realised our little fellow really wasn't well enough for the scheduled fourteenth and final operation next morning. However, it just had to go ahead.

It was just as well that this was his last operation. The thirteen previous operations had taken their toll. Frank would frequently say, 'He's tough but he's not bulletproof.' This was so true; being with him constantly we could see he was becoming weary of so much hospitalisation. He would never complain of more surgery when we would tell him, 'Tomorrow you have to go into hospital.' All he would say was, 'Will it hurt in one place or two?' We would always have to say, 'Two, maybe more.' Skin grafts were always being taken to be placed somewhere else on his body. Looking into the eyes of this now handsome, rugged and somehow wise face, we felt that we had to be completely truthful. He deserved the best from us; not simply cajoling and untruthful assurances that, 'It will be all right.' Yes, it would be all right eventually and he would survive but that was not the issue. His courage and fortitude deserved our deep respect and we would always honour that. The familiar smell of hospital brought on an aversion, not a rebellion. Yet he was certainly entitled to rebel.

His final operation was a rather minor procedure in a series to restore movement to his previously trapped fingers. Fingers that had been trapped in such a cruel and bizarre way by the accident. The recovery from that operation was different. He became withdrawn and one of the nurses said to us, 'He is very depressed.' This was brought home to us as we tried to comfort him in the recovery ward where, at one point he said, 'Mumma, let me die.'

My heart cried out for him. How could I comfort him? Had we been unreasonable to think that he could endure fourteen operations in ten months, a new country, a new family and a new language? The many changes this small child had coped with had brought him to the point where he was effectively saying, it's too hard, it hurts too much. 'Let me die.'

Following this bleak statement Safari's depression seemed to set in. We could see it and the nurses had mentioned it, his behaviour was different.

That last operation had come on the Monday after the Saturday night when he broke his wasted left arm and had to be admitted to RPA's Emergency Department at midnight.

By Thursday we felt we needed to act. We asked the nurses if we could wrap him up in a blanket, put him in a wheelchair and take him to Newtown, an easy walk from the hospital. They agreed and off we went, planning to go via a Lebanese restaurant, El Bahsa, where he was well known and always indulged gastronomically by the owners.

Leaving the confines of the hospital and out into the sunshine, Safari seemed to take an interest in his surroundings. As we approached the pedestrian crossing on Missenden Road a large truck stopped to let us cross. The driver recognised Safari and called out, 'Hi Safari, good on you mate, you're a great kid, Safari!' We crossed. Those words lifted Safari's spirits; he brightened up immediately, waved with his good arm and smiled. From that instant the depression was gone. He was back to his old self. We wheeled him into busy King Street and to the restaurant where he had a meal of chicken and vegetables. All was well and we bless that truckie, whoever he is. We were also very relieved. If plan A hadn't worked we had no idea what plan B was.

Frank and Safari were returning from RPA's Hand Clinic and it was convenient after crossing the Harbour Bridge to exit the Gore Hill Freeway at Artarmon and visit the Channel Nine studios at Willoughby. There Frank was to drop off Safari and Kilonzo's return air tickets to Danny Milosavljevic for some processing. At this stage Channel Nine had decided to accompany Safari, Kilonzo and ourselves to Kenya and video the homecoming for insertion in the 2002 series of *RPA*. Nine were very generous in offering to pay the fares for Lesley Coverdale, Dr Pennington and us.

At the studio gates, having Safari with Frank acted as an 'open sesame' with the security guards. There was no need to explain who we were. 'Yes, the *RPA* demountable is straight ahead past the parked helicopter,' the guard said, pointing to the helipad. Naturally, Frank and Safari stopped to check out the helicopter and were both enthralled. Dragging themselves away, they walked up to Danny's office in the demountable and were met with – as always from Danny – a warm welcome. He is one of those perpetually bright and optimistic characters whose enthusiasm is infectious. Danny was thrilled that his little star was there and all three proceeded on a tour of the station in a 'show and tell' to Danny's colleagues.

Frank later told me that the newsroom was a hive of activity with TV monitors showing TV feeds from all over the world. That day's newspapers were scattered like confetti all over journalists' desks and there was an atmosphere of expectancy all around. In a corner Danny found Brian, the station's helicopter pilot, who instantly suggested a ride above Sydney in his helicopter. Frank and Safari didn't need asking twice.

Down they went to the helipad directly underneath the huge TV broadcast tower and through the procedure of boarding the helicopter and strapping themselves in. Frank said that he and Safari sat in the back and Danny, not to be left out, sat next to Brian. Safari's eyes and ears must have been working overtime as he soaked up the activity of the preflight procedures, the huge array of instruments and the newness of the experience. Finally, huge headphones to cut out the engine noise were strapped to Safari's head and the chopper was up, up and away. Seeing the crisscrossed framing of the broadcast tower pass by as they rose into the air gave the peculiar feeling to Frank that they were climbing a giant's ladder into the sky. In a minute or two they were hovering alongside the top of the Harbour Bridge arch; the sight of that magnificent structure from their vantage point was out of this world. 'If it was out of this world for me, what was it like for Safari?' Frank wondered. 'Brian positioned us so that I could get a photo of Safari framed in the window with the arch of the bridge in the background.'

After chasing a visiting New Zealand warship up the harbour it was back to the TV station and the end of the dream. Frank thanked Brian and Danny profusely and reverted to the mundane task of driving home. Safari was for once speechless. How much fun can you have in one day?

A friend offered to organise an art exhibition to help raise funds for the Safari Appeal in October. The venue was Gosford's Regional Art Centre in East Gosford. It is a beautiful complex in a Japanese garden setting with the gardens and ornamental fish ponds meticulously set out in the Oriental way. The City of Gosford has a sister-city relationship and cultural ties to the Japanese city of Edogawa.

The Art Centre was ideal for our exhibition and we were very happy to accept the offer to arrange artist friends to exhibit and donate part of the sales of their works to the appeal. Well-known actor Penny Cook was invited to open the exhibition on 12 October and kindly agreed. The event was a wonderful success.

During the course of the opening night supper was served and Safari showed another aspect of his remarkable self. Dressed in smart beige long pants and crisp check shirt he took it upon himself to offer food to the guests. He derived such pleasure showing hospitality by carrying around food platters and offering them to the guests. His face was animated as he kept offering and urging people to, 'Take some, go on!' I could see his pleasure shining from his very being.

Now that we understand a little more about hungry seasons in the village and food shortages we can understand Safari's pleasure at being able to give food away.

A little later in the evening we could see him outside exploring the floodlit gardens and marvelling at the huge colourful ornamental fish in the ponds, perhaps contemplating what they tasted like.

A Sydney radio station, MIX 106.5, interviewed Safari and had kindly offered us a night of respite just weeks prior to our leaving for Kenya.

Safari was very interested in seeing how everything worked at the radio station and asked endless questions. Mardi Cole, the announcer, was very happy to answer all his queries and admired him greatly. On air, for a seven-year-old Safari made a reasonable fist of his first ever radio interview.

We were delighted to accept MIX 106.5's gift of a night at the Duxton Hotel at Milsons Point in the shadow of the Sydney Harbour Bridge and overlooking what must be the most magnificent harbour in the world. This gave us a carefree evening with a beautiful meal, excellent accommodation and a night without the phone ringing.

As I tucked Safari into bed I thought, how will he explain this to his family and friends back home? In fact, how would he explain the myriad things that he had experienced in that year in Australia?

By late October interest both from the public and the media had risen considerably and Frank and I were on a media merry-go-round. Channel Nine's breakfast program *Today* with presenters Steve Liebmann and Tracy Grimshaw invited Safari, Lesley and me to appear as guests. We were staying at Frank's girls' unit at Strathfield when Nine phoned with the details of the TV interview the next day and they suggested that they send a chauffeured car to pick us up and take us to the studio.

Early in the morning we were dressed and ready for our first appearance on live television. The black, chauffeur-driven limo arrived, we hopped in and met a charming man, Andre, the driver. Soon Andre was explaining everything in the limo to our curiosity package, Safari, who as usual wanted to know the lot. Andre patiently obliged and then, as all fell silent, he said, 'The little boy is from Kenya, I believe?'

'Yes,' Frank replied.

Then Andre said an astonishing thing. 'I frequently drive a man to and from his home in West Pennant Hills to the airport. He is a Kenyan in the tea business and his name is Raju Shah.'

'How very strange,' we remarked, 'we met the same man at an exhibition at Darling Harbour earlier in the year.'

And then Frank said, 'You know, quite often during the year I have been meaning to look him up. I don't know why, but I do feel that we have to make contact for some reason.'

On the *Today* show Safari stole the limelight, enthralling not just Steve and Tracy but the whole studio floorcrew as well. It was early in the morning and naturally Safari was hungry so he asked if he could have a bacon and egg sandwich. The order went down to the station canteen, up came a sandwich and Safari munched it nonchalantly on national television to an audience of millions.

Two days later we visited Raju Shah at West Pennant Hills. Frank knew from his youth the area where Raju lived. He said that it used to be full of peach orchards and blackberry bushes. It was known locally as 'Dingley Dell' but today is mostly filled with houses as a result of Sydney's urban spread.

Raju, his wife Madhur and son Deep's home is in a pocket of beautiful tranquil bushland. They welcomed us and invited us to a delicious Indian dinner. Safari was with us and Deep, a young man in his twenties, entertained him while we got to know Raju and Madhur.

Out of the blue Raju said, 'Have you got transport arranged when you arrive in Nairobi?'

'No,' we replied. It had been on our minds because we had a large number of boxes of aid for the village and were wondering how to get it all down to Kasaala. We had heard that Nine had been quoted prices they said were ridiculous from vehicle hire companies.

Raju said, 'I have a friend called Batuk in Nairobi who operates a fleet of minibuses to take visitors on camera safaris through the parks. If you like I'll give him a ring and ask him for a quote for a minibus and driver per week.' This was great; within a few minutes Raju was on the phone to Batuk in Nairobi and was back with a very good rate instantly. We accepted and our transport problems in Kenya were fixed.

That meeting with Batuk via Raju turned out to be so helpful that we wonder now how we would have coped without him. And it was all due to that chance meeting with Raju at the Body, Mind and Spirit Festival. And the prod from Andre, Nine's chauffeur.

It was the hundredth anniversary of Australia's Federation in 2001 and throughout the year the nation celebrated with parades and parties.

The City of Gosford celebrated Federation on Saturday 17 November and the Gosford Chamber of Commerce, who were organising the event, invited Safari to lead the parade through the main street of Gosford behind the mayor's car. It was very evident that Safari had risen to celebrity status.

The theme of the transport vehicles for the various celebrities was vintage cars and the one we were allocated was canary-yellow with an open top. Saturday was a clear sunny morning and for the parade I outfitted Safari in a bright yellow T-shirt with the words, 'Safari the Central Coast luvs U' emblazoned across the front. It was one of hundreds of T-shirts that our friends at the Central Coast Rugby League Football Club had produced and were selling to raise money for Safari. When he left Australia he wore this shirt in recognition of the people of the Central Coast.

Assembling for the commencement of the parade it was necessary for us to keep him almost hidden from the crowd, such was the interest. Frank and I along with Safari jumped into the old car not knowing what to expect but very excited. Someone placed Australian flags in our hands and the driver slowly led us into the main street in procession behind Mayor Robert Bell, resplendent in his mayoral robes, sitting in his car. As we approached the main street shopping area the footpaths were swollen with people twelve to fourteen deep shouting, 'Safari, Safari!' We were truly astonished by the warmth out there. I looked across at Safari; he was looking all around him, waving his flag. Someone would call, 'Safari, look here.' He looked and cameras would flash. He was amazed. Then, as I looked he slowly lowered the flag to his lap and just gazed at the people. As I looked at him I wondered, what was going through his mind?

On this fabulous day he rode in a cavalcade through town – and I'm sure that in some part of him the realisation of the cavalcade of affection from the Australian people also resonated.

The parade finished at the park behind the Leagues Club, where marquees and events had been organised. We were invited to a luncheon with parade dignitaries and had a lovely time. Later in the park Safari was invited to take the rostrum with Frank. Safari was so overwhelmed and shy, worn out and tired from all that had happened, all he could do was snuggle into Frank's neck as he held him and addressed the crowd. With Safari in one arm and a microphone in the other, Frank thanked the people for taking this little boy from Africa to their hearts.

The physiotherapy program continued unabated and Safari submitted. Vanessa and Rebecca tried to make it more playful and Safari loved the excursions into massaging shaving cream over the treatment table, practising picking up large Lego blocks, hardly aware of the therapeutic benefit. They exercised his left arm's extension and marked a corner of the wall with notches to track his progress, just like many parents do with their children's heights. Safari enjoyed looking back at the marks from weeks ago and revelled in his achievements. We all enjoyed seeing him progress. However, we could see the departure date looming and felt that he really would benefit from more physio, months more. Still, Vanessa and Rebecca did the very best with what time we had. And we noted carefully their techniques so we might continue the exercises in Kenya. We were going for an extended stay in the village and would have to manage as best we could.

One journey back from the Hand Clinic in Sydney culminated with Kate and Safari arriving in Gosford after dark. The chamber of commerce and the council had switched on tiny fairy lights that were scattered through the trees of Kibble Park in the centre of town. Preparations were being made for Christmas celebrations. As they drove along Safari gazed at the lights and said something to Kate that touched her deeply. 'You know, Kate, Australia is very beautiful. One day I'm going to take all this beauty back to Kenya.' Kate, taken aback, thought, this is pretty profound talk coming from a seven-year-old boy. Later she told me, 'Mum, it brought tears to my eyes and I couldn't answer him.'

Safari's initial fascination with our electrical lights had never abated. So we thought we would show him something quite spectacular before he went home, a house called 'Gracelands', in a suburb of nearby Newcastle.

For a long time the owners of Gracelands have each Christmas decorated their house with thousands and thousands of lights, producing every year an increasing spectacle. Every year people come to admire their efforts. The crowds got bigger until police crowd control was necessary. The idea has spread to other nearby homes and it has become a neighbourhood of competing efforts. People come from miles around to get a glimpse and of course there is also the ubiquitous Mr Whippy ice cream vendor.

It was into this kaleidoscope of light and colour that we stepped with Safari just a week before he headed home. There were lights all over the roofs and guttering and there were scenes from nursery rhymes picked out in lights. There were beautifully decorated trees and toy trains and cars moving to music. Safari was speechless, his eyes growing wider by the moment, not knowing where to look next. We thought at the time that he would always have within him this image, although perhaps never able to explain it to family and friends back home. It was outside their reality.

Chapter 10

The time of Safari's departure to Kenya was now fast approaching. Safari had received many, many gifts and couldn't possibly take them all home. He very carefully made the choices and packed his bag, taking home items such as patchwork quilts lovingly made by friends. We later observed his mother Ngayau running her hands over these in her dwelling in the village as she carefully packed them back in his suitcase. Later in the village we also saw Safari open his case and give almost all the shirts, shorts and books away to family and friends. It was as if he wanted to share out the love that he had been given. Safari was given probably 100 or more soft toys. He couldn't take them all home, and we talked over the idea of selling them on our street stalls and converting them to money to put away for his future. This he was very happy about.

Along with Jenny, Frank and I were due to fly out on 19 December, Sunday evening. Jenny had decided earlier in the year to join us in returning Safari to his family. The days before our departure were chaotic.

Kate and Frank's brother Richard decided to go to Kenya as well. Because we were to stay quite some time in Kasaala some groceries and other supplies were needed from Nairobi. A big shopping trip in Nairobi was necessary and our tight agenda with the film crew meant that we wouldn't have time to do all these tasks before travelling the 300 kilometres to Kasaala. Kate and Richard left the Wednesday before our Sunday departure in order to sort out these logistical details.

During Thursday there was feverish activity in Gosford's Kibble Park. The council and the chamber of commerce were organising the yearly Carols by Candlelight in the park for that evening. Trucks arrived with sound equipment and stages and Christmas bunting and lights to transform the park into a child's wonderland. This year's celebration was also the Central Coast's way of saying farewell to their hero.

As darkness fell, people arrived with their foldup chairs and blankets and party food. Chris King, well-known entertainer and local personality was Master of Ceremonies. Popular children's characters such as Humphrey Bear entertained the small children and people bought Glow Stixs to light up the venue in a moving ocean of colour. Safari was having a great time playing hide and seek with other kids. In a few days it would all be just a memory, a fantastic memory of Australia.

Friday was frantic. A Channel Nine film crew was coming up to film a segment for *A Current Affair*. It took all morning and we had fish and chips with them on the waterfront at Gosford while they filmed. Then a dash for Sydney to attend the last physiotherapy session and pick up solar lights for the village from BP Solar at Silverwater. With the Friday traffic we missed out on the hospital appointment and only just got the solar equipment in time. Some of the equipment had been specially airfreighted from Spain that day and for a while was lost between Sydney airport and one of two warehouses at Silverwater. We eventually tracked everything down with minutes to spare.

There was a steady trail of people calling to the house for last goodbyes. Thinking we would be in Kenya for three months there were many last-minute things to attend to, so we asked a good friend, Margaret Bushby, to do what we couldn't.

We were up early on Saturday morning, preparing to go to a motel in Randwick, close to the airport. There was excitement in the air – we were all going to Kenya, and more importantly Kasaala. Safari and Kilonzo were going home, far, far away. And still there was a steady stream of visitors. I couldn't even get the kitchen cleaned up after breakfast so I called Margaret. 'Please, Margaret can you come and give me a hand?' I pleaded.

'Certainly,' she replied, 'I'll come straight over.' Margaret and I have been good pals for many years and can call on each other at any time. We share a great friendship and understanding.

I didn't want to think about leaving. How would Safari be able to settle back into village life after all he had experienced? There was no-one really he could converse with about his life in a completely strange land. We knew that Kilonzo would rarely be around. His life for the moment seemed to be with Mary and their children in Nairobi, even though he was in a quandary over the competing interests of greater life opportunities in the capital and his responsibilities to care for his aged parents in Kasaala. How could Safari explain his helicopter ride or the pain he had endured, or all the pretty nurses that had kissed him or the electric lights that had lit up the room with a flick of a switch on the wall? And all the gifts and adulation of people in the street. Or the ocean and the boats on the harbour or a thousand and one things that were outside the experience of almost everyone at home. We could see that perhaps he would suppress the memories of these experiences because they could be too hard to explain.

Our very good friend Betty arrived and drove us to Randwick where she had arranged for us to stay overnight before we left Sydney.

We had been invited to meet the Kenyan and East African community of Sydney at their Kenya Day celebration at a park on Bronte beach. Bronte beach is one of Sydney's eastern suburbs beaches very close to the city. We had a lovely afternoon with these wonderfully warm-hearted people. They were very welcoming and greeted us with great friendship, sharing their food and drink; we felt that we had known them for years. The hospitality shown will never be forgotten.

They passed around the hat and presented Safari and Kilonzo with $1000. They were very spontaneous and so generous, keen to help us in any way in the future. Frank addressed the crowd and told Safari's story. He said that we were touched and thanked them for the way they saw Safari as 'their child'.

In the Africans' attitudes to Safari it seemed that caring for children is a community responsibility, not just a responsibility of the parents. It seemed to us that all of those people at Bronte felt they had some stake in his welfare. Many people came up to us and thanked us for looking after Safari as if he were their own child. We tried to explain that for us, taking care of Safari was a very real privilege; a privilege we had not expected at all when we made that snap decision to be involved. As the year had progressed and we learnt more of the situation in a poor rural village in Africa we felt that if we could be instrumental in helping his family and village then we would feel satisfaction.

That Saturday evening at Bronte beach Kilonzo and some of his countrymen went to the Africa Club in Sydney. We didn't see him again until late in the afternoon of the following day, just before the plane left. He hadn't returned to the hotel after the Kenya Day celebrations and was nowhere to be found the next morning.

On Sunday morning at breakfast we saw the first signs of Safari's recognition that he was going home. He devoured all the bacon in the bain-marie, perhaps remembering what it was like to be hungry.

At breakfast Frank's phone rang. It was Kilonzo. He didn't know where he was but was having a great time and was going to buy a camera. Frank emphasised, 'Just be at the airport by 5 pm.'

Our friend Clare Collins and her daughter Alice arranged for us all to have Sunday lunch at Star City on the Sydney waterfront and then to see Nikki Webster in a production of *The Wizard of Oz*. Safari was enthralled with the show. It was just wonderful to watch his face as the curtain went up and the music started. Those big brown eyes just got bigger and bigger and his feet were tapping to the music. It was magical for him. We later went backstage and met Nikki Webster. She was friendly and very generous in taking the time and care to explain certain aspects of the show to Safari.

Clare drove us to the airport. Frank's brother Howard, his car and trailer overflowing with the 44 boxes to go to Kenya, arrived and checked them in.

By 6 pm there was no Kilonzo and we were getting concerned. Sometime later he appeared looking very sheepish and smiling drunkenly. We didn't ask any questions but Kilonzo had obviously had a good time.

An SDA children's choir, 'Joyful Singers', had travelled from Melbourne to farewell Safari in song. It was a wonderful tribute from these small children and it brought tears to the eyes of Lesley and others. For my part, hearing the sweet voices of the children stirred my heart with many thoughts. I thought of my own dear family that I was leaving. I'd be so far away from them all. I pictured how Ngayau and John must have felt when they looked at their youngest son walking away from them at Nairobi airport eleven months earlier. He was not going on a trip with a predictable return; he was going for medical treatment with an extremely uncertain outcome. As John explained to us later when we met, 'I thought I would never see my son again.'

I thought of the generous-hearted people who had joined us at the airport to farewell Kenya's youngest ambassador. My grandchildren who had come to say goodbye allowed their tears to flow as they hugged me and as they embraced Safari. I held back my own tears to comfort and reassure them. There was time for more reflection on the plane.

The Channel Nine crew filmed our departure then left with us. Along with Lesley, Jenny and Dr Pennington we vanished into the immigration area.

Part Two
Kenya

Chapter 11

Our flight to Nairobi with Emirates was an adventure in itself. Frank and Safari were invited to the flight deck and so began a million questions from Safari who was absolutely fascinated by all the lights and gauges in the darkened cockpit. The flight crew were equally fascinated by this boy.

At our early-morning stopover in Dubai, Emirates' Media Relations Manager, Fay Thompson, met us. Fay was also intrigued with Safari and thought his story would be a great subject for their in-flight magazine. Photos were taken and a story prepared. Fay remains a good friend and we keep her up to date with Safari's progress.

In the plane Kilonzo was very content to doze with his headphones no doubt playing his pop favourites. By Singapore he was sober and keen to eat. Travelling home Kilonzo certainly looked a man of the modern world. A very short haircut, which is de rigueur for African men, and small curved sunnies topped off by jungle green multi-pocketed trousers and beige suede boots completed the picture. It was now not Kilonzo, but rather Mr Mwanzia who sat beside us.

The flight from our stopover in Dubai to Nairobi took five hours. Dubai is in the United Arab Emirates on the entrance to the Persian Gulf. Departing Dubai in the early morning light we could see the sandy landscape that reminded Frank of his two years on the Gulf in Saudi Arabia some 27 years earlier. Frank reminisced as we gazed out the plane window.

As the plane took off and climbed, the sand continued into the distance, contrasted only by the blue water of the Gulf. The sand stretched for what seemed an eternity with the landscape crisscrossed by straight desert roads and low hills. In the wadis or valleys between the hills often patches of green showed where some subterranean riverbed was giving forth life-sustaining water at an oasis.

We turned east to follow the coast to the Strait of Hormuz and the Gulf of Oman at the head of the Persian Gulf. Then turning south, the plane hugged the bleak coastline of Yemen, before crossing the Red Sea at Aden to approach the Horn of Africa and Djibouti.

The plane's course shifted ever so slightly and we banked gently to the right, taking us inland. We passed over troubled Ethiopia and then Somalia, home to the Somali friends we had made in Gosford; forced to flee their country as refugees.

Our first glimpse of Kenya came as we broke through the clouds close to Nairobi. The high plateau was covered in gently undulating hills. The land looked green and fertile and small farms dotted the landscape.

Kenya is a country of 35 million people. It was a British colony until after a bloody struggle it was granted independence on 12 December 1963. Today it is a multiparty republic within the Commonwealth and, because of its general neutrality and stability it has played a leading role in the quest for peace and stable government in the often turbulent East African region.

The capital Nairobi is home to 1.5 million people and is the hub city for East Africa. Kenya has 32 major indigenous African groups, of which the five largest constitute 70 per cent of the population: the Kikuyu, Luo, Luhya, Kamba and the Kalenjin. The principal ethnic minorities are Arabs and Asians, mostly of Indian descent. It is a predominantly Christian country and about 19 per cent follow indigenous religions and 6 per cent are Muslims. English is the official language and Swahili is the national language, which brings together the many tribal groups.

The name Nairobi is derived from a Maasai word, *Ewaso Nairobi*, meaning 'stream of cold waters'. It probably refers to the swampy nature of the land around the city. The city originated in 1899 as a supply station for the expansion of the railway into the interior of Kenya, then called British East Africa.

Close to the equator the mile-high altitude moderates the city's temperature to a mild mid-twenties during the day and mid-teens overnight. The sun is, however, searingly intense as it shines close overhead.

As we disembarked from the plane at Jomo Kenyatta International Airport, Safari was very animated. I could see that he was glad to be home at last in such familiar surroundings amongst his own people.

It was a great relief to arrive safe and sound in Nairobi. Frank had previously made arrangements with Emirates regarding the excess weight of the boxes of aid and the airline staff were extremely helpful. We had taken medical supplies; clothing for men, women and children; solar-powered lights; spectacles and many other things we thought would be useful in the village. We also decided that if we were to be there for three months we wanted to be comfortable so included was a large tent, which Boots Great Outdoors camping store at Erina had given us together with several blue folding chairs. Many times we see those blue chairs in photos and remember the family promising to keep them as 'Mumma and Pappa's chairs' for us to use when we visit. So nice to know that far away in a village in Africa one's chair awaits one!

We cleared customs with our 44 boxes very easily, which was just as well. Opening all those boxes and then resealing them after our exhausting 23-hour flight from Australia would have been onerous.

Kate and Richard along with the parents of Josephine, our Kenyan friend in Sydney, were waiting for us. They introduced us to Josephine's parents Reverend Daniel and Mrs Mbai and their daughter Kelu who had come to the airport to welcome us. Kate and Richard had stayed in Limuru, a rural town 30 minutes north of Nairobi, as their guests for the four days prior to our arrival.

Richard said later as we drove into the city that Daniel had showed them around Nairobi and the surrounding countryside in his car and that he was deeply moved by the confronting sight of the poverty and the tragedy of people very ill in the streets from disease.

Also waiting at the airport was Batuk Shah, our transport lifeline and friend of Raju Shah back in West Pennant Hills. Batuk's driver, Benson, was to transport us around the country. Batuk Shah, like Raju, was of Indian ancestry and born in Kenya. He was a pleasant man; a middle-aged and quick-witted businessman. He operated a tour bus business to the game parks under the novel name 'Nutty Safaris'. Now that we were in Kenya we were so happy and relieved that we had organised our own transport beforehand through Batuk's friend Raju.

And David Syme was there to take charge of 'the expedition' in the Africa he knew so well. Outside the terminal, although we were travelling independently, several ADRA vehicles waited and we were introduced to several ADRA Kenya staff before our entire party departed for the Hilton Hotel where Channel Nine had kindly paid for us to stay.

The Uhuru (Freedom) Highway took us the short distance into town, passing the construction site of the new US Embassy, built after the embassy building in the centre of the city was destroyed in a bomb blast in 1989. The new complex was very heavily fortified with a massive wall and a half-kilometre-wide buffer zone. As we continued it was apparent that security was a big issue for Nairobians. All the buildings – commercial and residential – were heavily guarded. This aspect of the city was quite confronting. We were warned to keep the car doors locked and keep the windows closed as thieves often crept up at traffic snarls and snatched watches and valuables from the unwary passengers. This was a place for the visitor to always be on the alert. And we as Europeans were obvious targets. The advice was always be on guard, never relax on the streets.

Nairobi traffic is chaotic and the smoke belching from diesel-powered buses and trucks made our eyes smart. The tension of the traffic and the glare of the sun made the foyer of the hotel an oasis. At the desk of the Hilton Hotel we confirmed our bookings and checked in Jenny, Richard and Kate.

It was by now late afternoon and we all went to our rooms and freshened up. I looked out from the large window in my room to the city below. Just across the square a large group of Africans were listening to a pop group parade their talents. The sea of dark faces was so strange. We were so unaccustomed to brown faces. Frank reflected that for Safari, coming to a country of white faces must also have seemed so strange. I guess we are all products of our own view of reality and our assumptions. We all know intellectually that Africa is black but not until we are presented with Africa do we at another level accept its equally valid reality.

Vehicles crisscrossed the streets and crowded into roundabouts five deep like dodgem cars at Luna Park. Nairobi life was hectic as if there were no tomorrow. I was worn out from the flight and from the heat but the day was not yet over and David Syme had some doors to knock on. He asked us to accompany him to the Australian High Commissioner's office to meet the Acting High Commissioner, David Livingstone.

Kilonzo excused himself and caught a local *matatu* or minibus to Banana Hills in the outer suburbs to be at last with his wife Mary and his girls at the coffee plantation where Mary worked and they all lived.

David Livingstone and Second Secretary Diana Nelson were nice folks. David was a youngish fellow, had an unusual hairstyle, halfway between mohawk and ponytail but as Charles de Gaulle once said, 'Vive la difference.'

On the way out we noticed that the High Commission was very close to the carpark of Nairobi University's mortuary. A daily stream of relatives drove their deceased car accident victims and others away for burial. How strange for us shielded from death to be witnessing other people dealing very practically with this aspect of life. Another lesson in our African education.

Refreshed after a good night's rest, next morning we met Kate and Jenny in their room. Safari had spent the night with them and Jenny told a funny story. 'At around 3 am Safari was awake and rearin' to go. While we were still asleep he wrapped my sarong around his waist, turned on the lights and woke us up.' Kate continued, 'He then started to show us by his gyrations how to dance with the village "dancing mummas".' The women of the village would be entertaining us at the homecoming.

We laughed at his tricks and went down to the dining room for our first smorgasbord breakfast. Delicious tree-ripened tropical fruits; pineapples so sweet it was remarkable, huge juicy passionfruit and so on. But for the traditionalist there was the English breakfast and of course porridge. The image returns of a tall, handsome, statuesque African woman, very elegantly dressed in pristine starched chef's whites and with resplendent chef's hat, serving porridge. Her appearance and true grace and politeness impressed me. There was none of a servant's obsequiousness about this woman and neither was there a contemptuous attitude. She was a proud African and it was good to see. She was a good introduction to Kenya and has left a lasting impression on us.

My mind wandered over what her life held outside work, when all of the Western trappings of wellbeing and affluence were removed. What was it like and where did she call home? It seemed so foreign for this proud person to live as she probably did, in difficult circumstances in the city.

Quite a lot of our time at the hotel was spent in the foyer. A busy hotel, a constant stream of travellers; acres of travellers' bags coming and going. Everything under the command of the bell captain, an older man in his smart maroon uniform. We got to know him, he knew that Safari was in our party. 'What happened to that boy?' he asked. We told the story and he was very interested. 'You must take that boy back with you for a good education,' he said in a firm tone. 'That is the best thing you can do for him.' The bell captain knew as we did that education was the key to a better life. We agreed and told him that it was for his parents to decide. He thanked us on behalf of Kenya for looking after Safari. He spoke almost as if Safari were his son. This personal concern by a stranger toward a child, one from his own culture, we found strange from our cultural perspective and it reminded us of how the Sydney African community at Bronte beach had thanked us for caring for 'their child'. In Africa, children belong to everyone and are the responsibility of all – not just of their parents.

Batuk arrived at the hotel foyer and we discussed our transport requirements and a deal was done. A little while later as we chatted to Batuk and found out something of his business and background, Kilonzo walked in accompanied by Mary, his wife. Kilonzo introduced us. Mary handed me a lovely bunch of pink and white roses and gave Lesley the same. We shook hands. Mary was a quiet, slim and youthful woman with a proud and at the same time gentle bearing. A quiet confidence shone that was most appealing. Her gift of flowers told me that she and Safari's family were so grateful for our help. She also was obviously proud of her husband Kilonzo and the vital part that he had played in the Safari saga. Mary and Kilonzo were coming to Kasaala with us for the homecoming celebrations.

Eventually everyone was ready and the party departed in several vehicles. We were all anxious to be under way and see for ourselves the real Africa. Safari, Frank and I together with Lesley, the Nine crew, Dr Pennington and David Syme travelled in the minibus that Channel Nine had hired. It was a bus with a pop-top, the type used to take people on game park safaris. From the safety of the vehicle I could imagine tourists, their hearts pounding, standing up and sighting their first wild lion and cheetah, elephant and gazelle.

The way south from Nairobi took us through areas of

which in our ignorance we knew nothing, not even the names of the towns. The road passed through fertile market garden towns growing vegetables for the population of Nairobi. It is easy to see how, even close to Nairobi, so many people are reliant on the seasons and agriculture. For many of the people of Kenya and indeed a good deal of Africa a crop failure means the threat of starvation.

Everywhere people walked in that steady, rhythmic loose-boned pace: a combination of what seems resignation and conservation of energy in the searing heat. It is this gait that says 'Africa'. There is none of the frantic 'have to get there' that we are used to in the West. Here it is the pace of self-survival. It doesn't seem a country beset with stomach ulcers. As we took all this in, Frank remembered Safari's words during the year, 'Calm down, Pappa.'

Men liked to wear jackets and always long pants, mostly with sockless shoes or thongs, called slippers locally. Countrywomen mostly wore wraparound colourful skirts. Some wore these with T-shirts from the West; sometimes with ridiculously inappropriate motifs. Heads were adorned with *leso* scarves. *Leso* scarves are pieces of fabric often matching the design and colour of the sarong-like skirts. The scarves are multifunctional. Occasionally they are worn as a scarf around the neck, sometimes a cloth to wrap a parcel or as padding under something heavy carried on the head. But mostly they are wrapped around the head as an adornment and tied at the nape of a woman's neck. Second-hand clothes from the West are very popular. In the towns many women wear good business suits. Rich or poor, people are conscious of clothes. In the countryside women are frequently seen walking, backs straight, with their belongings elegantly poised on their heads using leso headscarves as cushions. I was surprised to see so much synthetic fabric used in that hot climate.

The van paused in a village traffic jam and I gazed out the window at the scene. What caught my eye was a woman coming out of a grocery shop laden with shopping bags in each hand. She went to a quiet spot, put her bags on the ground, and opened up a large sarong. Carefully she placed half the bags in the cloth and made a parcel. Then she produced another sarong and repeated the process. The first bundle she tied on her back. The second she gracefully balanced on her head, and off she went, both hands completely free. I looked on in amazement.

As we passed through the towns and villages I could see that life was a struggle. Everything seemed to be ramshackle, make-do or constructed with the resources available. The buildings were meagre; the whole scene spoke of rural impoverishment. However, the people looked proud – walking or cycling, always aware and proud of themselves.

We seemed to be passing small allotments where farmers, backs stooped, weeded and attended to their crops. I asked David Syme, 'What season are we in, David?' He replied, 'There is no winter and summer in this equatorial climate. The seasons are distinguished by the rain or lack of rain.' He continued, 'We are in the rainy season now after a prolonged dry and the crops being harvested for the market are the quick-growing vegetables to fill in while the slower-growing grains come to maturity.' As we passed a small red brick grain storage shed he said, 'Wastage of grain through vermin is a big problem. As much as 30 per cent of a harvest can be lost through insecure storage.'

We fell silent and I daydreamed as the vibrant colour of lush bougainvillea swept past the window.

I was brought back to the present and my gaze went to Safari sitting across from me. He too had been surveying the passing scene. A scene new and fresh with interest for us but I felt that for Safari it was a scene that brought back memories; memories that were in his private domain. Then I saw him pass his right hand across his eyes and down his face to his neck as if trying, it seemed, to obliterate the scene before him. He repeated this gesture from time to time. Then he caught me watching him. He slowly shook his head from side to side as if in resignation. He knew and I knew, and there was no need to make an empty comment. We both understood the plenty of Australia and the harsh difficulties of Africa. He knew he had all of this to face and live amongst again. While Frank and I would return to the abundance of what our country had to offer he would stay. Most of us never realise just how fortunate we are, and yet there are many of us who still complain.

Our lunch break was to be at a large town called Kitui. It was quite a fair-sized place with electricity and telephone as the poles were everywhere. Ghetto-blasters in roadside stalls and cafés immersed us in African music as we jostled our way through the traffic. The road into town was the usual packed-dirt road; the claypan made rock-hard and smooth by traffic, much like the roads of outback Australia. In town the shop verandahs were raised up from the street either because the street had worn away, which is more likely, or they had been made that way to cope with the heavy rains. Up on the elevated and covered verandahs the shopkeepers would ply their trade and exhibit the goods meant to catch the eye of passers-by. There were foam mattresses piled up high. On other shop verandahs sat tailors, both men and women, treadling away on sewing machines making garments. Another popular line was cooking utensils strewn on hooks along the way. There were woodworking shops and machine shops and the names of some establishments both in Kitui and in Kenya generally were really hilarious. I remember seeing a 'Divine Glory Welding Shop' and somewhere a church called 'Jesus Manifestation Centre'. And in the outskirts of Nairobi a 'Jimmy Big Head Boarding Academy'.

We climbed out of the minibus and poured into a restaurant named aptly, 'Tourist Hotel', ravenous for lunch. The restaurant was a nice plain concrete building. Potplanted canna lilies guarded the entrance. Inside, fans adorned the ceilings and plastic tablecloths finished the tables. Men sat around indulging in the African male's favourite pastime: gossiping. Wonder who was doing the work while the men got the goss?

It was a lunch of delicious fried *sukuma wiki*, accompanied by boiled rice and washed down by hot milky tea. Lunch over and before boarding the bus we made our way to the loo at the rear of the restaurant. Safari had already been and came running up the path shouting, 'Mumma, don't go down there, it's disgusting!' I smiled and looked for myself.

Kitui is the district centre for the area that covers Safari's village and home to the office of the area's District Commissioner, who's name we believe was Francis Lenyagume. Mr Lenyagume administered the area we were entering, and David Syme had invited him or his delegate, District Officer D.J. Falana, to the homecoming celebrations.

He was a tall mid-forties civil servant, well spoken, self-assured and dressed in a blue-grey business suit. We filled his office in a police compound and he was pleased to be visited. David Syme introduced his entourage, Lenyagume acknowledged us and we left, not quite sure what had been achieved. David certainly seemed to have an excellent rapport with this powerful man in the area in which ADRA operated.

South of Kitui the road became bad, really bad, and the countryside lost the green market garden look of earlier in the day. Even with the lush vegetation brought by the rain it looked a barren place. Swollen creeks had washed away the road and invariably an overloaded truck was to be found stranded in the creek bed, labourers trying to extricate it with minimum tools and makeshift timbers. Some work was going on rebuilding creek crossings – perhaps an election was in the wind.

Continuing south we started seeing the weird bottle-shaped baobab trees, a sure sign of a dry area. We were in the heart of the arid Ukambani region, the lands of Safari's Kamba people.

Around a corner and a village called Ikutha swung into view. We were at our staging camp for tomorrow's invasion of the village of Kasaala – a place we had come halfway around the world to in order to deliver a small boy to the bosom of his eagerly waiting family.

Ikutha is not big. In fact it's very small; barely able to contain the meow of a cat! The town or rather the village is a scattering of shops and a communal market area with thatched low platforms for villagers to display their produce. The shops were made from baked mud bricks and roofed with rusty corrugated iron which continued forward to form a verandah supported by twisted saplings. The shop facades were rendered and painted in a pale aqua that made us think the paint shops had but one colour on offer. The Airview Lodge was to be our home away from home for the night. The sign on another nearby guesthouse boasted, 'The destination of your illusions.'

The ADRA compound lay alongside the village and consisted of a fenced-off area of a couple of hectares with a large single-storey bungalow-style building, solidly made from cement-rendered concrete blocks. The large corrugated iron roof gathered all the roof water and fed it to a large concrete tank. At the back there were garages for vehicles. There seemed to be about twelve off-road motorbikes and four four-wheel drive Landcruisers. A toilet block and diesel generator shed sat along the fence away from the living quarters. The living areas were large and spacious and beds were arranged neatly in the dormitory-style bedroom. Mosquito nets over each bed signalled that malarial mosquitos were a problem in the region.

At the entrance there were a number of empty offices, so we filled one office with all the boxes of aid that we had unloaded for the village people from our rented minibus.

We intended to distribute it on Christmas Eve, in a few days' time.

My daughter Kate and I sat on the ends of a couple of beds and discussed our feelings. Kate said, 'How do you feel, Mum, handing Safari back?' She sat quietly crying. Safari had crept into our hearts and Kate, Frank and I knew it. There was no going back now. We will always be part of his and his family's life; we will always be in contact. He has become an integral part of our lives. I tried to push my own feelings aside and be there for Kate, as I said, 'He belongs to his family, they have not had him for a year of his precious life and they have missed out on so much of what he has experienced.'

Safari had spent quite a lot of time with Kate, John and their girls and they had grown to love him. He had found ways of getting from Kate what he wanted. All he had to say was 'Oh schweetie' or 'Pleeese darlink' or 'Come on darlink'. I know it was very hard for Kate, she had been there for him in the difficult times in hospital. She was very genuine in her affection for him.

Yes, I was upset. We were to miss his voice and presence around our place. We would miss him as a small child in our midst.

Even now as I remember, I occasionally come across an article of clothing belonging to him, and a lump comes to my throat. A small pair of check pyjamas, underpants or a shirt. I look at them and put them away – our keepsakes, part of our memories, these small items seem to bring him close to us again.

One day at home, a quiet moment presented itself and

I seized the opportunity to talk to Safari about his living once more in Kenya. I explained as simply as I could that when we love someone, all the oceans and all the mountains can't really separate one from the other. Our spirits and the love which has brought us together will always connect us, and so we will always be together in that way. I said to him, 'These words may be difficult for you to understand.' However, I believe he did understand. Tears come to my eyes at his sensitivity.

That day sitting on the bed in Ikutha I was very upset inside. How was he really going to cope? Would he be able to settle? As Michael Murtough-Coombes, the Nursing Unit Manager at RPA's Plastics and Reconstructive Surgery Ward, said to us during the year, 'He has come here, but what's going to happen to him when he is taken out of the goldfish bowl and put back in the reality of Africa?' We asked ourselves this same question. Frank said, 'I knew exactly what Michael meant. In Australia he was a celebrity but Michael's concern was, who would be interested in being involved in his life and welfare after he faded from the scene?'

With all these thoughts and feelings we could not possibly just dump him home as if to say, 'Well, that job's done.' To simply say hello and a few other words to his parents and then say goodbye was not an option, we felt.

Safari was only six and a half years old when he arrived in Australia. He displayed some remarkable qualities for one so young – more than can be explained away by some who would say, 'Oh, African kids are tough – they have to be.' Sure he's tough and we may be thought to be one-eyed and sentimental by some of the aid professionals. To some people, he may simply represent the poverty-stricken of the world. But to us he is a unique human being. We have seen a microcosm of need. We make no excuses for our stand. A child can't be loved too much.

What were the parents of such a child like? What kind of family and cultural environment played a part in the qualities we and so many other Australians had observed? We were so keen to meet these parents who had instilled so much; we wanted to stay some time in their home and get to know them. And the parents also had a right to know who we were, rather than just to be told by Kilonzo second-hand about the people who had looked after their son. They must also be keen to know about Safari's future medical requirements and prognosis.

After a meal at the ADRA compound, we left with Kate for our accommodation at the Airview Lodge in Ikutha village. The air was hot and humid and, with nightfall, increasingly sticky. The mandatory mosquito nets were a strange intrusion and we restlessly passed the night.

Chapter 12

Early next morning we were up and about. Life in Africa starts very early with the locals rugged up against the damp cold air. Cold for them but only cool for us. At the compound we had a breakfast of boiled eggs, toast, fried vegetables and the usual spreads. It was very nice.

As the day progressed, the heat and humidity intensified. The air was electric with excitement. After breakfast we stood around waiting for our party to board the vehicles for the 20-kilometre trip to take Safari home to Kasaala. It seemed to take forever.

Frank and I were very appreciative of Danny's thoughtfulness that day. He knew we were anxious to hear the results of some medical tests being undertaken by a family member in Australia. He surprised us by arranging to bring a satellite phone from Nairobi so that we might learn the outcome as soon as possible. He knew that our planned camping trip to Kasaala for the next weeks would keep us out of touch with the rest of the world for some time and he knew our concern.

Frank and Danny tried every corner of the compound for reception and double-checked all the instructions but to no avail. We would just have to wait until we returned to Nairobi.

We travelled with Safari, Lesley, Dr Pennington, Danny, Chris and Tony in a pop-top minibus. Today it would allow Chris to get a prime position for his crucial first video of the arrival. There was to be no second takes today and we are sure he was anxious to get great footage of such a significant homecoming.

Because of the recent rain everything was lush and green. Later in the day in speeches at the village the assistant village chief reminded us that the usual appearance of this dry land was parched brown. Just two years earlier the December rains had failed and the whole area of 1.5 million people faced starvation. However, this day there was water everywhere.

The red sandy soaked soil provided a sharp and attractive contrast to the blue sky and the verdant vegetation. Vegetation that looked like it had been waiting for so long to at last display its beauty.

The rough dirt road was often covered with water and at times we wondered if we would make it across the swirling depths to the other side. Sometimes it seemed as if the road had been totally washed away. It was obvious that this was not a new experience for our driver though, he didn't seem perturbed at all. It certainly was a bumpy road and in some way it seemed to add to the drama of the experiences ahead of us.

As we approached the village, I noticed Safari became quiet, he looked at the countryside, an expression of recognition and of something else in his eyes. I had a feeling of his apprehension. Quietly I leaned over and said to him, 'What's the matter, mate?'

He replied sadly, 'Mumma, I don't want to be hungry any more.' I felt tears stinging my eyes and a lump came to my throat, my heart went out to him so very much. I thought to myself, my dearest one, I want to help you. I remembered the day he said, 'My Kenya mum, she say, "Drink water, drink water!" But I eat sand.' At home we nonchalantly say we're hungry; we don't really know what hunger is.

Shortly we saw and heard the welcoming party of women lining the sides of the road. They were the villagers of Kasaala, very brightly dressed, smiling and waving, some singing, and some ululating. Such happiness seemed to abound. All these people were craning their heads to get a glimpse of Safari.

The parade of vehicles pulled off the track to a small grassed paddock. The exuberant crowd followed, singing, and clustered around us. We slid the door of our van open and got out. Safari sat within the open door. He looked shyly at the crowd, then away almost in disbelief. Disbelief and awe at the people celebrating. He seemed to be self-conscious and embarrassed at being the focus of festivities.

The crowd of villagers had deepened now and it was time for us to walk a few hundred metres down a narrow track to the Kimanzi family *shamba* or living area. The crowd was growing and a light drizzle of rain started.

The singing and ululating was increasing in strength. People were beginning to crowd in on us. I could again feel tears behind my eyes and my emotions were beginning to rise.

Looking ahead down the narrow track that was deeply rutted from recent vehicles, I saw the figure of a small, lightly built man in a blue and white check shirt running towards us, arms outstretched in welcome and to balance himself on the edge of the ruts. It was our first glimpse of Safari's dad, John Kimanzi. His whole being seemed engulfed in unrestrained joy and excitement. His mouth wide open, his face beaming uncontrollably; he was surely the epitome of happiness.

The previous afternoon the TV crew had gone into Kasaala to set up for the filming of today's arrival. Danny had told us last evening that Safari's father was very excited and wasn't able to sleep. Chris Roles and Tony Clunes remarked that John was exceedingly animated, barely able to contain his emotions.

John approached us, his glistening eyes riveted on his son. He gathered him up in his arms, moaning, '*Jambo, jambo*, Safari' – welcome, welcome, Safari. He hugged him and put him down, looked at him almost in disbelief, and then gathered him up in his arms again. These gestures he repeated time after time. The eyes of everyone in our party seemed to glisten with emotion. Such a precious moment for father and son. The crowd strained forward, eager to catch a glimpse of this climactic moment, the culmination of so much pain, so much sadness, so much love, so much good fortune, so much goodwill.

Quick introductions were made on that bush track.

Lesley politely shook John's hand while she clutched an umbrella to ward off the drizzling rain. David Syme and David Pennington did likewise. Frank felt more moved to abandon a reserved and courteous handshake in favour of a warm embrace to communicate his feelings of affection. Soon it was my turn to greet John. *'Jambo, jambo,'* he kept saying as he hugged me tightly. Words were unnecessary; there was a mutual warmth and understanding that passed between us. We had brought his son home. Oddly, I didn't have the feeling that we were strangers, meeting there for the first time. I think Safari's talk about his parents through the year had brought me to know them in their absence. He had somehow united us.

Then John Kimanzi grasped Safari's hand and the two strode proudly the remaining few metres to the family shamba. We all followed. There Safari's mother Ngayau waited, quietly surrounded by her friends, a large pastel-coloured scarf covering her head. She picked him up and quietly pressed him to her neck and cuddled him. She was smiling at him contentedly as a mother would with a new-born child. She wiped away the tears of joy with the corner of her headscarf.

Introductions were made. Ngayau stretched out her arm to me and we three stood there together communicating in a silent embrace. Two mothers quietly crying with emotion, between them one very well-loved special boy.

A shade canopy supported by cut saplings had been erected beside the family house in the area next to the growing maize patch. This is where the celebrations would take place. We were so grateful for the shade as the hot equatorial sun unrelentingly beat down on us. Beneath the canopy were rows of locally made chairs, bent cleverly from small green branches and dried in place. There was a row of tables in front covered with brightly coloured tablecloths where we could rest the bottles of Fanta and springwater that we were so happy to receive.

As we sat there waiting for the District Officer from Kitui to arrive we familiarised ourselves with the various family members and local dignitaries. We met Safari's uncle Rashid and his wife Ruth. Kilonzo's wife Mary, who we had met in Nairobi, had come down for the celebrations. We met Safari's grandfather on his father's side, Mwanzia, and his wife Ndamaris, and Ngayau's mother and her friends. Apart from John, Kilonzo, Rashid and Mary no-one spoke English. It's amazing how much can be conveyed by gestures and smiles. Kilonzo pointed out the various village administrators – the Assistant Chief, Samuel Kilunda Mbaka, and the village councillors.

In the front row with Lesley, Ngayau and Kate, Safari sat between his mother and Kate. His grandmother came over and with all the interest of any grandmother pulled aside the collar of his red tab-fronted shirt to inspect his neck. I remembered dressing him in that shirt for a reason. Because his left shoulder was so small compared with his more developed right shoulder normal shirts with wider neck openings tended to slip off his left shoulder. I thought this might make him self-conscious on this special day.

His gran was satisfied. Another lady came up to the table and leaning over to Safari practised her English with, 'How are you?' I thought, Safari, you are surrounded by love.

Mary spoke about her ordeal in getting a couple of unpaid days off work and her story illustrated the reality of the corruption which engulfs every aspect of life. Her boss at the coffee plantation knew that her husband had come back from Australia with money in his pocket and he wanted some of it. So he demanded that Mary pay him a bribe of 3000 Ssh (Kenyan shillings) – about A$55 – to keep the job open for her for two days. In this country savvy operators know how to work the system.

Mr Falana and his police escort of two arrived and sat behind us with Kasaala's assistant chief. A man carrying a piece of paper and dressed in a suit jacket began calling the crowd to order in a tongue unknown to us. We were so used to being in an English-speaking world. Now we were the outsiders, unable to understand what was being said. There were no subtitles.

The celebrations began. The first speaker was Assistant Chief Samuel Kilunda Mbaka. The Chief, John Ngengo, was out of the village and unable to attend. Through an interpreter, Paul Nyrr, and before the TV camera the assistant chief opened with, 'We thank God for giving us a time like this. We also thank Him for bringing us visitors from Australia. We also thank God for keeping our boy and he is the cause of our being here. Together with that I take this opportunity to welcome all the visitors; those who come from Australia and those who are from our country Kenya. I want to tell the visitors they are in Kenya now.' The crowd clapped warmly and he went on to say, 'Feel at home. Welcome.'

There were speeches, singing of songs with our names woven in, girls and older women in groups dancing and a diminutive man with a pork-pie hat accompanying in an ecstatic way with a double-ended drum strapped around his shoulders. The younger girls wore black skirts and white blouses and with only drum accompaniment sang in harmony as only Africans can. The older women wore brightly coloured skirts and blouses or T-shirts. They surely would have gone into debt, just to look the part. Their tightly curled hair was sometimes worn naturally but most of the older women seemed to prefer coloured headscarves, intricately tied, to adorn their heads.

The presence of an Australian TV crew added another exciting dimension to the homecoming. Never before had the village been under such scrutiny. We could see that apart from obvious affection for Safari there was an element of expectation of help from Australians for the desperately needy people of this region. It was quite reasonable for these people to recognise that they had at last 'been found'. Indeed, in the speeches to follow, these expectations were reinforced. They knew that the people of Australia had opened their hearts to their son and to them as well.

All the time people seemed to come closer to the action. All the time Safari sat demurely between Kate and Ngayau. At times he could be seen looking shyly at a little girl nearby. We were soon to learn that she was his sister Ndamaris. These two children were close in age. Furtive glances passed between them for a while and shortly she came and sat down next to him. Without words and as they smiled at each other, Safari quietly took her hand and held it. Such a privilege it was for us to observe these intimate moments between sister and brother once more united.

From where we were seated we could see the family's corn crop growing. It was about 1 metre high and came up close to within 2 metres of our chairs. The children were standing on the edge of the corn watching proceedings but amazingly very few of the plants had been trodden. Such was their respect for this vital food source.

Standing amongst all the other boys was a little boy of about seven and I became aware that his eyes never left us. He wasn't staring, instead he just observed our every movement. I looked across several times and smiled; he just kept looking. For him it was as if the singing and dancing didn't exist. His gaze fixed determinedly on us – maybe he had never seen a white person before. We were not to know then that this boy was soon to step into our lives. His name was Amin and he was Safari's orphan cousin.

It came Safari's parents' turn to address the gathering. Safari stood between his parents in the same slightly shy, slightly bored way that seven-year-olds all over the world adopt at these sorts of occasions. He was probably thinking about when he was going to be able to exit stage left and play with his brothers and friends, compatriots he had not seen for such a long time. Still, he stood there, lifting his red shirt to wipe perspiration from his face and unconsciously revealing to the world his scarred stomach and the wires to his radio microphone.

John's opening words were, 'Firstly, I thank God.' He continued by thanking everyone involved for the gift of help that had come to his son and to his family. Then he said, 'When I last saw Safari at Kenyatta International Airport I did not know whether this child would come back the way he is and I was worried inside myself. Because of God and those people in Australia I am very happy in my heart and I just want to thank you very much.'

Ngayau continued, 'I greet you all. My name is Ngayau Kimanzi. This child is my son and when he got burnt I was just helpless. I am very grateful to that Mumma who first saw Safari. I feel like donating Safari to her. I want to say that this child belongs to her for life. I would also say that Janet and Frank as well as David the doctor, this is your son as well. What has shocked me is him speaking a language I cannot understand even a word. But I am very grateful to see him.' The crowd clapped loudly. Safari, his hands folded across his chest, drew lines in the sand with his foot and looked down shyly.

Frank and I then spoke and expressed our admiration and love for Safari and our admiration for his parents in their difficult years. Frank introduced Danny, Chris and Tony to the people and said that through their special skills the character of Safari had been shown to all Australians. He said that Dr Pennington's great skills had transformed his life from a life with no hope to a life with a wonderful future.

Mr Falana also spoke: 'This occasion is so heartening, you know so emotional, so moving and yet for us who are receiving so sweet.' He acknowledged Safari's bravery and said that he had heard that one in three Australians knew who he was and knew of Kenya and Kasaala. Through Safari and his popularity in Australia many people in his community would benefit, he said. He closed by saying that Kasaala was a peaceful place and extended an invitation to stay and visit.

The celebrations concluded with a very late lunch. There were hot goat casseroles, spicy rice, chicken, salads and fresh fruit. All this courtesy of the generosity of Channel Nine. When the decision was made some months earlier to accompany Safari home they told us that we were their guests and that all airfares and hotel expenses would be met by them. They looked after us extremely well.

During lunch Frank got talking to Mr Falana. Frank touched on the subject of staying a while and mentioned that we had come prepared with tents, food and a minibus. He said that we had come to experience the hospitality that Mr Falana and the assistant chief had extended in their words to the crowd earlier in the day. However, to his great surprise Mr Falana was uneasy with the plan. In fact he seemed to be making reasons on the run that discouraged the idea. 'What if you broke your leg?' he queried. Frank replied that we had transport so it would not be a problem. Still Mr Falana seemed uneasy with our staying in the village but said nothing further.

Earlier at lunch we had spoken to the Assistant Chief of Kasaala and he was very willing for us to take up his invitation to stay. It was puzzling. Still, there was no explicit ban. Maybe he was just considering our welfare and it was concern we were hearing.

The meal continued. We spoke to John's brother Rashid and his wife Ruth. Ruth spoke no English but Rashid stood out as a very strong and capable family member. They had no children but he took his role as uncle to Safari and all his other nephews and nieces very seriously. We were seeing an aspect of the extended family system at work. He also wanted to know all about Safari's surgery and what the future held for him medically. We presumed Dr Pennington would tell the family later what lay ahead. He also wanted to know of Safari's life in Australia and we could tell he treated him like a son.

We told Rashid and Ruth that we had many stories to tell and videos to show, albeit in miniature on the view-finder of the video camera. We had the complete *RPA* program and other videos of Safari at play and at home in Australia. We said that we were staying several weeks so there would be lots of time to get to know the family.

Rashid was very happy to host us in the family shamba and showed us where we should erect our tent. Danny was also keen to video our tent camp in Kasaala for his viewers. Frank mentioned the strange warnings about how we would handle an emergency. Rashid laughed. 'We are not quite so isolated from the world here, you know, Frank. The bus for Nairobi leaves Kasaala every morning at 7 am.'

The sun was starting to fall behind the trees and we were keen to get unpacked. The rest of our party was anxious to get back to Ikutha to spend the night before returning in the morning when Dr Pennington was to remove a large lump on the face of Safari's elder sister Kanini.

As we started to unpack the minibus, one of the police-men who had accompanied the District Officer came up, his rifle at his side, and to our surprise told us we couldn't stay. His English was not good but I challenged him, saying, 'Why can't we stay?' He didn't give a reason but just insisted that we were not allowed to stay. He was a very tall man, much taller than I was. I persisted, but to no avail. Then I saw him playing with his gun, raising it and lowering it. Frank could see the futility and not wanting to force Mohammed into an embarrassing position said, 'I know you are just carrying out orders, Mohammed.' Frank then offered his hand to Mohammed and they shook hands. John, Rashid and Kilonzo were as astonished as we were but the rapidly approaching darkness left us no time to discuss things with them.

We left with the rest of the party for Ikutha. Our minds were a maze of questions. Why were we not allowed to stay? Why was the village administration so very welcoming, yet others hostile?

The bus arrived at our 'hotel' in Ikutha, the Airview Lodge. The security gate closed and with neither air nor a view we were ensconced for the night. It was the same place where we had sweltered the night before. We were so looking forward to an airy mosquito-netted tent. A cool place, not a concrete block, hot all night from the day's blazing sun.

At the ADRA compound we had eaten dinner but kept to ourselves our thoughts and questions from the day's dramatic ending. Not feeling particularly sociable Kate, Jenny, Frank and I retired early and discussed our theories in the privacy of our room at the Airview. In any event, whatever happened next would be governed by the results of those important medical tests in Australia.

Chapter 13

The morning following the day of celebrations and speeches we had our breakfast of toast, boiled eggs, vegetables and tea and readied ourselves for the day. Tony Clunes wired us up with radio microphones for the day's filming just as we had done many times before in the foyer of RPA on Monday mornings.

We bounced and splashed along the slippery, boggy road to Kasaala, which at that time of year might more aptly be called the Challenge Highway. Soon we were at the village again.

The village health clinic was the first stop and here Dr Pennington was to hold a clinic to see if he could assist villagers in need of his help.

One such person was Safari's grown sister Kanini who had a lump on the side of her face which was unsightly and needed removal. Dr Pennington, David Syme and Lesley stayed at the clinic with the film crew to carry out the minor procedure while we walked the 400 metres to the family home. We knew that John and Ngayau would be anxious to speak to us, something that had not been possible in the hurly-burly of the previous day.

The next hour was to be a most special time and will remain with us always.

We sat beneath the shade of a large leafy tree with Jenny, Kate, Richard, Kilonzo's wife Mary, Kilonzo, John and Ngayau. Ngayau had prepared her family's welcome just for us and we felt so privileged. She with her best tablecloths had prepared a couple of tables surrounded by chairs. She went to the house to bring back a tray of cups and a large pot of tea. Ngayau spoke no English but her actions were a beautiful gesture of hospitality. After the excitement and activities of the day before, we now had a chance to just sit and imbibe the nature of Safari's mother Ngayau. She was a very gentle, softly-spoken person. She wore a pale yellow floral blouse with a multicoloured sarong around her waist. On her head she had a scarf similar to the fabric of her blouse wrapped in the African way. Her crinkly hair was very short and her face smooth and exquisitely coffee-brown. As I looked into her face I could see sadness – a sadness surely born of the hard life of an African woman. Sadness at the deaths of other children and the hopelessness of the future. A look indelibly imprinted on her face and her persona even though this day was a day to rejoice in her son's seeming resurrection. It was a look that could not be so easily erased despite the day's joy and promise of hope for the future.

Safari wore a light blue knitted shirt and sat easily and quietly on his mother's knee, his scarred neck peeping from under the skewiff collar. Ngayau leant forward in her chair in what seemed an attempt to add extra importance and emphasis to her words. Quietly she spoke a few words we didn't understand. Ngayau turned to her right, nodding to Mary to indicate that Mary should translate. Mary translated, 'I just want Safari to have a chance in life.' I quietly nodded, understanding. I knew exactly what she meant and how she felt.

The tea was very welcome and we chatted about our families and learnt a little more of Safari's brothers and sisters. Safari had four sisters and two brothers. His two elder sisters Penina and Kanini were about nineteen and sixteen respectively and Penina had a baby, Ann, about eighteen months old. Every time that Ann laid eyes on us she screamed. Perhaps it was the sight of white faces, strange and alien to her.

The boys Museveni and Musembi were older than Safari, about fourteen and twelve respectively. They both went to the local primary school in the village, a school with about 800 students. Safari had a sister Nyamai, slightly older, and his younger sister Ndamaris who was the little sister I had seen holding hands with Safari the day before.

Ngayau continued to talk as Mary translated. She explained her labour and the circumstances surrounding the birth of her lastborn son. As Ngayau's story unfolded, I imagined the scene that day.

In the cool morning air just before dawn on that day in August 1994, she and her husband John set out on foot to the markets at Ikutha 16 km away. It was a pleasant time of year and the family had a little spare cash to spend on food items their own garden did not supply – things like sukuma wiki, tomatoes, potatoes and beans. Although she was near the end of her time, Ngayau kept pace with her husband in that relaxed and rhythmic African gait. I imagined her woven basket balanced on her head and her back straight in the way I had seen so many African women walk.

The journey was not just for food but to socialise, to catch up with friends at the market town. There were always crowds of people from the surrounding villages. The atmosphere was one of people happily greeting others together with serious bargaining between buyers and sellers of wares or surplus crops.

The communal market was a crude array of simple low platforms each a metre or so square. Knarled tree branches formed the uprights, bound together with local grasses woven carefully into a thatch to provide a low counter for displaying produce.

After shopping and exchanging news with other farmers, the two set off home in the afternoon – again on foot along the 16km track. They arrived home on dusk and Ngayau helped the older girls Kanini and Penina prepare the evening meal by the light of the hut's cooking fire.

After tea John and Ngayau retired to their sleeping hut. It had been a long, tiring day but a satisfying one.

Ngayau continued her story and, guided by her gestures, I could picture the scene.

Ngayau said she was restless and couldn't settle in bed. Time after time she got up, walking awkwardly, swaying from side to side with her folded arms supporting the small of her back – just as mothers-to-be do all over the world.

Ngayau then returned to her husband's side. Eventually towards midnight Ngayau knew her time had come. She asked her husband to fetch his mother from her hut 100 metres way. Ndamaris came immediately and after a short labour a boy was born.

Because the previous day had been such a happy event – a *safari* or journey to the markets – the couple decided to call their new son Safari; Safari Makau Kimanzi.

As I write these words another special scene comes to my mind. Recently when we visited Safari and his family in Kenya, John greeted his son at his school in Nairobi. Although tired from the daylong bus trip from the village, he held him close and said with reverence 'this is my lastborn, my beloved son.'

Back on that day after Safari's welcome, sitting under the tree with his family, John soon came to the matter that was foremost in his mind. He asked us if we would take Safari back to Australia for a good education. We were not surprised at his request, as Kilonzo had said during the year that he thought we might be asked.

We agreed. But we felt that Ngayau and John should be aware of certain disadvantages to such a plan, which needed to be stated but which we were sure they already knew. Frank pointed out that if Safari came to Australia he would get a good education but they would lose their son. He would lose his language and culture and whilst we would always make it possible for him to return during the school holidays, there would come a day when he might say that he preferred to be with his Australian mates. All this they understood, but still thought his best chance in life lay in an education in Australia. Frank also explained that Kilonzo had spoken in Australia of the possibility of their request and that we had made some enquiries about the matter. That day, as we sat and listened to John and Ngayau's dreams of an education for Safari in Australia to break the cycle of poverty, we were unaware that our attempts to fulfil their wishes in the way they imagined were to be thwarted.

John brought up another matter that concerned him as we awaited our party's arrival from the clinic. He produced from his pocket a small invoice written in green ink listing a number of items bought for the celebrations. There were chickens, a goat, bags of rice and maize and vegetables, all amounting to 6700 Shs, about A$120. John explained that because on the day prior to the celebrations no-one had come forward with money to pay the shopkeepers for the food he had borrowed the money to pay the bill. He pointed to a couple of people sitting to one side, waiting for their money. The amount of money was for him huge. It had been a tremendous worry to him since before the celebrations.

Frank took the bill to David Syme who had by now returned from the clinic where he had acted as assistant to Dr Pennington in Kanini's procedure. The oversight was corrected.

The operation on Kanini's face had been very successful and only a very neat scar showed where the growth had been. Kanini was shy but we are sure, very happy.

Kate alerted us to David Syme leading John and Ngayau along with Paul Nyrr, the ADRA interpreter, to a quiet spot away from the crowd. We followed and were astonished by what we heard. Ngayau said through the interpreter, 'David Syme, can we have your permission to send Safari to Australia for education?' David's response was that to do so would cause huge legal and political problems.

Frank said, 'Why can't he come back to Australia?' David replied that donations had specifically been given for Safari's reintegration into Kenya.

Frank said, 'I suppose your books are open to scrutiny,' to which Syme replied, 'Certainly.' With that, he hurried away and left for Nairobi where he was to take an early flight to Thailand. There he was to be the marriage celebrant at his daughter's wedding.

Hearing this discussion I felt bewildered and confounded. What was going on? I couldn't understand why these people had been spoken to in this way. I kept asking myself question after question. Our thoughts were many and confused. Our reaction to what we had just heard was at first disbelief. Even Ngayau's words, 'Can we have your permission' had a profound effect on us.

Calming down a little later we gathered to mutely watch TV along with the crowd. Danny, Chris and Tony had brought a small TV from Australia and with it connected to a vehicle battery and placed in the shadow of the front door of the family home proceeded to present the *RPA* program featuring Safari. Everyone sweltered in the hot afternoon sun but the villagers watched with interest. Danny took pity on Frank's plight and offered his leather hat to shield the sun.

The day was drawing to a close and Tony removed our radio microphones and packed up. We said farewell to Safari and the family fully expecting to be back in a few days. But in fact we were not to return as we had promised. The news from home that evening meant that we had to return to Australia almost immediately, on the next flight in three days' time. We left my good friend Jenny to stay on in Nairobi and return to Kasaala later in the week.

We felt that we were breaking our promise and were concerned that Safari might see it as betrayal. Still, we were depending on Jenny to explain things to him and to his family.

That evening in Nairobi Frank, his brother Richard, Kate, Jenny and I took a risk and furtively challenged the dark and foreboding streets. We walked to a restaurant two blocks away. In the security and comfort of that restaurant we discussed all that had swept over us in the last four days. Still bewildered at the unexpected turn of events, we retreated to the hotel for the night.

Next morning we met Batuk Shah in the hotel foyer and laid out our plans for the use of his minibus and driver Benson for the rest of Jenny's stay in Kenya. Kilonzo had come down from Banana Hills that morning and was anxious for us to meet his children and see where Mary worked. The arrangements made, we all clambered into the Nissan Urvan. Benson, with one hand on the wheel and the other on the horn, headed off to Banana Hills and the coffee plantation.

The inner city was bleak. Streetboys sniffed glue and begged for money. Diesel fumes choked our breath. The roads were paved and guttered but showed the signs of neglect with garbage strewn about. From *dukas* – makeshift roadside stalls of galvanised iron, cardboard and ply – poor traders eked out a living. Fruits and vegetables were displayed on counters made from newspaper sheets on the footpaths. This was a proud city slowly falling into neglect with the passage of time. There were deep open culverts beside the footpaths to handle the monsoon rains. Here and there men stood in the culverts, backs politely to the road, relieving themselves out of necessity.

The minibus moved on, through the wealthy suburbs and the whitewashed-walled villas of foreign embassies. We climbed steadily until the pollution of the city lay behind us. At Gigiri we passed the huge UN compound off to the right. Nairobi is the centre in East Africa for aid and we passed many aid Landcruisers, from white UN-badged vehicles to World Wildlife Fund cruisers, administering in an antlike fashion the bureaucracy which is the aid industry.

The affluence of the diplomatic quarter receded and the ordinary African farming and market stall world emerged. Ramshackle dukas, plying groceries and utensils; a rickety one called 'Stage Kiosk', its wall billboarded green with a Sprite ad that commanded the passer-by to, 'Obey your thirst.' The tiny shed-like 'Life Centre Hotel' spruiked an ad for Tusker beer. People waited at informal bus stops for the plethora of overcrowded matatus, the public transport minibuses. Matatus sped by with weird macho-sounding names painted garishly on their sides and windscreens: 'Kosovo Conflict', 'Death Wish' and 'Love Bus'. As if to add to their dramatic presence, at night their interiors glowed with luminescent greens and blues.

A small abattoir swayed past on the left, every part of the grisly act of slaughter on display. Its purpose and reality was not hidden and sanitised as we in the West are accustomed to, but unashamedly part of life. We passed a carpenter's shop with the product range on display out front. Two items said it all: a baby's crib and a coffin.

Locals had told us that in recent years with the pandemic of HIV/AIDS, coffins were on display everywhere. The plush quality and shine to the caskets spoke of peoples' reverence for death and its ceremony and their preparedness to give the deceased an exit from this world which in many cases was much more extravagant in a material sense than anything they had experienced in life.

Up the road the music of the bazaar lifted my spirits. It was vibrant, earthy, rhythmic, and immediate. It was the soul of Africa and so eloquently described in some intangible way the essence of the people. Living in the moment, enjoying what is now. It made me think how wise they are, because for all of us all we have is 'the now'. Great thinkers like Paramahanda Yogananda and others throughout time have reminded us of this. The people outside my window of comfort were living this truth. Safari, we had observed since we met him, exemplified this very natural and wise way of accepting life and embracing all it had to offer, both positive and negative. Such a different view of life, I thought. We in the sophisticated West believe we can dominate nature. Here it seemed people accepted nature rather than trying to bend it to their will. Was it of necessity, or freely embraced, this acceptance of nature and 'the fate of destiny'?

There were many churches – some mainstream, most evangelical – little more than tin sheds but all loudly promising 'salvation' and a better 'life hereafter'. It was obvious that whilst people accepted and embraced all that this life presented they also had hopes and aspirations. For these people, opportunity was severely limited here on earth and evangelists both conventional and savvy were addressing in their own ways the population's hope of a better life after death.

A pop music radio station played on the van's radio. A very African rap music song finished and a very beautiful example of African harmony replaced it. Frank commented on how the sound reminded him of the equally powerful and beautiful a cappella singing of the Welsh. We sat, touched by the universality of the music. There are threads in human existence, in art and music, that transcend culture and race and encourage us to acknowledge our common humanity.

The song changed to one with a strong political message. The words were forceful and blunt and were a reflection of what we were seeing with our new fresh African eyes:

Africans are dying of starvation
Politicians are paying for corruption
Feel the power

Why all the suffering down in Africa?
We gotta find a solution

Power, power to the people
To the children
The next generation

Both Frank and I looked at each other and silently out the window. Safari, along with the young people outside our comfortable bus, was the next generation. What was his and their future?

I was shaken from my thoughts as we turned off the road we had been climbing out of the city. Benson stopped for Kilonzo to get some groceries for Mary. At the roadside market people milled around, we *wazungu* or white people were a novelty. Turning around, we caught sight of the city of Nairobi beneath us, 16 kilometres away. Here amongst the local people who spent their lives out of the city, we were something new.

In a few minutes we were heading along a minor road to the plantation. We passed a rudimentary sawmill. Kilonzo pointed it out and said, 'My brother, Safari's dad, used to work here until earlier this year. He came because the rains failed at the end of 1999 and he could not grow enough maize to feed his family in Kasaala. However, nine months ago he lost this job.' Frank asked why John lost his job. Kilonzo explained that the sawmill had lost its logging permit because of the government's environmental concerns. It seemed to me so unkind to John and his family for him to have to spend months here, away from his family, to be able to put food on the table. I was coming to a real appreciation of how the other half live.

The air at that higher elevation of Banana Hills was still crisp and sunny at 10 am. Rolling hectares of coffee trees swung into view next door to the sawmill. We were at Kilonzo and Mary's home. Kilonzo explained that before independence in 1963 the plantation had been developed and owned by a British company, but had been sold into African hands when large numbers of British farmers left Kenya. An access track ran beside young coffee bushes barely half a metre high in the carefully weeded rich soil. It all had a look of commercial order and efficiency. Ahead were a simple concrete blockhouse and a boomgate. Standing beside the boomgate waving to us was a woman in a guard's uniform of dark blue trousers and long-sleeved shirt in police blue. The outfit was a little baggy on her diminutive frame. A dark blue tie completed her look of quasi-authority. It was Kilonzo's wife Mary welcoming us. Although a shy and gentle person she was warm in her greetings and welcome and suggested immediately that Kilonzo take us to their home within the estate where we would meet their girls. She explained that she couldn't leave her post but said we should go with Kilonzo and he would serve us tea.

The plantation track rambled on past mature trees laden with red coffee berries, past an irrigation dam and into an area of concrete houses with galvanised iron roofs. This was the housing area for the estate's workers. Kilonzo took us to his home, a simple three-roomed rectangular building the size of a double garage. A small concrete washroom and toilet was near the front door. Two little girls in neat cotton dresses sat shyly on the front door step. They must be Kilonzo's girls Janet and Lucy, I thought. Kilonzo said something to them in Swahili. The girls came shyly forward and we were introduced. Kilonzo said we were the first white people Lucy had ever seen and she was especially shy.

I could see that Mary was very proud of the home she

had created. The middle room was the living area. The simple lounge chairs had doilies as antimacassars and the otherwise drab concrete walls were decorated with scenes from calendars and coloured magazines, not in costly frames but simply glued to the wall. In one corner an area was neatly set up as a kitchen. White plastic buckets held flour, grains and foodstuffs. Curtained boxes hid utensils. There was no electricity, running water or sink but Mary had managed very well; very well indeed. The room in which the children slept was very simple, a large cot with sides was Lucy and Janet's bed. They slept together. Across the room were several rows of rope strung across as hangers for the children's clothes. The room was very clean and very tidy, everything neatly in its place.

As Kilonzo made us a cup of tea he announced that since returning from Australia and seeing Pappa cooking he had decided to help Mary by being the family's cook. She had her hands full. Kilonzo said that she worked six days a week from 6 am to 6 pm and was paid A$100 a month, which included the use of the house. I noticed as we arrived that the clothesline was full of drying clothes that the family had worn the day before. On her own she had been up early enough to get breakfast for her children, wash their clothes and then walk the kilometre to the boomgate, all before 6 am. At the end of the day's work she would get home in time to cook tea before dark and help the girls with their homework, then walk to the corner shop where we had stopped for Kilonzo to bring some groceries. It was a good 3-kilometre walk. In all of this I had seen a happy, relaxed, cheerful soul, very accepting of her lot in life.

As we left Kilonzo tagged along for a lift to the grocery shop. We stopped at the boomgate to bid Mary a tearful farewell. We promised to keep in touch and we told her of Jenny's plans to return to Kasaala. Mary wished us well and we continued on our way, farewelling Kilonzo at the corner shop. I felt a sadness that our friendship with Kilonzo and Mary was at a temporary hiatus but knew that our lives would continue to be intertwined.

Back we went, along the road to the hotel. Past the dukas, the churches, the whitewashed diplomatic suburbs.

Danny and the crew suggested that we all go to a local Indian restaurant they had discovered for dinner. So our party of Richard, Kate, Jenny, Frank and I bundled into two cabs and relaxed for the evening in the company of friends.

However, work still needed to be done in Kenya. The 44 boxes of aid for the village that generous people in Australia had entrusted to us had to be distributed. Bank accounts had to be established for the family members and most importantly Safari and his family had to be assured that we were not just 'here today and gone tomorrow' people. Jenny had courageously volunteered to take on these responsibilities and see the job through. She would be relying on Batuk's minibus and Benson to help her through this difficult assignment.

All this was discussed at the Hilton privately between just the five of us. We were sending Jenny back to the village where Frank and I had been welcomed by the villagers but ejected by the District Officer and we didn't know whether it was just a ban on Frank and me or on Jenny as well. We were also mindful that Jenny would be going back into an area where she would be the only white woman amongst a million Africans. Still, we were all confident that from what we had seen of the family and the villagers she would be entirely safe and that they would take good care of her. And Benson was a reliable man, capable in the country he knew well. We were never to be disappointed in Benson.

With our plans in place the entire group, Jenny included, prepared to leave for the airport. We travelled in Benson's bus and the others drove in ADRA vehicles accompanied by ADRA officials from their Kenya office in Nairobi. We were all well aware of the enormous responsibility we were setting on Jenny's shoulders. She would have to act alone and while we have great faith in Jenny's abilities we knew it was a big ask.

Once on board the plane for home I had time to reflect on the events that had taken place since we arrived in Kenya and all the associated emotions. I was touched deeply by the hospitality the family and villagers had shown us. They had gone to so much trouble. Their welcome was so warm, so sincere, so genuine and they were so poor. I thought of Ngayau's plea for us to take Safari back to Australia, for that 'chance in life'. The villagers' invitations to stay being overruled by the District Officer really puzzled us.

Kate, too, was upset. She could see the lack of educational opportunities and had heard Safari's parents' plaintive wish. She just couldn't stop crying. Saying goodbye to Safari was extremely difficult for her.

At Sydney we collected our baggage and bid farewell to the group. It was such an effort. We were at home in the beautiful city of Sydney and it was Christmas Eve. The airport arrival hall was dressed in red and green and people were carrying parcels wrapped in Christmas paper. Around me there was a feeling of happiness and excitement in the air. People called out, 'Merry Christmas' to each other; people were becoming relaxed with the Christmas holiday season approaching. I felt none of this.

The appearance as if by magic of Frank's daughter Helen was such a welcome sight. We piled into her little Mazda and hurried home.

Back in Gosford the cupboards were bare. Expecting to be in Kenya for quite a while, I had let stocks run down. So we needed to refill the refrigerator. Wandering through the supermarket I recognised at a deeper level, not just intellectually, the chasm between the assumptions and expectations of people in the developed world and the reality of life in the developing world. Wandering along the aisles packed with food in such variety, I thought, we are so lucky, so fortunate, so blessed. There was even a complete aisle devoted to the needs of our pets. A sense of guilt, of shame, of the vulgarity of it all went through me. Frank and I spoke about this 'culture shock' and agreed that all of this plethora of consumption must have been overwhelming for Kilonzo and Safari during their stay. We were returning to permanent plenty; they had arrived to only temporary affluence. Their stay in Australia was but a dreamlike reprieve from ongoing hardship.

At home Frank and I prepared lunch and had the quietest

Christmas meal in our lives. We felt we needed this quietness to reflect on all that had taken place in the last seven days. To think through all the various attitudes we had witnessed and the African experiences we had been exposed to.

Later in the afternoon we caught up with the family. Sitting amongst them I thought of our many blessings and all that we have. Whilst a material disparity exists between our Kenyan family and us, the sense of family that we saw within the Kimanzis was every bit as real, strong and buoyant as ours. And our strong sense of unity with the Kimanzi family had been forged through their child Safari. Safari, Frank and I felt, had been a catalyst for so much. We were not to know it then but he was to become a catalyst for so much more in the future.

I looked across the table at Kate; she was busy in the role of hostess. I knew how upset she was but she was pushing aside her own feelings to make sure everyone was having a happy time. I thought of the care and love she had freely given to Safari. Her compassion through his pain, her kindness shown in so many ways. Yes, I am proud of my daughter and the depth of her feelings.

What was that boy doing right now? My mind went back to the day of celebrations in Kasaala. There Kate expressed her love for Safari to the family, the villagers and to the camera. She said that Safari was the son she had never had. Safari has in my daughter Kate a staunch champion who will be there for him through thick and thin regardless of what the future holds.

Chapter 14

Meanwhile back at Nairobi airport we had left Jenny standing on the footpath with the realisation that we had gone and she was on her own. When we spoke later about this abrupt severance she said she was not sure how to describe the feeling. It was not fear, just the abruptness of that unexpectedly quick parting followed by an intense feeling of aloneness. 'In a way I was in shock,' she said. She was still trying to accommodate her feelings as Benson drove her back to the hotel.

The next day, the Sunday before Christmas, was a quiet reflective day. Jenny went to the local branch of Nakumatt supermarkets where a life-sized gyrating mechanical Santa Claus sang 'The Yellow Rose of Texas' and provided her with some light relief. Back in her hotel she quietly sat, occasionally gazing from her vantage point at the activity on the street below. A church service was taking place down in the square. All day in the searing heat from 9.30 in the morning until dark, preachers preached, people sang, worshipped and danced with seemingly endless energy and enthusiasm. She had arranged for Benson to come the next morning to meet her and travel up to Banana Hills to pick up Kilonzo and the girls and for all to travel to Kasaala for Christmas.

In the morning after changing some of Kilonzo's and some of her own Australian dollars and after picking up the others they headed for Kasaala down the main East African artery, the Nairobi to Mombasa road. Kilonzo had asked Jenny to change a small amount of money for him and she was quite surprised to hear the reason why he didn't want to go to the currency exchange office himself. He explained that questions would be asked. 'Where did you get this money? This is too much money for a simple Kenyan to have in his pocket.' Even though the amount might only be A$50 or $100.

At Ikutha Jenny and her band called into the ADRA compound to find Monica, a local lady and ADRA employee, and collect the mountain of food, equipment and the boxes of aid from Australia. They managed to pack about half into the bus and told Monica that they would be back in the morning for the remainder. At this point Monica told them that Safari had not been well and had been taken to the Kasaala health clinic. They were all anxious to get to Kasaala to find out the full story.

Darkness was falling as the bus rolled into Kasaala. Jenny hurried to Safari's parents. John said that Safari had overdone it on his skateboard from Australia. His hand was sore and a little swollen and he was alarmed, not knowing what to do. Jenny was greatly relieved but quizzed John and

Ngayau to find out if they or Kilonzo had been given any instructions about the physiotherapy for Safari's hand. They said they had not.

After quickly unloading the bus Jenny realised it was too dark to attempt the task of erecting the new tent. Besides, there was a second load of boxes back in Ikutha to be loaded. She decided to return with Benson and Kilonzo to spend the night at the Airview Lodge. Without a mosquito-netted tent there was too much of a risk of malaria to spend a night in a mud hut in Kasaala.

Christmas morning arrived and for breakfast that auspicious day Jenny opened a tin of Molly O'Rourke fruitcake. It was a sweet reminder of home and of the special day.

Jenny, Benson and Kilonzo picked up Monica from her home and drove her to the compound where they filled the bus with the remainder of our Australian aid and headed for Kasaala.

Once the bus was unloaded the first job was to set up the spacious tent that Boots of Erina had kindly donated. It was a large igloo-like structure, and it was not obvious at first reading of the instructions how it all went together. This puzzle was the villagers' 'entertainment for the day' as they stood around watching Jenny, Kilonzo and Benson struggle with the instruction sheet. Buckets of sweat later the tent was up and the villagers dubbed it and its smaller version 'the big and little turtle' as they sat in the shade and watched.

Everyone stood around expectantly. Word had swiftly circulated that the group had come bearing Christmas gifts. Eventually Jenny got the message that the great pile of Christmas presents should be opened there and then. Safari and Kilonzo allocated the solar rechargeable torches that Eveready Australia had kindly donated, with Kilonzo giving instructions on their use. We had sent boxes of books, pens and some fun things for the children, clothes, and sunglasses – the list went on. Safari and Kilonzo were in charge of distribution and Safari simply loved the act of giving. I could imagine his pleasure as I had already seen his enjoyment in offering food at the art exhibition in Gosford.

Christmas Day was a full day with lots of activities. By far the cross-country skateboard with large wheels that Kate had given Safari to take home was the biggest hit. It was such a great source of fun and excitement. Hardly a moment went by without someone pushing or being pushed. The shamba had a slight incline and incessantly they went up and down, up and down, absolutely thrilled by the experience.

Villagers came and went all day, stayed a while in the shade of a tree, chatted amongst themselves and those who knew English approached Jenny for a chat.

We had sent some basic medical supplies: adhesive dressings and bandages and some vitamins that a friend with a vitamin business, Annette Watts, and her husband had donated. Jenny had great difficulty explaining to John and Ngayau the purpose of these pills but with Kilonzo's help the idea took root. A man from the Central Coast, Jim Richardson, had parcelled up 22 dozen pairs of second-hand spectacles and John became the village optometrist. Older people suffer eyesight problems no matter where they live and this gift of better sight was most appreciated. It didn't matter at all to the men if they looked like Dame

Edna Everage. The other major item we had for Safari's family was solar lighting equipment for the homes. This was the equipment we had raced to pick up from BP's warehouse in Silverwater. It needed expert installation, which Frank himself had planned to do but now it would have to be done some other way.

Jenny's most prominent memory of that first day and evening in Kasaala was of the oppressive heat. She perspired constantly; it never seemed to give up. Her discomfort was a constant source of amusement for the Kenyans, who at night when it was fractionally cooler would put on jackets. Jenny, however, would still be sweating.

Safely in her mosquito-proof tent Jenny spent her first night at Safari's home. Early the next morning she noticed through sleep-bleary eyes that she had a visitor. Standing at the door of the tent was Safari. He wanted to know where his Australian Mumma and Pappa were. Jenny sat him down and they had a little chat. She explained that they had to return unexpectedly to Australia. As always, rational explanation worked and Safari understood the situation. When I imagined that morning I remembered Frank's and my explanations to Safari about medical procedures, and how mature his understanding of the realities and his acceptance of what lay ahead. However, he was definitely not a child who could be or should be deceived. He always deserved better. 'Do what has to be done but please tell me about it first,' seemed to be his creed.

During the night Mary had arrived. She had been unable

to get time off work to come down with the others in the bus.

That day Jenny had a chance first-hand to observe Safari at home with his brothers and sisters and his close cousin Amin. There was always a sense that they were safe exploring and playing. Amin was never far away; he and Safari were the best of friends but complementary in nature. They were the same age. Whilst Safari was loud, boisterous and a born leader, Amin was shy, retiring and willing to follow his cousin. The year that Safari was burnt had been a devastating year for the family. Amin's parent's, along with a sibling, had died of TB and were buried next to Safari's paternal grandfather's shamba nearby.

Jenny spent time with John and Ngayau with Mary translating and John's brother Rashid. Rashid and his wife lived 200 metres away. Rashid and John spoke excellent English.

The day wore on and Jenny surveyed with interest the scenes of village life. Trips to and from a source of water were made by the eldest girls Penina and Kanini. They carried 20-litre plastic drums hanging on their backs from straps on their foreheads. Using a plastic bowl, Ngayau washed up the cooking utensils, washed clothing and, using some stainless steel vacuum flasks we brought, made endless cups of tea for visitors.

Rashid came around with some fresh honey from his hives, which was a lovely treat. It was a very hot day, a little cloud in the morning helped a lot but the equatorial sun was so intense and the moisture from the recent monsoon rains made it very humid. Jenny would have loved to curl up in a cool place and sleep. The tent was definitely out – it was sweltering in the confined space. There was only one thing to do: sit in the shade of a tree and move as the sun moved across the sky.

The kids were happy. Like little girls everywhere Janet, Lucy and Safari's sister Ndamaris played with dolls and skipping ropes. Jenny asked Safari's elder sisters Penina and Kanini to plait her hair. When they touched her soft hair they burst into peals of laughter; they had never felt anything like it, such a contrast to their thick, wiry hair.

Jenny spent some time with Ngayau, Penina and Kanini explaining the importance of applying cream to Safari's scar tissue after his evening wash. She demonstrated how a crepe bandage was to be used to steadily draw his fingers into a fist and so stretch the tendons that had been immobilised for so long. This was always an extremely painful procedure and the women needed to be assured of the correct method and that pain was unavoidable. Jenny said later that she was so grateful that we had shown her how to explain it all.

It was a marvellous time of the year to be visiting the village (apart from the heat) because it was so green. The rains were nearly over. 'The crop of maize was only within a couple of weeks of harvesting so I was surrounded by six-foot cornstalks,' Jenny said. 'It was almost surreal walking through the maize between John and Rashid's place, it was magical.' It reminded her of scenes from the movie *Field of Dreams* with people moving in and out through the head-high cornfields. It was so lush and so beautiful.

In hindsight, ignorance was bliss, because lurking in those cornfields was the ever-present danger of deadly snakes.

Jenny spoke with Kilonzo about going to the bank the next day to open accounts for him and his brothers and his father. This way money could be transferred to their accounts. The money would enable them to buy more land and so become more prosperous farmers. The nearest bank was at Kibwezi, two hours' drive away. They arranged to leave at 9 am the next day.

Kilonzo's brother Michael did not have a current ID card, a minimum requirement to open a bank account. Jenny had been told that an ID card takes months to get from the District Office in Kitui. She discussed the problem with Michael and he was content for his share of the money to go into Rashid's account.

Jenny and the men went to the counter of the Kibwezi branch of Kenya Commercial Bank and asked what was needed to open an account. A photocopy of current ID and a coloured passport photograph was the reply – but passport photos took five days to develop and a photocopier was not available. Jenny decided the easiest thing was for her to take all the IDs back to Nairobi and photocopy them at the Business Centre in the Hilton.

She decided to withdraw cash on her Visa card and give them 2500 Shs (A$45) each, as an advance on the monies that were to come. As usual, this was easier said than done. The transaction could only be completed at the town of Mtito Andei, about an hour away on the main Mombasa road. They all piled into Benson's bus and headed for Mtito Andei.

While Kilonzo and Jenny were sitting in the bank, he told her in detail of the family's plans to buy more land, which would enable them to grow more maize, plus generate an income by selling the excess. This sounded like a great idea and she encouraged him.

John expressed his concern about Safari's hand being overworked by pushing the skateboard, and told Jenny that he had decided to hide the skateboard for a while to give his hand a rest. Jenny took the opportunity to ask John if it would be possible and helpful to get a donkey to ease the burden for the girls, who had to trek 2 kilometres each way to obtain water for the family. He was very pleased about the prospect and said a donkey could be bought in Ikutha.

The bank manager at Mtito Andei was able to confirm Jenny's Visa transaction and give her some cash. Happy that something had been achieved, they started back home.

It was 6 pm when they arrived back at the village and they had been gone since 9 am. It had taken all day and still the accounts had not been opened.

The next day Kilonzo and Benson went to Ikutha to find someone who could undertake the installation of the solar lights. Getting the lights installed was a priority. The plan was to install the solar panel on the roof, a light in each of the three rooms of John's house and a lead running across to the amenities block. It was too risky to put lights in the thatched huts in case of a short-circuit and fire.

The amenities block consisted of two cubicles with concrete floors, and was painted white with blue trimming, the same as John's new house. The toilet cubicle had a hole dug and two foot pads for squatting, the other cubicle was plain for washing. Jenny guessed it was modernity not generally found in a village and felt it quite a privilege to have this privacy. John had built his new house in 2001 with money he borrowed from locals. He repaid them with cash Kilonzo brought back from Australia.

The remaining solar equipment was five portable solar lights. Each unit was not much bigger than a briefcase, consisting of a solar panel on one side with a light and switch on the other. These were the lights that BP Australia had gone to so much trouble to bring in especially from Spain for us. Jenny laid these out in the sun for four hours to charge and waited eagerly for nightfall to try them out. They were fantastic, lasting 2.5 hours of continuous use and projecting their light for quite a distance. Jenny endeavoured to take some photos, but it was difficult to portray the contrast and difference they made. In the cooking hut, the light illuminated the entire area. Penina and Kanini were thrilled; they were given one for their own hut. It was amusing to observe that just like teenagers everywhere, in their rooms – in this case a hut – light shone out under the closed door and there was talking until all hours of the night. The other lights went to Mary and Kilonzo, Ruth and Rashid, Ndamaris and Mwanzia.

Jenny spent several days in Kasaala, and has many precious memories of her stay. Night was a relaxing time, listening to Kamba music playing on the radio for hours and dancing under the stars with the older girls.

During her stay at the village everyone treated her wonderfully – calling around, staying and talking, waving greetings, *jambo*, whenever she was passing. Always she felt in a protected and loving environment.

On Sunday 30 December 2001 it was time to leave. Jenny packed everything from the tent into John's house and said her goodbyes. Together with Kilonzo and Benson she was driving back to Nairobi. There she was to organise the paperwork for the men's bank accounts before going on a 'mini-safari' to Amboseli National Park and Mount Kilimanjaro for a day and a half.

The children and women were up and dressed for church. It was funny for Jenny to see all the brothers and Amin proudly wearing Safari's shirts. There was great excitement when they could get a lift to church in the bus on the way out of Kasaala.

Kasaala to Nairobi is a five-hour drive. The Mombasa road and Kenyan drivers are a lethal combination. They have so many fatal bus accidents. The condition of the road is indescribable – huge potholes and in parts it was nearly like being on a railway track as there were deep grooves carved out by the numerous trucks that travelled up and back from Kenya's seaport of Mombasa to Nairobi and beyond. And the drivers were so impatient, overtaking at any time, as if they were the only ones on the road. Without exception, Jenny felt safe and grateful for Benson's skilful driving.

Back at the Hilton that evening, Jenny sent a long email to us at Pinetop spelling out all the happenings down in the village and of course, reporting on Safari. And taking a long hot bath!

The next morning, New Year's Eve, Jenny found out just

how difficult it was going to be to open a bank account. Coming from Australia she expected it to be a relatively simple operation. The bank was in the money business; she wanted to give them money, easy. What could possibly be a problem?

Off they went to the bank armed with Kilonzo's passport photo and copy of his identification card. But further information – work references and verification of the source of the money were required, as well as the name of a relative who already had an account. After approaching three banks and receiving the same response, Jenny asked to see the bank manager.

She briefly told him the Safari story, how the money was coming from Australia, and why it was being given to subsistence farmers. To the bank, it was essential the money was coming from a legitimate source, not from selling arms or equivalent. She also advised him about the rest of the family's desire to open more accounts in Kibwezi.

Finally, Jenny asked if a letter from the Australian High Commissioner verifying her story would satisfy the bank. In particular, would it be sufficient for the bank manager in Kibwezi? Yes, was the reply.

Time was getting short. Everything was shutting down for more holidays. They raced back to the Hilton, Jenny rang Diana Nelson, the High Commission's Second Secretary, and explained the situation and what was required. Literally within the hour, a letter was delivered to the Hilton. The accounts would now be able to be opened at Kibwezi.

After a memorable few days which included New Year's Eve celebrations and her mini-safari, Jenny returned to Kasaala with Kilonzo and Benson. When Benson drove into the family compound, both John and Ngayau came straight up to her and gave her the most unexpectedly spontaneous welcome with huge hugs. She felt overwhelmed and surprised. While she was staying with them, she did her best to respect them and their culture and was very aware of not overstepping any boundaries. To receive this reaction to her sudden arrival spoke volumes to her; it represented their acceptance of her and appreciation of all she was doing for them on behalf of everyone back in Australia. It brought tears of joy to her eyes.

The next day Jenny arranged with Kilonzo to see each of his brothers and father separately and talk with them about the money we would be sending over from Australia, and to answer any questions.

In the meantime, the girls (Ngayau, Penina and Kanini) asked Jenny to accompany them to church. They walked there, taking the short cut along a track through the maize and neighbouring compounds. Once again, ignorance was bliss. Jenny had no idea of the potential danger from snakes.

Jenny and the girls sat at the back of the crowded church, but of course everyone was aware of Jenny's presence. The preacher frequently made comments, which resulted in everyone laughing and twisting in their seats to look at her. Penina and Kanini thoroughly enjoyed themselves, whispering and giggling to each other. Jenny was asked to come to the front of the church and address the congregation while the preacher translated. Once outside, it was a relief to take a deep breath of fresh air, still hot and sultry, but fresher.

The afternoon was spent under the shade of the trees, talking to each of the men individually – Kilonzo, John, Rashid, Michael and their father Mwanzia – describing what money was coming, how it was calculated and why it was being deposited in the bank.

Later in the afternoon, John came up with a big smile on his face and sat next to Jenny, saying, 'Girls very happy!' For a moment she had no idea what he was talking about, then the penny dropped – the donkey. He was obviously thrilled and so were the girls. John and Jenny then talked about exactly where a donkey could be purchased.

The next day was Monday and bank day again. Quite a few villagers wanting a lift into Ikutha accompanied the group. With the weight of everyone aboard, the van for the first time got bogged, even though Benson was so good at navigating the large waterholes and muddy tracks. Although the rainy season was over, most nights there were heavy downfalls, which kept the roads waterlogged. With so many people to help, it was easy to push the van out.

It was market day at Ikutha, so they dropped Ngayau off. Her priority was to buy a donkey, while the others travelled on to Kibwezi and the Kenya Commercial Bank.

Finally, the four bank accounts were opened for Kilonzo, John, Rashid and Mwanzia with a deposit of 10 000 Shs (A$180). Jenny checked the bank fees involved and illustrated how to operate the accounts, as well as organising another cash advance of 2500 Shs (A$45).

Back at the family shamba, there was great excitement, as John and Rashid arrived with the donkey, which had been purchased for 600 Shs (A$11). It still had a foal suckling, which would be returned to the owner later.

Jenny didn't cook any meals for herself while she was in the village, due to the exhaustive heat. However, she was very aware of the situation and wanted to make a contribution to the household chores. One day, she made the effort and cooked up a big pot of bean curry, vegetables and rice. And as luck would have it, the timing was perfect. All the men were out, only Ngayau, a few of her friends and the girls were sitting having a chat. Such a great opportunity to thank the women, as they certainly were the ones doing all the work.

Gestures were made, as no-one spoke English. Jenny brought the food to the table and individually served them and they sat in companionable silence eating. The meal finished, Ngayau started to collect the dishes, but Jenny insisted that she was doing the dishes. They all smiled and giggled. Jenny said she didn't think they were used to being waited on, even if only for one meal!

A little later the kids arrived home and there was enough food left to feed them as well. Jenny was fulfilled and happy with the results. This certainly was not something she could have planned.

Every time Jenny went into Ikutha she bought fresh eggs, as these were one of Safari's favourites. There was heaps of powdered milk and chocolate, which Kate had bought. A morning routine was hard boiling the eggs and making a large jug of chocolate milk. Safari delighted in handing this out to the other kids.

We left a lot of food: bags of rice, tinned food, flour, sugar, salt, spices, tea – all the basics and more, as well as cutlery, plastic dishes, pots and pans, and a huge teapot. As Jenny was on her own, most of these things were stored in boxes in John's house and she forgot all about them. One day while Ngayau was serving the morning cuppa out of their leaking teapot, which required holding a cup under the spout to catch the spillage, Jenny remembered the identical teapot Kate had bought. She dug it out of one of the boxes and gave it to Ngayau. She was over the moon, and what a pleasure it was to see her wonderful, smiling, proud face the next time the tea was served!

Inevitably the time came for Jenny's return to Nairobi and on to Australia. Benson, Kilonzo, Janet, Lucy and Safari were to accompany her to Nairobi. Jenny suggested the departure be low-key. But this was not going to happen. People started arriving at 7 am; everyone wanted to bid her *kwaheri* (goodbye).

Dismantling the tents was a big task. Frank had emailed Jenny to advise of Australian quarantine restrictions and the necessity for all African dirt to be washed off the tents. Before dismantling started, all the kids piled into the tent for photos, a swarm of smiling faces and thumbs up. 'Everybody – Benson, John, Kilonzo, Rashid, Michael and others – were fantastic in the washing of the tents. What a chore!' Jenny said. 'I certainly could not have done it without them.'

As the bus drove out of the family compound for the last time, Safari's grandfather, Mwanzia came over to the van to say his goodbyes. Jenny leant out the window to take a photo of him, he said something and everyone laughed. Jenny turned around and asked, 'What did he say?'

The answer was, 'Not in these old clothes, you don't!' He had his pride and did not want his photo taken in his old torn, working jumper. We are all the same, it doesn't matter if we come from a little village in Kenya or from a large city like Sydney. We all like to look our best for the camera.

With two days to wait in Nairobi for the flight home, Jenny decided to spend the time and her money on a safari. And she thought Safari might like to join her and see some of his country's animals. He was very excited.

Outside the hotel Benson picked them up and they were on their next great adventure. The countryside was beautiful as they drove through Thika with its coffee and pineapple plantations, lush green rolling hills on both sides of the road. They crossed the equator; another great photo opportunity. Further north the road passed Mount Kenya to Samburu National Park.

That afternoon, Jenny and Safari embarked on a game drive. Safari thought it was excellent standing up at the back of the van and looking out through the raised roof at the passing parade of animals. They saw cheetahs, leopards, a lioness and cubs, oryx, giraffes, gazelle, ostriches, zebras, waterbuck – the list goes on.

Back at the lodge there was a nightly feeding of crocodiles, which Safari also loved. He was happy to stand on the other side of the fence. Another of Safari's loves on this safari was the food; he ate and ate, enjoying himself immensely. He had his fill of meat, three times a day.

There was, however, some concern on Jenny's part, as she noticed one of the scars on Safari's left arm at the elbow was open and weeping. She was not sure what to do, as they were a long way from any medical help, so she dressed it regularly with aloe vera and kept it covered. She kept a close eye on it, and felt a great relief as it slowly showed signs of improvement and healing.

The next day began with another early start and a game drive. This time Jenny and Safari saw some elephants, much to Safari's delight.

He was so happy, singing the welcome song from the village, as they were driving around. He loved seeing the animals and Jenny enjoyed sharing the experience with him.

Back at Nairobi, as planned, they met up with Kilonzo, Mary, Janet, Lucy and Ngayau and spent some happy hours together at the city's Giraffe Centre and Animal Orphanage.

All too soon, it was time to repack the suitcases, rewash the tents in the hotel bath and fold them up, again with Kilonzo and Benson's assistance. Then as surely as night follows day the moment came to say goodbye. Kilonzo suggested they go downstairs to say goodbye, but Jenny could not go, the goodbyes had to be in the room. She was far too emotional for public goodbyes. Kilonzo started to pick up his bags, and she told him to put them down and gave him a hug. A big hug and kiss for Safari. Next Ngayau and Jenny both lost it again, crying and hugging, they just held onto each other. The boys had left, the porter had collected the bags and they were standing in the doorway. Ngayau was loath to let go of Jenny, slowly releasing the hug to holding Jenny's hand and eventually letting go and walking down the hallway.

Still crying, Jenny closed the suitcases and the porter returned to collect the luggage. Jenny left the Hilton and left Ngayau, Kilonzo and Safari standing mute in the foyer.

Jenny, Benson and Batuk drove in silence to the airport. The next hurdle was dealing with her mountain of luggage and how to get it back to Australia. There was lengthy dialogue at the check-in counter, resulting in one of the tent bags being left with Benson, but there was still far too much luggage. Luckily for her, an Emirates flight attendant, who had been on the flight across with Safari, joined in the discussion and the excess was waived. Emirates had been marvellous on the way over and now continued to support Jenny's homeward journey.

Jenny counted out her last Kenyan shillings and bought a bottle of beer while she waited to board the plane. Although weary and emotional she felt immensely satisfied to be able to help the family and of course spend special time with Safari.

Jenny rang us from Mascot airport, and caught the shuttle bus to the Central Coast. By the time she had dragged her suitcases to the bedroom, we were at her front door. It was tremendous to see her; it seemed like such a long time since we waved her goodbye at Nairobi airport. So much had happened and we had so much news to catch up on.

Part Three
Unfinished Business

Chapter 15

Towards the end of January 2002 the family matters that had brought us back so suddenly at Christmas were being taken care of and we were in a position to be able to consider the matter of Safari's education.

During 2001 we had made some new friends in the Blue Mountains when we went to Katoomba for a few days in March while Safari was off our hands in hospital. Looking up an author of a number of spiritual books that had taken our interest we met Howard Murphet who lives at Hazelbrook in the mountains. Howard, a man in his mid-nineties, greeted us warmly and from the moment we met him we were captivated by his warmth, wisdom, acuity and youthfulness of mind and spirit. But particularly by his wisdom.

We have become very good friends of Howard and his circle. They share with us the same philosophy of life and are 'seekers of the truth' along life's journey.

On later trips to Howard's, Safari came along. It was a

meeting of two extraordinary individuals. Safari was somewhat in awe of this very old person. As he had for Frank's parents Alma and Ted, he displayed a natural reverence for the elderly and frail.

We had also met a friend of Howard's, Yvonne, that day in March 2001. The talk revolved around Safari and what was going to happen to him educationally when he returned to Kenya. Yvonne said that she knew of an unusual and very good school in Zambia that she had seen described on a videotape. She offered to send us a copy, which she did.

Things were almost always hectic that year and when the tape arrived we left it to one side for some time before finally sitting down to watch. Even then we must have been somewhat distracted, as the contents didn't really sink in. We were watching and listening with half an eye and half an ear.

After Christmas, a relative quiet had returned to our lives. With Jenny over for lunch one day after her return from Kenya, we revisited the video.

It described a school in Zambia, in the northern town of Ndola, near Zambia's border with Congo and 300 kilometres from the capital, Lusaka. Zambia, before independence was known as Northern Rhodesia and is 1500 kilometres to the south of Kenya. In 1992 a couple from Sierra Leone, Drs Victor and Genevieve Kanu, opened a school in Ndola. The Kanus were both educationalists with master's degrees from Oxford and New York universities and were on a mission to introduce a new approach to education in Africa.

The school they created from an empty tract of land took students that no other school would accept because of their poor grades and antisocial behaviour. The initial intake was all boys, although that has changed. They were drawn from the neighbouring high-density townships where schools were shockingly and routinely vandalised.

No tuition fees were charged. The school was open to students from all areas of society regardless of income, class, creed or religion.

They exposed the children to an ethics-based education, 'Education in Human Values'. The students were encouraged to develop a positive attitude about themselves, and not to think of themselves as dropouts or inferior. They were encouraged to respect all religions, respect themselves and their parents as well as the traditions of their country. Pupils were taught about all religions but because Zambia is a predominantly Christian nation there is a strong inclination towards Christianity. That unity of faiths approach to religion and Education in Human Values is espoused by the Indian social reformer and educator, Sathya Sai Baba and his principles of Love, Peace, Truth, Right Conduct and Non-Violence are emphasised. The fundamental underpinning to the teaching is the teacher's own living of the Values. The teacher needs to be an example at all times, inspiring the pupils.

The purpose of education, the Kanus emphasised, must not be for making a living, but for living a life that is meaningful.

In all aspects of their school and after-school life the students are encouraged to live the principles and not just give lip service to them. The Values are woven into every aspect of life. As an example, a maths lesson in division might incorporate the social idea of sharing and class discussion would follow. The students accept responsibility for the cleanliness and maintenance of the school and thus learn a sense of ownership and social responsibility.

The results of the program were and continue to be, extraordinary. Academically in government-run examinations the students achieve outstanding results with 100 per cent pass rates year after year.

We were very impressed with what we saw on the video and thought that if Safari's parents were agreeable that Safari's father John and Frank might go to Zambia and visit the school to see for themselves. We decided that Frank could do the necessary work alone and that it would be best for me to attend to the ongoing family matters in Australia.

The video had some contact email and phone details. We gave the phone number for the school a try, and eventually we got through.

Mrs Kanu answered the phone and we quickly introduced ourselves and explained the situation. Then to our complete surprise she said, 'Oh, there's no need to come to Zambia, there's a sister school in Nairobi.' She gave us the contact details and we were so relieved to have a starting point in our hunt for a school. If the Nairobi sister school met all our expectations then Safari would indeed 'have a chance in life'.

A few days later on 25 February Frank flew out for Kenya. Waiting at Kenyatta International Airport in the scorching sun were John, Kilonzo, Safari, his cousin Amin and Batuk's loyal driver Benson with the Nissan minibus which was to be their transport in Kenya.

Amin had a runny nose and Kilonzo remarked casually that he probably had a small dose of malaria. Frank was at first taken aback by such a casual attitude to what we consider such a serious disease but later realised the position of people dealing with hazards like malaria which are part and parcel of their life. Frank also noticed Safari had a small ulcer in the scarring of his inner right forearm. Amin's 'malaria' didn't develop but Safari's ulcer was soon to cause Frank some real concern.

Where do you stay when you are in Nairobi and on a budget? Luckily for the well informed there is a plethora of perfectly adequate hotels to be had, right in town. All one needs is a little local help. Batuk found Frank a really nice hotel called Azee House. At one-fifth the tariff of the Hilton and with meals included, why would you go anywhere else? Kilonzo, John, Safari and Amin were staying with friends in Banana Hills and after Frank was installed in the hotel he set about contacting the school that Mrs Kanu had recommended.

Along the road giggles and chatter came from the rear of the minibus. Sneaking a glance Frank could see Safari and Amin perched in the back thoroughly enjoying not only the treat of a ride in a bus but each other's company as well. They have always been inseparable friends. Amin's eyes shone with a true sparkle that was quite infectious as they bumped along.

The school was about 70 kilometres out of Nairobi in Maasai territory at a place called Kisaju. It stood on 20 hectares of land. Half the land was under cultivation growing vegetables for the school kitchen. The rich loamy dark soil was irrigated by beautiful sweet water from a deep well. The buildings were large and well built from concrete and with primary and secondary school classrooms. The secondary classrooms were unoccupied as the school had been in existence for only a few years and students had not progressed beyond primary level. Frank learnt that a generous benefactor in England with an interest in providing free education for poor Kenyan children had funded the school.

Frank and the party met the school's principal, Shastry, and his wife Sita who lived at the school. Shastry explained that the students were local Maasai children, boys only at present. The school had a policy of taking only one child from a family so as to spread the school's meagre resources over an area of great need. The thinking was that if one child from a family was educated then the benefit would spread to the family as a whole.

John was very impressed with the school and keen for Safari to be enrolled. However, when Frank said that Safari had never been to school before, Shastry explained that the school did not have a kindergarten level which it seemed Safari needed and that he would have to give him a test to see if he could fit at another level. Of course Safari could not read or write so the outcome was predictable.

But Shastry was keen to give Safari the best opportunity. The school was in holiday recess until the middle of April. If Frank were able to give him some coaching in rudimentary handwriting and arithmetic he would strongly consider enrolling him. Shastry was concerned that unless Safari had some skills it would divert too much of the teacher's attention from the rest of the class.

John was disappointed at the news but keen for Frank to coach Safari, so they left for Nairobi armed with a list of suitable books to get from the market. Frank said to me later, 'Jan, I never thought in my life that I would be one day finding the ins and outs of the Kenyan education system and teaching a little seven-year-old Kenyan boy to read and write!'

While John, Kilonzo and Amin caught a bus back to Kasaala 300 kilometres away Safari and Frank set up classroom in the hotel. Azee House is situated in an area of Nairobi called Parklands where large villas from the colonial era sit among large acre blocks of land in a suburban setting with strangely familiar trees: eucalypts. The area was at one time swampy, as was quite a lot of Nairobi, and eucalypts were brought in from South Africa and Australia to drain the land. All the properties are security-walled with 3-metre-high concrete walls topped by razor wire. The gates are high and made from steel and guarded by uniformed security guards called *askaris*. Some properties have triple levels of security within the walls. Nairobi residents are very security conscious. Unemployment is high and the resultant poverty on the streets no doubt forces some people to adopt robbery as a means of survival. For others, crime is just a way of life. For the visitor, the issue of poverty and highly visible security is very confronting.

Inside the security wall Azee House was very pleasant. The askaris were the tall, thin, ever-watchful Maasai. Seemingly so suited to shepherding, whether of cattle or people, they fill this urban role all over Nairobi. They are to be seen in their characteristic passive but watchful stance, armed only with a stick, the Maasai badge of office. They are not bored by the long, slow days but always on the lookout for lions; whether they are real lions on the plains or urban 'lions' in the Nairobi streets.

Azee House proved to be the ideal place to be with Safari. It is a family business and the guests range from businessmen from all over the region to visitors for the nearby highly regarded Aga Khan Private Hospital.

Safari in his inimitable way soon crept into the hearts of all the staff of the two-storeyed hotel. And they befriended him, not because when they met him they knew anything about his saga or the way he looked but just because he has that engaging and irresistible personality. From the reception desk staff to the odd-job man to the waiters and all the kitchen staff, Safari wended his way, introducing himself and asking a thousand questions about this and that. It was the ideal set-up. While Frank went about some things he had to do, he knew that Safari was being looked after by a dozen new uncles and aunts, and a tall, no-nonsense guard to keep him from straying outside. These couple of days Safari spent familiarising himself with his new surrounds while Frank went out shopping with Batuk for schoolbooks, stationery and all the other learning tools needed to start school. He was so fortunate to have Batuk's help; he knew everything about Kenya and Nairobi, especially the business world.

While Frank and Batuk were in the schoolbook section of Nairobi markets, in the maze of alleyways Frank decided to get some exercise books to take to the village primary school as a small gift when eventually he made the trip south.

I had made the suggestion to Frank before he left Australia that it would be a nice gesture to take some exercise books to the schoolchildren in the village school. Jenny had told us that there were about 850 children in Kasaala Primary School.

Batuk used his influence to get us the very best price in town and they loaded up the minibus with 2000 exercise books, 1000 rulers and 1000 pencils and erasers, chalk and pencil sharpeners. It was quite a load but when they eventually distributed them to the children in Kaasala, Frank said, 'I will never forget the pleasure and gratitude in the eyes of students, the teachers and the parents at this simple gift. I am sure that for some it was the first proper stationery they had ever had. Slate boards had probably been their only writing tools.' Frank was to spend seven days in Kasaala when he handed out the exercise books. He said how touched he was by the response to the gift. 'When I walked across the primary school's playing field an ocean of children came running towards me, greeting me. The image of so many children bursting towards me intent on meeting me was quite strange. For a moment I knew how a pop star might feel. I met the teachers and gazed on as the various classes lined up and the children received their little gift – such a little gift but one that was received with such gratitude.'

At the hotel Safari and Frank settled down to some intensive study interspersed by little breaks for him to explore the hotel and cajole the staff into meeting his requests – which were mainly culinary in nature. Frank has enduring memories of Safari in the dining room at mealtime, a small boy sitting neatly at the nicely set table being doted on by John Kihara, an elderly waiter who had been with the owners for 40 years. John just loved feeding Safari and Safari just loved receiving John's largesse. And John knew that our little carnivore loved meat. Another memorable image is of Safari delicately wiping his mouth with a napkin. Frank remembers thinking to himself, I could take this little fellow to Buckingham Palace and he would acquit himself very well. Frank has also mentioned the other days when they were out and had a meal at a roadside café with Kilonzo, Benson, John and Amin. There it had been completely different; no knives and forks. Instead, wash your hands as you walk in, then feel the goodness of the food with your own hands – or in Safari's case, hand. His left hand was not yet functional.

In his usual display of cultural and social ambidextrousness Safari was completely at home in either situation.

The staff were initially puzzled about Frank's relationship with Safari as I am sure the people in the street outside were when the two of them would walk to the little group of shops at the next corner for Safari's daily treat, chicken 'n' chips at the local fast food shop 'The Hungry Bite'. Frank said he explained the story a thousand times; people were so interested. One day at the bus stop near the shops a *kondo* boy, a bus conductor, hanging halfway out of the seriously overcrowded matatu cried out a greeting as he passed, 'Jambo! White man helping black man – very good.'

At the hotel Frank was asked to show the *RPA* program that he had recorded on his video camera and staff and guests crowded around the TV in the lounge and experienced the saga of Safari's journey to Australia. Meanwhile Safari was elsewhere in the hotel pursuing his own agenda. To him that pain and suffering was all history; what interested him was the present.

It was not any easy job teaching Safari to write – Frank's first task. He had little idea of how to form letters and Frank had little experience with youngsters. He said, 'In my teaching days all my students had been adults and teenagers and I was out of my depth.' Luckily, a lady, Professor Bali who was a trustee of the school at Kisaju and also the principal of Visa Oshwal Girls' Secondary School, helped him. Prof. Bali put him in touch with a girl who taught at a local kindergarten. Vivian came to the hotel after work and taught Safari handwriting. She was very good and he was progressing well.

Since Frank's arrival, Safari's ulcer had rapidly and dramatically worsened. Frank was treating it with Dettol and dressings from the local pharmacy but it seemed out of control and he was concerned. It was very angry looking and weeping badly despite his attempts at bathing it in antiseptic. However, the school came to his aid yet again. Another of the trustees was the professor of infectious diseases at Kenyatta Hospital and she arranged for Frank to see a specialist with

Safari. Daniel, the hotel's driver, took them to the Kenyatta National Hospital which was on a slight rise overlooking Nairobi's Uhuru Park and they spent what seemed an eternity queuing up to get an appointment.

The corridors were crowded with outpatients, many of whom looked like they needed to be in-patients. There were many children with their mothers and almost every one had burns injuries. Frank said he couldn't remember seeing a broken limb. Burns amongst children are very common amongst the poor and are caused by the lack of electric lighting and the common use of open fires for cooking. Many of the burns were bad and Frank wondered what Safari's body would have looked like when he was burned as a toddler. The children were mostly stoic and their mothers' eyes showed the resignation and suffering that is Africa. Suddenly our little ulcer appeared trivial by comparison.

The doctor looked at Safari's ulcer. Apparently the scarring on the forearm of his right arm had become inelastic and with flexure had cracked the skin. An infection had taken hold in the broken skin and a sore had developed. The doctor scribbled instructions on a card for a dressings nurse in a clinic down the hall. Frank had with him the video camera with the *RPA* program tape and was able to satisfy the doctor's interest in the surgery done in Australia. Frank could tell that in looking at the footage of Safari before surgery the doctor had seen it all before – many times before. He did remark, however, that in his view Safari needed more professional physiotherapy in order to regain better function in his left hand. Frank said that he agreed but that he was imitating what he had seen done in

Australia at RPA as the next best thing.

They left the doctor's rooms, sought out the dressings nurse and joined the queue. Frank said, 'I will always remember the burned child she was attending to as we entered her room. Terribly distressed, the child – I can't remember whether a boy or girl of about four – had burns to the entire chest and neck and was having the dressings changed. The dark skin was missing and the body was covered with the blotchy red and white of burns tissue weeping clear lymphatic fluid. The child sat on the mother's knee and by the mother's side a sibling watched on impassively. The mother's face had that same look of resignation and a look beyond despair that I had seen on other faces in the corridors outside.'

Frank watched the dressings nurse carefully, noting what she did and what products she used. He asked questions and in five minutes knew enough to assume responsibility for redressing Safari's ulcer. The nurse was quite happy to demonstrate what to do and to have someone else lighten by one her patient load.

Off they went to a pharmacy for Betadine and recommended dressings. Twice a day the dressing was changed and the problem gradually subsided. On reflection we wonder now what would have been the outcome had Frank not arrived when he did. What if it had gone unattended? Safari was not one to complain; in fact never during the twice-daily procedure did he ever wince with discomfort.

During the coaching period Frank made contact with the trustees of the school. The committee met in the Sathya Sai

Centre in the suburbs of Nairobi and on Sunday 3 March Frank went in to discuss Safari's coaching progress.

As he walked out into the bright noon sun he looked down the flight of stairs from the centre to the carpark below and was struck by the sight of an unknown European man standing there alone, slight in build and with the fair complexion of an Englishman. He was dressed for the sun in a white safari suit and panama hat. Nairobi is naturally full of dark faces but the bulk of non-Africans are of Indian extract so to see someone so pale and familiar was unusual.

Frank walked up and introduced himself. The man's name was Chris Hawley. He was very softly spoken; a reticent Englishman transported from Oxford or Cambridge to the outer reaches of the Empire and doing his best to 'keep out of the midday sun'. After explaining that he and his wife Margarita had lived in Nairobi for 30 years he asked Frank what had brought him to Kenya. Frank briefly told the story of Safari and explained the current education problem. Chris simply said, 'There is another similar school to Kisaju in Nairobi, you know. And it does have a kindergarten class.' It was music to Frank's ears! He went on to say, 'My wife and I are associated with the running of it – why don't you come and visit?' Frank hopped into Chris's little VW Beetle and did just that.

Along the way Chris and his wife Margarita explained their involvement with the school Frank was about to visit. Chris and Margarita, who was Spanish, had moved to Nairobi and before retirement Chris had worked for Coca-Cola Kenya as their accountant. They had raised a family and now had grandchildren in Nairobi. In their retirement they devote their lives to the children of the school. As they drove along, the picture of the school and its history emerged.

In 1995 they felt the need to help address in some way the poverty and destitution in the slums of the city. Starting in a single room offering a home but no schooling, in 1997 along with five trustees they established the formal structure of a home and a school at Uthiru. Fifty orphans from the slums were taken in and given love, a home and education.

These children were integrated with 130 poor neighbourhood children as day students to avoid the orphans feeling institutionalised. The local community was involved in the school and made to feel part of the school's life. This idea of helping the community at large as well as the students is an ongoing part of the school and home's plan.

Educationally, Chris and Margarita said, the Sathya Sai School at Uthiru follows the Government of Kenya school curriculum and uses the same Education in Human Values approach, which has been so successful in Zambia. In fact the Zambia school has become the focus in the region for the teacher-training program in Education in Human Values. The teachers at Uthiru are all qualified teachers and the Principal, Daniel Otieno, is a graduate from Moi University in Nairobi. When Frank met Daniel later that day he was very impressed by his quiet professionalism and dedication to the school and to the philosophy of Education in Human Values.

The school is located in the rural suburbs at Uthiru, 10 kilometres out of Nairobi on the road north to Uganda. Market gardens and banana groves on undulating hills with pleasant views cover the school area. It was away from the hustle, squalor and smog of the city and a perfect place for children to learn.

The school was in two parts. On one large rented lot the present temporary school and home coexist. Further down the narrow lane about 200 metres away the school's trustees had purchased a similar block and were in the process of building a permanent school of concrete. The trustees were pragmatic and because they struggled financially were frugal with the funds they had to work with. As a result the buildings at the first site were galvanised iron classrooms and dormitories. Even a tent had been pressed into service as a classroom.

When they arrived at the school, Safari was shy and stood near the car watching the boys play in the distance with a soccer ball. Soon the ball was accidentally or purposely kicked in his direction and he returned it with a well-aimed and resounding thud from his right foot. Instantly the other kids realised that this new kid on the block had some soccer savvy and the ball was soon booted back and forth. Thirty seconds later he was in the game. Ten minutes later lunch was served and Safari was handed a bowl of beans by one of the staff. He really enjoyed it. The coup de grâce came when someone offered him half an avocado and a teaspoon to scoop out the flesh. A little later when Frank thought it time to go back to the hotel he said, 'Safari do you want to go back to the hotel now?'

'No' he replied 'I'll stay here.' So Frank left him with his new-found friends.

The trustees at the little school at Uthiru also help where possible a very poor school in the Nairobi slums. Margarita took Frank to visit this school that they helped. It was a small building in a low swampy area – the classroom floor turned to mud when it rained. The building was of very rickety weatherboard construction with a very low ceiling, such that Frank had to crouch to enter. Inside it was full of happy kindergarten faces, faces that seemed unaware of their lack of even the most basic requirement of adequate shelter. The children and the poverty-stricken volunteer teachers welcomed Frank and Margarita eagerly as if their school was completely functional.

Frank videoed the scene before they left. Margarita explained that if they have a surplus of food they share it with the children and teachers of the little school in the swamp. Frank was impressed by this and by the dedication of the teachers who themselves had so little but who were prepared to do what they could for these extremely disadvantaged children.

Frank was very happy with the outcome of his visit to the school at Uthiru, and anxious to tell the family and have them come up to decide for themselves.

Chapter 16

A few days later Benson picked up Frank and Safari along with Kilonzo, who had been visiting Nairobi, and they all drove to Kasaala. On the outskirts of the capital they stopped at a Nakumatt supermarket. There they loaded up with food that Kilonzo knew was not available in the village. Frank wanted to give the family, particularly the children, a few treats.

Before Frank left he rang me and told me about the school he had found. We were both very pleased and hoped the family would approve. I suggested to Frank that if Safari went to Uthiru then maybe the school at Kisaju could allocate the place that they had reserved for Safari to Amin. Because he and Safari are very close friends, together in the loneliness of Nairobi they would form a common support and bond for each other. In the years ahead they would no doubt adopt city ways and move away, to a degree, from village ways. But through all this they would have each other to fall back on, to feel secure.

We felt very strongly about the benefits of the Education in Human Values program and we thought that Amin especially, as an orphan, should be advantaged. Before leaving for Kasaala Frank rang Shastry, the school principal at Kisaju, and put the request to him. Shastry agreed to consider Amin after first giving him an entrance test.

The drive south took the group through the terraced hillsides and the blooming cascades of bougainvilleas to the town of Machakos some 70 kilometres towards Kasaala.

After a stop for lunch at Machakos they returned to the Nairobi to Mombasa road and the insanity of the traffic, and continued the journey south, going to Kasaala via a different, more direct route to the one we took in December with Channel Nine.

They were on the road which was the artery from the Indian Ocean coast to Central Africa. This traced the route of the Mombasa to Uganda Railway that Britain had built in the colonial past to gain access to the interior of this rich land and which has played a large part in the romance of Africa. It is a single track and today operates on a much more casual basis than in its heyday.

Driving down the road they passed towns that are associated with the building of the line and towns that developed at the train stops. The architecture of the towns often reflects an Indian influence in its construction. Hindu temples are also sometimes to be found; these add an Eastern flavour to the African landscape.

As the four travelled south, on their right they saw off in the distance the magnificent snow-capped peak of Africa's Mount Kilimanjaro bursting like a pyramid from the plateau to 5895 metres. Kilimanjaro lies just inside Tanzania's border. The area is traditional Maasai land, which extends to the north and becomes the savanna grasslands around Kisaju. The flat vista was dotted with the occasional giraffe grazing gently on the upper foliage of an acacia tree. It formed a stage for the mighty Kilimanjaro to make the proud statement: 'This is Africa.'

Further down the road the vegetation changed to the iconic African baobab trees with their strange bottle-shaped trunks. That day the groundcover was lush and green but Frank thought that at the height of the drought this must indeed be a desolate landscape. A time of year where the black soil opens its pores and cracks violently as if begging to be drenched with rain. The black soil needs only water to provide in abundance.

They left the Mombasa road at Kibwezi, the town that Jenny visited to open the family bank accounts. Benson filled up the tank, the travellers filled up themselves and headed off on a back road to Kasaala, now only 60 kilometres away.

The area around Kibwezi is still quite a high plateau of red soil at over 1200 metres. Soon they crossed the swift-flowing Athi River, swollen by the rains. As they crossed an elevated bridge they could see down below on the riverbank people washing and carrying on with their lives. The river is home also to crocodiles and the dangerous hippopotamus, which hide beneath the banks and attack unwary animals and people. It is said that hippos kill more people in Africa each year than any other animal. For everyone in rural Africa who lives in the environment there are dangers, a reality that was to be brought home to us with tragic clarity less than a year later.

The van bumped and slid along the red murran dirt road past small, river-irrigated farm holdings growing the white maize, which is the staple crop for so many. They were in the heart of Kamba territory, Safari's tribal group. Small hilly outcrops appeared amongst the red soil and they could look down to their right to the wooded valley of Tsavo National Park, famous for its elephants and in earlier times, lions. Down there on the edge of the park lay Safari's village of Kasaala – so small it doesn't appear on the usual road maps yet it was to produce a child who has made such a big impact on people so far away.

The village of Ikutha lurched into view. Stopping only for some kerosene for the family, the group made the turn to the right for the last 20 kilometres of track to Kasaala.

At the village Frank got a warm reception. Ngayau, Kilonzo and Mary, John's brother Rashid and his wife Ruth and the grandparents all welcomed him to the family shamba. He pitched his dome tent – the same tent that Jenny had used – then went to see John's father, Mwanzia, and his wife, Ndamaris, who lived a little distance away. They spoke no English but took him immediately to three graves adjacent to their house. It was a tragic site of two adult graves of mounded earth with a child's grave in between. Through Rashid, Frank learnt that they were the graves of Amin's parents and a sibling who had died of TB when Amin was a baby.

Frank spent time talking with and getting to know the various family members. The hot sun moved across the sky and in synchronism they moved their chairs to keep under the shade of a tree in the family shamba. Ngayau and Safari's sister Penina brought a constant supply of hot sweet milky tea to cool everyone down. Friends and neighbours came down to say hello.

The family activities of the day went on. The girls fetched water; the clothes were washed in plastic basins with Blue Omo and hung out to dry. Dishes were washed in Blue Omo after the family duck and drake had pre-cleaned them. Kids were washed in Blue Omo. Everything capable of being washed was washed in Blue Omo. Everything was done squatting on the ground; no-one seemed to have varicose veins. The maize grew nearby and when dry it was stored in the huts. When needed during the year it is prepared by breaking off the now brittle kernels by hand and pounding them with a heavy stick in a hollowed log to make flour for ugali.

Meals were prepared and people gossiped. The men sat and talked. Sitting there in the family's place Frank learnt something of life in a remote African village where some things remain as they have always been. The subsistence farmers are bound to the soil and very reliant on the weather. If the monsoon rains fail then the outlook is very bleak but if they are abundant then the harvest is bountiful and the community prospers. John said that in recent years the El Niño effect had made for very unpredictable weather and that the village was very concerned. In 1999 and again in August 2004 when we visited the family, drought and starvation struck in Kasaala and the surrounding Ukambani area. When John and his brothers came to Nairobi to meet us we were shocked by their gaunt appearance; their hollowed cheeks and the outline of John's skull beneath the veneer of skin that described his face. All of their trouser's were pleated at the waist by belts drawn toward such narrow bodies. John was unable to eat a full-sized meal immediately and was anxious to get back to his hungry children with food. There had been a double disaster in Kasaala and the surrounding area; as far north as Kitui. Maize poisoning, the result of grain contaminated by a fungal disease had killed many people in the district. John told us that several children in Kasaala had died from maize poisoning. The reality of our Kenyan family's situation brought home to us in a very confronting way again the harshness of the life they and their countrymen endure daily.

Rashid explained how a villager's thatched hut is made. Simple, it requires nothing that cannot be drawn locally from the environment. No need for money to buy galvanised iron for the roof or nails for the timber or cement for concrete, yet it is a very effective structure and one easily replaced should the need arise. The poorest man with no more tools than a *panga* or machete can build a shelter for his family.

The typical hut is about 4 metres in diameter and at the entrance about 1.5 metres high, reaching up to 3 metres at the peak of the conical roof. The circular walls are made by cutting slender branches from a tree and burning the ends before burying the burnt ends to form a large circle in the ground. Rashid explained that charring the wood prevents termites attacking it. Other sticks are woven horizontally through the circular array of verticals in a knitted fashion. A post made from a carefully selected straight sapling is put in the ground at the centre of the circle to form the roof pole. Villagers, we are told, are very careful to conserve the trees in the forest that are used for the centre poles. They do not waste them for charcoal or firewood.

The knitted fabric that forms the walls is then plastered with red mud which, when dry, forms a surprisingly robust structure. The roof is formed by arranging sticks from the centre pole to the walls as rafters and weaving layer upon layer of grass fronds to form a watertight thatch. Rashid took Frank inside his thatched hut and he was surprised by how cool it was.

Similar huts with raised floors were used for drying and storing the maize harvest or as chicken coops. Others were used as cooking huts – the grass roof allows the smoke to dissipate. However, a proper chimney would be a really good improvement as everything, including the tea, had a smoked flavour. Inside the cooking hut the stove is traditionally three stones built around a wood fire. The cook squats on the earthen floor.

Water-gathering is an enormous and unrelenting task. Safari's two eldest sisters Penina and Kanini had this job and it took the majority of their time. People unable to afford a bicycle – and the bicycles favoured are heavy robust Chinese models – carry water in 20-litre plastic containers. They tie tapes to the drums and with the drums hanging from their back, strap the tapes to their foreheads. Carrying these full of water as far as 10 kilometres each day is hard work. Better-off families with a means of transport are able to do this with considerable ease. So we can understand the girls' delight to have the donkey Jenny purchased.

The social time of the day is in the evenings. People sit around a fire and reflect on the day's happenings. One evening Frank suggested that he show the family the videotape of the *RPA* program that he had on his camera along with the tape of the Central Coast's farewell to Safari in Gosford's Kibble Park. Everyone watched the farewell first and the family were in awe that so many people could be assembled to farewell their son. They recognised the Christmas carols and sang along happily. Frank said he felt honoured to be a part of this intimate family gathering.

John couldn't watch the *RPA* program – there was just too much blood for him – but the women and kids watched intently. Frank was glad that he could show the details of Safari's incredible journey to these people who were surely the most deserving viewers in the world. No-one commented on the program except Rashid who said that what had happened to Safari in Australia was a miracle and that the family was so grateful.

After the TV was finished John returned to the circle of family, friends and relations who dropped by. Ngayau and her elder girls made hot milky tea for the visitors and Frank lazily chatted to Kilonzo and his brothers under a clear, cloudless sky. There was no artificial lighting save the filtered glow of the portable solar fluorescent light through the thatching of the cooking hut, and as a consequence there seemed so many more stars in the sky.

John had his new transistor radio playing. Safari, his brothers and sisters and cousins were dancing excitedly to the vibrant rhythm, the urgent drumming, and the perfect harmony of 'Yele Yele' by popular Ghanaian musician Afro Moses. They danced instinctively, they danced with abandon. For them life was full to overflowing. It was such a privilege to be part of the life of Safari's village family that night.

Frank learnt more about Rashid and John's brother Michael. Frank and I have never met him, although Jenny did. Michael is a bushman and prefers to live off the land in the bush rather than be a farmer. He has a hut next to his father's shamba but is seldom there. To survive in the bush as he does, shunning the comforts of village life must make him an interesting character.

The family dog lazed around and at night-time warned off intruders. It had rabies and didn't seem mad but the family said it could infect with its bite. He never bit anyone but was unhappy if people quarrelled, when he became angry and a danger. He and the duck and drake were good at warning of snakes nearby.

Twice daily Frank dressed Safari's ulcer and was quite surprised by how slowly it was healing. In fact it hadn't completely healed by the time he left Kenya in early April. As he went through the twice-daily dressings ritual, invariably a crowd gathered. He took the opportunity to demonstrate the importance of cleanliness and the prevention of reinfection. Words were not much help as few spoke English. He would set all the dressings, Betadine and scissors out on a small table and pedantically go through the ritual of removing the old dressing and rubbing it in the dirt to indicate that old dressings must not be reused. Then, with a fresh piece of cotton wool from its package held in one hand, he poured the Betadine over it and began cleaning the wound. The process was repeated with fresh pieces of cotton wool. Hopefully the crowd learnt a little about the importance of cleanliness and wound dressing.

Frank spoke to John and Ngayau and Rashid about the offer of a place in the Sathya Sai School in Uthiru. He had a copy of the Zambia video in his video camera and they all watched it and talked about the type of education that they could expect at Uthiru. Frank explained that the Uthiru school was much poorer than Kisaju but that he thought the people operating it were very good and used what resources they had very wisely. They listened and Ngayau and John decided that they would return with Frank the next week and have a look for themselves. Frank was very pleased to hear Ngayau come forward and say that she would come as well, for he felt that she needed to be a little more assertive than the traditional village wife is. She was a normally quiet, reserved person and it was good to see her coming out of her shell. Frank reminded her of her words to David Syme before Christmas when she had felt she had to ask his permission to send Safari to school in Australia. Frank told her strongly that she had no obligation to ask anyone's permission on issues relating to her son's education. Frank said, 'I think my words resonated and led her to say she was coming along rather than ask if she could.' We feel great sympathy for the downtrodden African women and admiration for the feisty ones.

Rashid was also particularly keen to watch the Zambia video and learn all he could about this special kind of education. Rashid watched and listened intently to the video and concluded that it was a good school. If the Nairobi schools were modelled after the Zambia example, he would be very happy for the boys to go there. John and Ngayau likewise were happy to be advised by Rashid and a collective decision was made to check out Uthiru for Safari and Kisaju for Amin. The education of these two extra boys was all we thought the schools could manage.

On Sunday Frank went with Rashid to the little village church where the family worshipped. The church was in the African Inland Church tradition and was a simple building made from concrete blocks and a pitched corrugated iron roof with exposed rafters of tree limbs. The pews were simple, made by local carpenters and there was a simple altar. In true African tradition there was no set service time and parishioners arrived in dribs and drabs by the rear door so as not to disturb the service.

Soon the church was packed. The choir stood adjacent to the altar and their a cappella singing raised the status of that simple church to that of a cathedral. Frank told me later of that day: 'I'm sure there is nothing in the world to match their voices as they sang in Swahili the hymn "Bringing in the Sheaves".' It seemed so appropriate for a rural church community to be singing a hymn about harvesting. At the end of the service, which was in the village tongue Kikamba, there was what appeared to Frank to be some sort of an auction involving a woman in the congregation. Afterwards he asked Rashid what was going on. He said that the woman's husband had recently died and that various parishioners were pledging bags of maize to help her out. What Frank witnessed was true community spirit in action. Without the community help this woman with no family would be in dire straits.

After the church service Frank walked around the town. It seemed that Sunday was relaxing and socialising day. People were dressed in their finery and the children dressed up for Sunday school. Safari was there with his yellow T-shirt with 'the Central Coast luvs U' printed on the front. Many people came up to Frank to chat.

The next day Frank visited the village health clinic and the chief of the village. His office was then adjacent to the health clinic in the same building. Chief Jonathan Ngengo is a pleasant authoritative figure and he wins respect and friendship easily.

The village medical officer, Silas Nthaka, is a man in his early forties who apart from attending to the health needs of the village is a respected member of the community. Silas is dedicated to his job. He told Frank that in an average day he sees 60 or so patients with all kinds of illnesses from children with diarrhoea to malaria to people with HIV/AIDS to people with snakebite. Silas, in telling Frank this, opened his gas-powered medical supplies refrigerator. As Frank looked inside it was virtually empty. Silas said simply and resignedly, 'But I have very few medicines.' He was trying to do so much with so little in a poor country and had been waiting for ADRA to do a promised upgrade to his clinic. In waiting, patients were suffering, some seriously; this was the reality. Silas also said that the shortage of water in the village leads the people to underutilise water and as a result contract diseases through compromised hygiene. Frank promised Silas and Jonathan that we would help represent them.

As the tropical dusk fell rapidly the heat of the sun abated. People started filling the streets, doing their shopping and socialising. Socialising and shopping are inseparable and one is always an excuse for the other.

As dark replaced light numerous kerosene candles lit up the shopfronts. No sophisticated kerosene pressure lamps but just utterly simple homemade lamps, recycled tin cans with a wick poking out. No doubt the same kind of candle that had started the whole Safari saga. Frank mused that this simple flame had two aspects. It had been destructive yet in another way it could be thought of as a spark to light the light of love in the hearts of people who had come within this little child's orbit.

Suddenly the street was awash with sound as the daily bus from Kitui sped into town with its horn blaring. Bus crew all over Kenya are flamboyant people. The conductor was flapping like a flag in the wind at the open door of the bus. The driver changed down ten gears, flattened the throttle and red-lined the engine in a show of bravado. The bright yellow battered Mitsubishi, complete with 'Wendy's Team' and a heart emblazoned on the windscreen, had arrived. It looked like the passengers would get more value than just the bus fare.

Frank checked into the Kasaala Guesthouse for his last

night in the village, as he would not have time in the morning to pack his tent before making the bus trip to Nairobi with John, Ngayau, Safari and Amin. We heard recently that Rashid was subletting the guesthouse from his friend Benson and had renamed it 'the Channel Nine Hotel'. It was a concrete blockhouse with passive solar heating guaranteed to keep the unwary visitor piping hot all night. Oh, but it had a mosquito net and the loo was down the passageway so who was one to complain?

The bus crew overnighted at Kasaala where they relaxed then sobered up to resume the road battle with their trusty Mitsubishi steed. In light of their spectacular arrival Frank was wondering how the trip to Kitui would be along the less-than-perfect road or more correctly, track. One thing he knew for sure: the crew would be positive and certainly assertive.

Next morning, some time after 7 am, the bus was eventually ready to leave. Departures are never on time – someone running late might be missed. The family arrived: Rashid to bid farewell; John, Ngayau and the two boys to travel.

Within half a kilometre of setting out, Frank was absolutely convinced that the bus would self-destruct. 'The metal panels drummed furiously, the windows rattled furiously in their tracks; no-one could speak above their noise, why didn't they break?'

The bus was very popular. Soon it was standing room only. The roof space was not wasted – furniture, luggage, bicycles filled it to the sky.

Along the way Frank kept track of where they were by looking for the names of places on the shops of the little dusty villages the bus passed through. After what seemed an enormous distance the bus stopped at a small town and a sign said 'Mutomo Butchery'. Frank was amazed, this was Mutomo. This was where Ngayau had brought Safari to hospital when he was burned, 50 kilometres from Kasaala. The bus journey had been exhausting; how must it have been for Ngayau, walking home for two days and sleeping by the roadside at night, with a heavy heart, carrying her fragile child home to die. Frank looked across at Ngayau and through John asked her incredulously, 'Ngayau, you carried Safari home from here?' She simply nodded her head slowly once or twice.

There was no standing room left. Sitting at the back, Frank saw a multitude of dark arms hanging on the centre chrome grab rail. His eyes stopped at a strange sight. At the very front there was a wrist manacled to the rail with a handcuff. It was a prisoner being transported. Apart from being a furniture van this bus was also a paddy wagon!

The bus route wandered through mostly scrubby countryside that showed little evidence of farming, in sight of the road at least, until closer to Kitui and more populated areas. They crossed riverbeds and passed trucks that had broken down or slid off the track. Workers seemed none too perturbed by the Herculean task of getting them back on track. It is not in the culture to get all hot and bothered about things. People just accept it as yet another challenge and get on with it. They even seem to enjoy the experience and the comradely banter and laughter.

At Kitui bus station John led them to a big coach for the shorter trip to Nairobi. The bus station was just an open-air turning circle for buses surrounded by stalls selling food to the travellers. It was lunchtime and they stocked up with a huge bag of delicious tree-ripened bananas. The shorter trip was luxurious compared with the 'Wendy's Team' experience and sitting high up in the coach Frank gazed over the landscape dotted with terraced rolling hillsides under cultivation. Soon the coach was at another provincial town, Machakos, to briefly pick up and drop off passengers. Women came through the bus selling hard-boiled eggs with salt wrapped in small pieces of paper. Frank, Safari and Amin had their fill.

Within an hour and a half the chaotic streets of Nairobi loomed. The bus made a right-hand turn at one point and was overtaken as it did so. There was a strange metallic sound and Frank looked at the window beside him. Brushing along the row of windows the full length of the bus was a bundle of reinforcing steel carelessly skewed out from the side of a passing truck. No windows broke, it all happened and was over before anyone could be alarmed and Frank was sure that neither driver was aware of what had happened.

The bus entered the main Nairobi bus station. It was a huge paddock adjacent to the vegetable markets, a daunting place which looked dangerous. Frank rang Batuk to ask him to pick them up. Batuk warned that they were in a rough part of town and to be careful until he arrived. They found a quiet place against a high wall and circled the luggage.

All was well, Batuk arrived in his red BMW and he drove them to the hotel where Safari and Frank had been staying earlier. Frank booked a room for John, Ngayau and the boys and one for himself and they all relaxed with hot showers and a delicious hotel dinner. John and Ngayau enjoyed their night of comfort. Frank felt privileged to treat John and Ngayau to this touch of what for them was sheer luxury.

The next day they all made for the school at Uthiru. They caught a matatu for the 10 kilometres to Uthiru. Matatus form the backbone of the affordable public transport system in Nairobi. They are small Toyota Hiace or Nissan Urvan or similar vehicles. With seats for maybe fourteen people, they seem to hold 140! The local joking comment is 'And room for one more.' The conductor is also a trapeze artist as he collects fares, gives directions, banters other road users and alerts the driver to potential new customers on the roadside. Invariably as one person got out, two got in. Matatu men are all characters and no doubt love their devil-may-care lives.

Safely at the school Frank introduced John and Ngayau to Principal Daniel Otieno. They were both very interested and over three hours asked many questions. One of the teachers spoke Kikamba and they listened keenly to what she had to say. School was on vacation so there were no operating classes to observe but Ngayau and John were very happy and told Frank that they would be very pleased for Safari to be enrolled.

John and Ngayau sat around on a seat along the school's simple boundary fence. They were relaxed – African style; doing something doing nothing. John chewing on a piece of grass, his wife occasionally saying something to him briefly and he grunting pleasantly a response. Ngayau several times looked at him and smiled as he stared at the ground. Hers was a gentle lively smile that flashed her teeth white against her brown skin. Frank thought it so nice to see her smile then as it revealed that under that often poignant look there was a happy soul with hope for a better future.

They both had an air of quiet confidence, of accomplishment, of pride that the most important thing in their life, their child's education, was at last becoming a reality. They were so happy with the school and so pleased to be part of the selection process.

Frank's thoughts returned to the list of things to be taken care of before he left for home in a few days' time. There was the matter of Safari's physiotherapy. His left hand needed ongoing exercises to stretch the tendons of his fingers. Tendons shortened by years of immobilisation needed to be painfully stretched twice a day for half an hour. The last couple of weeks had been frantic and the treatment neglected by Frank. But now he was leaving Kenya and Mary, the teacher Daniel had assigned to look after Safari, needed to know how to carry on the physiotherapy.

Frank gathered Safari and the family in Daniel's simple office. There John and Ngayau sat each side of Safari on a wooden bench and waited while Daniel fetched Mary. The demonstration began and unfortunately it was always painful for Safari. It was also painful for Frank to be inflicting pain and this dominated his thoughts, although he did not speak of it.

Safari knew what to expect and bravely offered his hand, which Frank proceeded to gently wrap with a crepe bandage to try to coax the fingers into a fist. At this stage of his recovery the ability to make a fist was poor, really only the fingertips would bend. Safari never flinched; he was so brave. However, his eyes told another story and he began to quietly whimper. Ngayau's eyes glistened and she too was feeling the pain, the mother's pain that had been so much of her life since the accident. Her left arm went to his shoulder and she tried to comfort him. With her right hand she took a corner of her headscarf and wiped away their tears. Mary, John and Daniel looked on in great respect at Safari's stoicism.

After a few minutes the pain subsided as the bandage stayed in place with a clip.

True to form, as the pain eased Safari hopped up, left the room and joined Amin and the other children in kicking a soccer ball.

Half an hour later Frank, John and Ngayau left with Amin for the second night at the Azee House hotel in Nairobi, leaving Safari at the school. Frank was intrigued to learn how John and Ngayau would react to leaving Safari alone at the school and how he would react in return.

Contrary to our experience of a child's sometimes dramatic first day at school, at Uthiru that day there were no hugs, no show of emotions; just a gentle exchange of waving hands at a distance and shouts of '*kwaheri!*' Safari seemed more interested in his soccer pals and the game, and his parents looked serene. Serene and, I guess, as it is in Africa, happy to entrust their child into the hands of another trusted community member.

All that remained now was for them to visit Kisaju and see if they approved of it for Amin.

Batuk drove the group to Kisaju the next day. Amin now with papers from Kasaala primary school releasing him and papers signed by the village chief was ready to sit for the entrance test. He passed with flying colours and Shastry was very happy to accept him. However, as Frank and the family sat there in Shastry's office a quietness came over Amin. He began to realise that this strange place was to be his home as well as his school and that he would be here by himself. He began to cry silently and Frank instantly realised that they couldn't leave him by himself. In any case it was still the school holidays and the school was closed for another two weeks. Amin would have to come back later.

Frank was due to fly back to Australia in two days' time on 3 April so he needed to make arrangements for Amin very quickly. They drove back to Uthiru and spoke to Daniel, Margarita and Chris about his concerns. They kindly suggested that the both boys be enrolled with them. Frank was relieved and so appreciative that in spite of their own overcrowding problems they had made room for Amin.

Earlier when visiting the school Frank noticed that there was no kitchen – the cooking was done in the open. Large cauldrons over open fires cooked ugali, beans, rice and vegetables. The children helped with the cooking, making chapatti bread on hotplates over the fires and preparing the vegetables. The diet is vegetarian in keeping with the Education in Human Values philosophy of non-violence and the children are well nourished. When Frank spoke that night to me he described the school and mentioned the lack of a kitchen. I said, 'That's no good. I'll call a committee meeting to see what we can do.' As a result Frank suggested to Chris and Margarita that they accept A$4000 to build a new kitchen. They were very grateful but Frank was surprised when they spoke of the question of donations and help. They said that it is part of the school's philosophy not to canvas for help. They said that when help was needed that it would come and that it must come from the heart. We have respected this philosophy and follow it in our efforts to help the school.

With Amin and Safari's education in good hands it was time for Frank to return home. He took John and Ngayau to the sawmill at Banana Hills where they were to stay a few days with friends before returning to Kasaala. There they bade farewell. For Ngayau it was the last goodbye; eight months later she was dead. That last year of her life, however, must have been the happiest. She had seen her son returned healed and she had, courtesy of the generosity of the Australian people, some money in her purse to put food on the table. She had solar-powered lighting in her home and, most importantly, she was assured that her son was at last getting 'a chance in life'.

Part Four
The Widening Circle

Chapter 17

By the time Frank arrived home from Kenya on 5 April 2002, many community groups had phoned, asking if we could speak at their venues about our experiences with Safari. This had all happened through word of mouth following the talk I gave at St Peter's Church in Springfield, Gosford while Frank was away in Kenya. We gladly accepted all invitations and have spoken at hundreds of places all over the Central Coast and beyond. People were and are so interested to hear about Safari and his year in Australia but also about his family and village. They always ask the question, 'How is he getting on now?'

Since we left Safari in Kenya we have realised the extraordinary benefits of that marvel of the communications age, the email system. It has allowed us to keep in touch on a daily basis with Chris and Margarita and Safari's principal, Daniel. Daniel writes us beautiful quarterly newsletters filled with information and refreshing views which add to our appreciation of how the school operates and how its philosophy of values education works and brings rich benefits to the children.

Margarita wrote to us with news of an excursion Safari's school had organised for the children the previous Sunday.

A friend of Margarita and Chris in the US had recently been married and she and her husband wanted as a wedding gift to give the children at the school a good time in their name. So the school hired a bus and driver from the Kenya Wildlife Service to take them on an outing to Nakuru National Park.

Safari and Amin along with 54 orphan children, the teachers, Chris and Margarita Hawley and their grandchildren filled the bus. The children were so excited as the adventure began.

Nakuru National Park is 160 kilometres north of Nairobi and only 40 kilometres south of the equator. It is quite high at 1800 metres on the Mau Escarpment; Nakuru means in Maasai 'dusty place'. Lake Nakuru is famous for its bird-life, especially flamingoes and pelicans. At certain times of the year the lake is host to one of the world's most spectacular wildlife sights, that of millions of brilliant pink flamingoes as far as the eye can see.

None of the children had ever been to their own country's world-famous park before and to see lions, buffalo, zebra, rhino, Rothschild giraffe and smaller animals like Thomson's gazelle and warthog and others was an absolute treat. This park is also home to the near-extinct black rhino. All these animals that to us say 'Africa' but which the children had only heard about, never seen.

They took a lunch of apples, bananas, sweets, chapattis

and pita bread with vegetable filling, washed down with the passionfruit juice for which Kenya is famous.

Amin, Safari and all the other children had a wonderful time and they talked about the things they saw over and over in class for months to come. Because hiring a bus for so many is expensive the school is not able to have these excursions very often. But, as Jenny had also discovered with Safari, children are enormously appreciative and truly enraptured by the experience.

In June 2002 we received an email message of disaster.

After school on Monday the children helped with the school chores of mopping out the cement-floored classrooms and preparing the evening meal. Some peeled vegetables, some mixed the dough for chapatti and some folded clothes that had been out drying on the school's long wire fence. Safari and his cousin Amin pitched in with the others, carrying water from the bore to the kitchen. They liked to work together; the two boys continued to be inseparable friends. Part of the philosophy of the school is that the students feel a sense of ownership, which comes with contributing to the upkeep and the day-to-day tasks, which are within their capabilities.

The work over, the boys started a game of soccer in the large open area behind the dormitories. All the boys loved soccer. The grass was brown for it was the dry season and all the vegetation looked dead.

As with all he did, Safari played with gusto and was enjoying the game until disaster struck. He fell heavily on his left arm and the bone in his upper arm broke. It was the same arm that he broke in Australia ten months earlier when he bumped into a small girl while playing. The bones in that arm had been immobilised since babyhood and this fact, coupled with Safari's earlier poor nutrition, meant that they were ridden with osteoporosis. The break was very painful but the school's doctor came and bandaged it with a splint and gave Safari some painkillers to ease his suffering and help him sleep. It was not possible to get him to Nairobi hospital that evening so he spent an uncomfortable night and the next morning Margarita Hawley took him to the hospital for an X-ray and a plaster cast. The X-ray showed that it was a clean break and the doctors expected no complications. On their way back to the school they stopped off at Margarita's home where she made him a toasted cheese sandwich for being a brave boy. He was very happy with that.

When Chris and Margarita emailed us with the news we realised that something had to be done about his osteoporosis. As luck would have it a friend in Sydney was travelling soon and was able to take a large quantity of calcium tablets over, along with some soccer clothes that had been donated. Strangely, at the time of Safari's accident I had felt a sense of foreboding. The feeling dissipated but its significance was apparent when we heard the news from Chris and Margarita.

Towards the end of 2002 we dropped in to Timbertown on our way back from Rockhampton in Queensland. Timbertown is a tourist village with an early Australian theme, situated near Wauchope on the mid-north coast of New South Wales.

Although we were unaware of it as we browsed through the bric-a-brac of yesteryear, our visit was to trigger a new project.

I was recognised by a woman who was a dedicated viewer of the *RPA* program. Before I declared myself the woman kept saying, 'I know you, I know you, just let me think, I know you.' After the connection had been established we discussed Safari's bravery and courage. We also talked of our mutual interest in patchwork quilting and I expressed a fantasy wish of being able to provide each of the 60 orphans at Safari's school with their very own patchwork quilt. The children shared a communal wardrobe and I felt they needed something to call their very own.

Frank and I were amazed when Heather Miller, the lady we met in Timbertown, phoned a week later and said, 'Janet you are going to have your wish. We, the Wauchope Quilters, are going to make the 60 quilts.'

Being a patchwork quilter, this seemed to me to be a mountainous task. But Heather had expressed my wish to her quilting group and they were happy to take up the challenge.

We contacted the editor of the *Australian Patchwork and Quilter* magazine and they promised three quilts, as did Hobby Craft at Pennant Hills. Heather put the story on the Squilter's website and in just a few days quilts were promised from as far away as Yeppoon in Queensland, Port Macquarie, Sydney, the Central Coast and many other places. Soon we were caught up in the fever of patchwork quilts. The generosity of the people involved was astounding. Donations of fabric and wadding came from trade houses as far away as Western Australia. We were astonished when one day a quilt arrived from Kalgoorlie in the Western Australian gold fields.

The Wauchope Quilters were exceptional, working consistently day and night on the quilts. My dear friend Heather gave so much of herself in doing this work, with the help of her husband, Noel. Within three months more than 60 quilts were completed. A warm-hearted and generous woman from the Central Coast's Lakes Baptist Church hand-crocheted many rugs which we included with the quilts.

Then, a bombshell.

On Monday 9 December 2002 I was out shopping with Jenny. At home the phone rang and Frank answered it.

It was Lesley. She said, 'Frank, a terrible thing has happened. Safari's mother has been bitten by a snake in the village and has died.'

Frank was dumbfounded.

Lesley went on to explain that David Syme had just phoned her and told her that Ngayau was walking home from the village market when a snake had bitten her. She said that David Syme had emailed us and the details would be in the email.

After Lesley hung up, Frank rang us with the tragic news. We were all numb with shock.

The exact circumstances became clear when we spoke to

our friend Silas Nthaka, Kasaala's medical officer, in October 2003. Silas was the first person to attend to Ngayau.

It was the last day of school before the Christmas holidays for Safari and Amin. Safari's father John had caught the 7 am bus into Nairobi to bring the boys home for the holidays and was due to return to Kasaala with them at 7 pm. Apparently Ngayau had been waiting in the village for the bus but when seven came and it had not arrived she decided to walk to her home, less than half a kilometre away. She took a short cut along a path that was seldom used and overgrown with grass. It was here that what is believed to be a green mamba bit her on the ankle. Terrified and panic-stricken she ran back towards the village centre and the health clinic. She collapsed at Silas's feet vomiting and terribly distressed. By the time the bus arrived at 7.30 the venom had taken hold and Ngayau was unconscious. Safari and Amin saw her lying there and must have known that their mother and aunt was dying.

The same bus was commandeered and Ngayau was driven the 50 kilometres over the extremely bumpy road to the small mission hospital at Mutomo. Some 24 hours later she died. This was the same hospital that had been associated with tragedy for the Kimanzi family years earlier. Safari spent time here after he was burned and it was the hospital from which Ngayau carried him home. Walking for two days, sleeping by the roadside, she was bringing him home, she then thought, to die in the arms of his family.

We immediately wrote a letter to John Kimanzi expressing our shock and sympathy.

There was another aspect to Ngayau's death that left me empty.

Over the eleven months Safari lived with us I had become aware of his sense of deep compassion, his kindness and desire never to hurt anyone or anything, his ability to have complete trust in everyone and also to be happy all of the time. I pondered over this and came to the understanding that these values come from his family – in particular, I thought, from his mother. I had planned to spend time with her in the village to really get to know her. This didn't happen on our first visit; however, it would have been a priority the next time we visited Kasaala. When I was told of Ngayau's death I realised I would never really know her. Today I feel the same empty sorrow of not knowing this woman who had imparted so much wisdom to her son.

ADRA advised Channel Nine and they broadcast the sad news of Ngayau's untimely death. She was only 43 years old. We had many phone calls as a result from people questioning the lack of facilities at the health clinic that ADRA had promised to upgrade. Most said, 'Why haven't ADRA fulfilled their promise of refurbishing the clinic?' We had no answers but agreed with the callers that answers were needed from ADRA. The Sydney and Central Coast newspapers carried stories airing our concerns.

Public questioning was such that we decided to hold a silent demonstration outside the offices of ADRA in the heartland of Seventh-day Adventism; Fox Valley Road, Wahroonga on Saturday 21 December 2002. The media was invited and Channel Seven among others came along.

Wahroonga is a leafy upper-middle-class suburb in the north-west of Sydney and Fox Valley Road has been for many years the home in Australia for the Seventh-day Adventist church administration and the church's private hospital business, the Sydney Adventist Hospital. The hospital, the church administration buildings, the ADRA headquarters and the Wahroonga Cathedral are grouped together in the valley.

The demonstration, which included a number of friends in the East African community in Sydney and the Central Coast, was silent and peaceful. It was held for one hour, during which time we carried poster-sized prints of a picture of Safari on his mother's knee taken the day after he returned home. The crowd understood when Frank said that it had to be a demonstration of our feelings of sadness that ADRA had not yet taken up the opportunity to help a pitifully poor community – one typical of the many throughout the world that ADRA profess vocally to be the champions of. It must be a demonstration that Nelson Mandela would be proud of. Many people that day showed their support.

Channel Seven sent a reporter and cameraman. It was realised that our story deserved more than a 20-second sound grab on the evening news and later we were put in touch with an investigative journalist from Seven's *Today Tonight* current affairs program, Michelle Tapper. Our concerns about ADRA were put to air on 8 January 2003.

Michelle required us to present to her our case against ADRA. Our case was simply that the villagers and the village administration had told both Frank and Jenny that one year after Safari's return, ADRA had not implemented any of the promises they had made to the villagers and the generous Australian donors.

Chapter 18

The morning of the demonstration Frank awoke at about 4 am with an idea, one which wouldn't go away.

What if a 'Centre of Excellence' could be established in Kenya, in Kasaala? Frank had learnt from his time with CSIRO that 'Centres of Excellence' are very specialised research centres, set up to address the issues relating to a particular narrow area of research. In the medical version it would incorporate a teaching function to efficiently disseminate research results to the wider medical profession. In Kasaala, an area particularly prone to snakebite cases, it could be a field station to study methods of management and treatment of patients and to train doctors from all over Kenya and indeed all over East Africa.

It was not a crazy thought. We knew that the inspirational Australian Professor Fred Hollows had successfully established in Eritrean caves factories for manufacturing intraocular lenses for cataract patients whilst a war with Ethiopia was raging in the countryside. Here was an opportunity. ADRA was promising to upgrade the medical clinic in the village. Why couldn't it be upgraded to the standard of a functional snake study and toxinology facility? Also a Centre of Excellence would by its very nature be able to offer first-class general health facilities to the community that ADRA had been going to help.

Seeking more information on snake toxinology, the following Monday after the demonstration Frank rang the Australian Reptile Park at Somersby, near Gosford, as a first step in our learning process. The person he spoke to said, 'You need to speak to Australia's leading snake toxinologist, Associate Professor Julian White at the Commonwealth Serum Laboratories in Melbourne.'

A call to Melbourne revealed that Dr White was at home in Adelaide where he had an office in the Women's and Children's Hospital and the person Frank spoke to at the Serum Laboratories gave him his mobile phone number. He immediately rang and it was as if Dr White had been waiting for his call. Frank explained quickly about Safari and his mother's death from snakebite and our wish to do something towards establishing a Centre of Excellence. Dr White said he didn't watch much TV, had never seen Safari on Nine's *RPA* program and knew nothing of him but was very enthusiastic about Frank's idea for a centre for the study and treatment of snakebite in Kenya. 'It's a great idea and nothing like it exists in Africa, a continent plagued by snakes. As a matter of fact, I'm running a Toxinology World Congress to be followed by a ten-day training course for doctors in Adelaide in September. As a first step, it would be great if you could arrange for as many Kenyan doctors as possible to attend.' So started our collaboration and friendship with Julian White, yet another wonderful person brought into our orbit by Safari.

Our interest in achieving something really substantial by way of a toxinology centre nevertheless had to be woven alongside our other commitments.

Subsequent emails and phone conversations revealed that Julian, extremely busy organising the September meetings but always with the time to listen to our questions, needed some help in attending to the myriad of detail. We became his ad hoc secretarial help.

The concept of ourselves establishing a Centre of Excellence in Kasaala we felt was way outside our capabilities. But ADRA with their presence in the area and their organisational structure was well qualified to establish such a training and research centre. The question was, however, would they be interested?

We were unsure, based on our earlier encounters with their Executive Director, David Syme, whether we could get his support. So we contacted the Chairman of the ADRA Board and Secretary of the SDA Church in Australia, Dr Barry Oliver. Dr Oliver is a theologian with a doctorate from the SDA Andrews University in the US.

In our letter to Dr Oliver we set out the concept and the manifold benefits of a Toxinology Centre of Excellence and the support the idea had from Australia's foremost toxinologist. We pointed out the successes of Australia's Professor Hollows working with great results in much more extreme circumstances. We set out the case enthusiastically and suggested that ADRA might, in establishing this African centre, take ownership of the idea and receive well-earned praise. It was in Africa, an untouched area with real benefits for a modest practical input and we felt from our discussions with Julian White that it would receive support from the Kenyan Ministry of Health.

Dr Oliver's response was noncommital. A decision would have to come from the ADRA board and the next board meeting was not until June, some months away. We were not confident of their support but took the decision that we should go ahead anyway and try to get doctors to the September training workshop. Together with Dr White we put a proposal to the Kenyan Ministry of Health via the Kenyan High Commissioner Mr Loyatum in Canberra. We were already quite well known to His Excellency and his staff and had a very good working relationship. So when we put the idea forward that we were looking for the names of a number of Kenyan doctors that the Kenyan Ministry of Health thought might benefit from the training, Mr Loyatum quickly furnished a list.

In our discussions with Julian White we learnt that AusAID within the federal Department of Foreign Affairs and Trade offered financial support for overseas professionals with their International Seminar Support Scheme. However, it was late in the year and insufficient time was available to make the necessary application. We approached our local member of parliament, Jim Lloyd, and asked if he could help process Dr White's late application. Mr Lloyd was very happy to help and as a result we had AusAID support for three doctors. Our committee felt that we should sponsor Silas Nthaka.

By this time Dr Oliver and ADRA had had their meeting and decided not to support the Centre of Excellence in Kasaala, citing a letter their Kenya office had from the medical director who oversaw the area. Dr Gitau was very interested in a facility but said that in his opinion it would be better placed in the provincial centre of Kitui. There it could serve more than 600 000 people. We agreed entirely with Dr Gitau and wrote to Dr Oliver saying so. Still Dr Oliver did not warm to the idea of ADRA being involved in a significant way. They would be prepared to sponsor one doctor, preferably Dr Gitau, who they knew. Dr Gitau was not on the High Commissioner's list; in fact he was about to be promoted to another area of the Ministry of Health. Dr Oliver allowed us to nominate a replacement. We nominated the incoming Kitui Hospital Director, Dr David Musyoka.

The number of doctors who were to come to Adelaide in September 2003 was now set at five.

We suggested to Julian that we drive to Adelaide to meet him and to ensure the Kenyan visitors were met at the airport and ferried to their hotel and generally chaperoned about. He was very happy about this arrangement. Frank and I had never really spent any time in Adelaide so it was also a chance to visit 'the city of churches' and ramble around the district's wineries.

We wrote a letter to Silas Nthaka telling him and the others who might travel with him how to collect their domestic tickets and change planes at Melbourne airport for their flight to Adelaide. We knew the email addresses of only two of the travellers: Dr Anisa Omar and Dr Eugene Erulu.

On 9 September 2003 we set out for Adelaide via my daughter's home in Euston where we stayed overnight before completing the 1500-kilometre journey.

At Adelaide airport the next day, as the arrival terminal filled I searched for dark faces that looked like they might be from Kenya. A tall bespectacled man and a shorter much fairer woman, both in their mid-thirties, appeared likely so I walked up and said, 'Are you Eugene and Anisa?' They looked at me quizzically and just shook their heads in denial. Strange, I thought, scanning the crowd for more likely candidates. None presented so as the terminal emptied I approached the couple again. Speaking very slowly and precisely I said, 'Are you Doctors Eugene and Anisa?'

Immediately they chorused, 'Yes!' Eugene looked at me and said, 'We expected a man,' in an excellent educated accent.

Anisa and Eugene instantly in quite an extraordinary way became our friends; there seemed to be rapport and understanding that we all submitted to, almost as if it was a meeting of old friends. They were tired from the long flight and we headed for their rooms at the Hotel Adelaide via a McDonald's for an early-morning heart-starter with a cup of coffee and scrambled egg breakfast. Eugene was African and Catholic and Anisa was a fourth-generation Yemeni Kenyan Muslim. Eugene worked in private practice at Watamu near Mombasa on the Kenyan Coast and Anisa was a specialist paediatrician and the director of the 200-bed regional hospital in nearby Malindi. Watered and fed, we took them to their rooms at the hotel and arranged to pick them up at 1.30 pm.

We went away somewhat puzzled but not really surprised that the others had not turned up yet. Two hundred metres from the hotel was Adelaide's Women's and Children's Hospital where Associate Professor Julian White had his office. There we introduced ourselves and reported that we had two out of five visitors so far, which we thought was pretty good. Julian was a very pleasant, quiet, erudite man with a trim beard. Frank said that he reminded him of many scientists he had worked with at CSIRO. A man who was completely modest and approachable but who obviously knew intimately his area, that of toxinology. Always happy and patient and keen to explain any aspect of his work, he was obviously dedicated to his field. When we asked him why a toxins unit was located in a children's hospital he explained that historically children were the group most likely to accidentally poison themselves so the facility usually has its roots there. Very logical, we thought.

We wandered around the beautiful broad avenues of trees and the elegant old buildings and parks that make Adelaide so pleasant and well known. We soaked up the atmosphere, waiting for our charges to recuperate from their long flight over from Africa. It was a cold blustery day, pleasant though in such a quiet, proud, mature, Australian city.

Eugene and Anisa were hungry when we met up again so we strolled along past the coffee shops and pubs near the hotel and decided to ensconce ourselves in a pub that offered a nice open fire and colonial atmosphere. Anisa and Eugene were frozen by the wind reaching up from the Southern Ocean. It was nothing like the warm breezes from the Indian Ocean that they were accustomed to. We sat there for hours over some beers, each of us telling our story.

We explained our association with Kenya through Safari and our association with snakes through his mother's death and our feeling that we must do something to prevent others suffering her fate. Her death must not be in vain. Eugene and Anisa confirmed our thoughts on the problem of snakes for village people. They agreed that it was not a problem of the magnitude of HIV/AIDS or even malaria, which kills thousands of infants in Kenya each year. However, they said it was not a problem they as doctors could ignore; every life is precious.

They told us their story. Anisa was in her early forties and her father had been keen to see her educated and career orientated – a view not common in her Muslim community where a woman's role is traditionally seen as mother and homemaker. As a result she had trained in medicine and paediatrics and was now director of the government hospital in Malindi. The hospital, she explained, served a population of 350 000. Anisa was not married and had no children of her own but had adopted two girls in need. She seemed to us to be wedded to her job as a doctor. The hospital was, as Anisa's brother-in-law told us recently, 'Anisa's heart'.

Eugene was a general practitioner in private practice in Watamu, a small town just to the south of Malindi. He and Anisa were colleagues and had a common interest in the issue of snakes and snakebite treatment. In Watamu there is a world-famous reptile park operated by octogenarian

James Ashe and his young wife Sanda. They have been in Kenya many years; James was once the curator of the Kenya Museum. They keep the country's deadliest snakes as tourist attractions and also as a source of venom. They send the milked venom to a laboratory in South Africa to be made up into anti-venom. Eugene and Anisa had collaborated with the Ashes and world snake toxins expert Professor David Warrell to produce a brochure. Eugene said much could be done to address the problem by education. He said also that their friend and colleague Professor Warrell would be lecturing at the Congress and that we would meet this remarkable man who was intimately involved in the study of African snakes and clinical treatment regimes.

The afternoon drifted on and darkness fell. We were totally absorbed in our newfound friends.

Eugene and Anisa had already started calling us Mumma and Pappa. We were certainly family, African style. The following evening we invited them to the flat we had booked in the centre of town for a few nights. We entertained them with pizza and wine. Anisa's pizza was pork-free and chilli hot, mine vegetarian and Eugene and Frank were happy to be omnivores as long as they had jalapeno chillies on top. We settled down to a further session of 'getting to know you'.

Anisa's mobile phone chimed SMS messages continually and Anisa solved problems and answered questions from her hospital and her adopted girls. Anisa's uncle had passed away and Anisa without children of her own had taken the role of surrogate mother. She said, 'You know, it's very cheap to SMS around the world and you can say a lot in 160 characters.'

Eugene had a video with him that he had made just

before they left Kenya. It showed the world-renowned 'Bio Ken' snake farm at Watamu that Eugene and Anisa's friend's James and Sanda Ashe operated. They were both English and from the video James, clad in nothing but an ankle-length loincloth, looked quite amusing. However, as we learnt, James and Sanda were very well-respected world experts in African snakes. They spoke about and showed glass-caged examples of highly venomous snakes such as the feared black mamba, the green mamba, and various vipers and cobras. Just looking at the video made me feel uncomfortable; I am never comfortable with snakes and lizards or even their images.

Eugene's video report then crossed to a walk through Anisa's 200-bed government hospital in Malindi, on the Indian Ocean coast 130 kilometres north of Mombasa. Eugene explained that Anisa had only recently come into the job of director of the hospital and that since her arrival she had transformed it from a neglected facility into a clean, neat and tidy but still terribly underfunded hospital. The camera followed Anisa wearing a white hospital coat as she walked along the covered walkway between wards, past poor villagers standing around, waiting, no doubt, to see their relatives. The plain cement-rendered structures with corrugated iron roofs amongst very tidy tropical greenery were impressive – not in a way that says affluence but in a way that demonstrated what can be done with a little money and a lot of practical, hands-on help. Anisa's hospital was poor but proud. As she was filmed entering a ward she asked after the day's progress with the ward sister. The ward sister was dressed very well with freshly laundered blue-edged white uniform and starched cap. She reported that they had a number of children suffering burns.

Inside the ward the floor was covered in pastel-coloured lino tiles and the walls were decorated with children's themes and the alphabet. The children's cots were all full. Speaking to camera, Anisa excused their antiquity and shortage but said they did the best with what they had and that the decorated walls cost nothing and added hope and light to an otherwise grim medical reality.

Mothers and aunts gathered around pitiful children badly burned and covered with insect netting. The mothers helped the overtaxed nurses, soothing and caring for the children. Frank remarked that the looks of despairing resignation reminded him of the faces in the hospital at Nairobi when he took Safari to have his ulcer attended to. It was the look of the archetypal long-suffering African woman. As I watched the children's small brown bodies covered in the white-red of burns, my mind went off in a sombre direction, imagining how Safari must have been on that terrible day when he suffered the same fate. I looked in the eyes of the mothers, superimposing Ngayau's face. What was the fate of those in the video?

Anisa said that there was a severe skilled staff shortage, with a ratio of one nurse to 80 patients, and two doctors apart from herself. She doubles as clinician and administrator.

The video ended and we sat silently for a moment. I thought of the wonderful resourcefulness and dedication of Anisa and her lack of the facilities she so richly deserved. We talked for some hours with Anisa and Eugene and discussed what was needed. Eugene showed us the snake education brochure that he and Anisa along with James and Sanda Ashe and Professor Warrell had prepared. They were thinking a prevention program would be cheap and effective in reducing the problem. The brochure gave very good practical information and amongst other facts told of the snake's place in the scheme of things in controlling the pests that would otherwise ravage the villagers' crops. Anisa and Eugene wanted to have more brochures printed and distributed to villagers to show them how to avoid being bitten and the appropriate first aid for a snakebite victim.

We sat, listened and wondered, intrigued. What could we do to support two such dedicated professionals working under difficult conditions? How could Mumma and Pappa help without spreading ourselves so thin as to be ineffective anywhere? Frank and I discussed this later and, always the comedian, he suggested that we ask Santa Claus for some extra hours in the day.

Within two days the other three Kenyan visitors had arrived at Adelaide airport. They were doctors David Musyoka from Kitui and Kelly Okumu who came from a town called Saiya close to Lake Victoria in North Western Kenya. Accompanying David Musyoka was Silas Nthaka. Kelly and David were both young men recently graduated and beginning their medical career.

We picked them up from the airport thoroughly exhausted from their long trip and after settling them into their accommodation we left them to rest. Later in the day we took them the short walk to Adelaide's Women's and

Children's Hospital and introduced them to Professor White.

For the remainder of the week we saw very little of our new Kenyan friends; they were all totally immersed in the training.

The following Sunday, their first free day, we invited our guests to an Australian barbecue at the Adelaide Shores Caravan Park. We all pitched in and cooked a wonderful lunch and in the warm Adelaide spring sun relaxed on the lawns to enjoy it. Over some cold beer and wine we told our story about Safari and the reason for our interest in snakebite treatment after Safari's mother's death. They in turn told of their lives and their work.

Kelly worked in a government hospital and David told us that he had recently been made director of Kitui district's government hospital; the hospital administers the area that includes Silas's medical centre in Kasaala.

Silas gave us news from the village and from Safari's family. As we sat there on the grass in the warm sun he explained in detail the events on that tragic day that was the trigger for Safari's story. We listened intently, anxious for every detail. Hearing these details first-hand was important to us, and also very upsetting, as we each had our own mental picture of Safari's suffering.

Silas also explained the terrible guilt Ngayau carried because she wasn't in the hut when the girls bathed Safari. Her guilt was such that ever since that day she tried to keep him hidden from the gaze of people. Maybe this explains the sadness in her face often picked up by the camera. Silas said that before this accident Safari was a particularly beautiful baby and his parents very proud.

I watched Silas as he recounted Safari's accident. Then he went on to give the details leading up to Ngayau's death.

Our hearts went out to Silas. Here was a man dedicated to his work, skilful and resourceful. In both these circumstances he just didn't have the facilities or the medications to give these patients what they needed. I said to him, 'This must be very difficult for you, to feel such helplessness?'

He nodded silently and said, 'Very often I just try and comfort them while they die. In the month before I came here I saw five patients with snakebite.' He looked down for a moment and then continued, 'I thank God that none of them died.'

ADRA had by now completed some renovations to the centre, including a new roof, and had bought some medical equipment plus a small fridge. But medicines were often in short supply.

Silas went on to tell us that at night he had no light to work by. Frank then said, 'Well, we have some plans to do something about that.' Frank then spoke of plans we had to send Silas back with some solar-powered lighting. Frank said that he would like Silas to come back to Gosford with us where he would show him how to install some solar panels that BP Solar had kindly offered to donate – solar lighting similar to that which we had installed in the family's house. Frank jokingly said, 'Silas, when I'm finished you will be the village electrician as well as the village doctor.' Silas laughed.

The barbecue picnic ended on a nice note with other people in the caravan park. Their curiosity soon led them to ask about our group. Most remembered Safari from the

TV and were fascinated with the story. They had many questions to ask our African friends.

All too soon the course was over and all except Silas caught their flight back to Kenya. Silas travelled back with us to Gosford experiencing the vast expanse of Australia along the way. The countryside had a green flush from recent short rains. We had to remind Silas that it was not often so green and that by and large Australia is a dry, brown land.

Back home my friend Margaret Bushby billeted Silas for the few days that Frank needed to get all the lighting equipment organised and to show him how to do the installation. We also used the time to show Silas the sights that had been part of Safari's life for the time he was with us. Silas enjoyed his time on the Central Coast and all too soon flew back to Kenya.

Chapter 19

Sometime during the hustle and bustle of arranging the Kenyan doctors' visit to Adelaide in September 2003 I had a surprise call from a woman in the tiny Central New South Wales town of Trangie. Jean Richardson introduced herself and of course the subject quickly focused on Safari.

Jean and her friends in the wheat and cotton farming town of 1000 people had all been touched by Safari's special qualities and felt moved to support him. They were keen to arrange a function to help raise money to help Safari's school in Nairobi.

A suitable date revolved around the farming calendar to choose a time where the weather and the cropping and planting cycle would be most appropriate. Finally the weekend of the first week in May 2004 was set in concrete.

We drove the 600 kilometres; over the Blue Mountains via the picturesque Hunter Valley and through the coalmining towns of Cessnock and Kurri Kurri. This was the area to which immigrant Welsh coalminers like Alma's family had come for a better life at the turn of the twentieth century.

Crossing the saddle of the Great Dividing Range we headed towards the wheat lands of the Western Plains. The road followed the rail line used for carting the huge quantities of grain, past the railside silos. By afternoon the large Western Plains town of Dubbo loomed into view.

The drive out of Dubbo took us along the dead flat and dead straight highway past vast holdings empty of crops. The land was parched and the hardy gum trees and native grasses were covered in the dust of the drought. Forty minutes later, after a drive across a flat expanse and past Narromine the Mitchell Highway crossed the rail line and we were in the tiny hamlet of Trangie – population, according to the Main Roads sign, 1100. Some wag had crossed out the last two zeros and written 21.

It was getting late so we skipped a lap of the main street and headed for our hosts' wheat and cotton property of Carlisle, 12 kilometres towards Nyngan.

The drive in to the 5750-acre property of James and Sue Winter, where we were to stay, was at least 4 kilometres. Frank cheekily remarked to me that they must be people who prefer to be away from the noise of the traffic on the main road. On our right the stubble showed that a crop of wheat had been recently harvested. In the middle of the field a small mob of kangaroos surveyed the evening, ears pricked at our arrival. Driving through Trangie we had passed a railway siding and a huge tarpaulin-covered pile of grain, evidence of the size of the area's recent wheat crop. A crop diminished by the four-year drought. We said to ourselves, 'What must a good year yield from these vast wheat lands?'

In typical Australian style, Sue and James's homestead was set in an oasis of gum trees. The roof of the large verandahed house swept down with an expanse of galvanised iron. A bore watered the manicured green front lawn. The working homestead was surrounded by equipment sheds, huge tractors and large acreage implements. It all projected the image of a place made comfortable and self-sustaining and able to provide an escape and a shelter from the heat of the harsh Australian summer.

Sue was a slightly-built woman in her early forties; attractive and very friendly. We quickly learnt that she was a woman with great knowledge of the industry that she and her husband were involved in. She regularly drove the gigantic machinery and was a dynamo of energy. The home that she and James had created was very beautiful and modern. Her use of ornament around the garden showed a woman used to making creative use of what was available.

James was not home. He had gone to Moree, five hours' drive away, to bring some equipment from another farm they were associated with. As well, he would collect his mother, who was keen to be part of the celebrations on the weekend.

Sue showed us her preparations for the Safari picnic. The garden had been transformed into an African game park. Lions peeped out from behind shrubs. A life-sized giraffe grazed on a gum tree and beautiful paintings by a local artist showed zebras at a waterhole, cheetahs and Australian bush scenes. A room was set aside to house the generous donations for the auction. Sue was very animated, and so glad to be part of and hostess to this event to help Safari's school. Much attention to detail had been given by the committee.

Over a cup of tea Sue quickly told us of our accommodation and what she needed to do to be ready for Saturday night's festivities. She also told us of the plans for the next day, Friday. The schoolchildren of Trangie wanted us to view and judge their artwork, once again on an African theme. It was by now getting dark so after this very pleasant getting-to-know-you session with Sue we settled down for the night.

In the cool of the next morning the long winter shadows clung to the trees. Kangaroos grazed nearby and a small group of peacocks picked attentively at what seemed very little on the ground along the farmhouse fence. The two cattle dogs played chasings around a tree, bounding playfully and hiding from each other in the bushes.

Both Frank and I agreed Safari and Amin would love the feel, the smell and the ambience of this rural Australian setting. We could just imagine them both riding wide-eyed on the huge tractors and being so keen to lend a helping hand to the grown-ups and show them that they were becoming grown-ups, too.

Breakfast over, we headed back to Trangie to meet Peter Macbeth, the Principal of Trangie Central School.

The school was a broad complex of neat weatherboard building with two flag poles – one flying the Australian flag and the other the red, black and yellow Aboriginal flag. It was heartening to see and we felt that this school held great promise for an inclusiveness that stretched to Africa. We were soon to have these feelings validated.

Peter Macbeth was a tall, friendly man with the countenance of a headmaster and a manner which, while completely approachable, commanded respect. Frank said later that Peter seemed to be a similar vocation-motivated person as Safari's headmaster Daniel Otieno. Peter's bright eyes from beneath fashionable elliptical glasses welcomed us to his school. On the way to the staff room a display case showed items of Aboriginality, a further acknowledgement, we felt, to the area's original inhabitants. In the staff room Peter introduced us to his colleagues and we commended him on his school and its friendly inclusiveness and acknowledgement of Aboriginal Australia – something not often found in rural Australia. Peter briefly explained his teaching career. It was very interesting. His wife was a Californian and he had taught in America for several years. He had also taught in extremely isolated schools in Australia. For him Trangie was a welcome small town with the kind of facilities that he truly appreciated.

Peter soon quizzed us about Safari's school. What was a day in the life of an African school really like? Frank explained briefly the school and its philosophy of Education in Human Values; Peter was keen to know more so we promised to link up the two principals via email.

Tea and cakes over, we accompanied Peter to the school's large new assembly hall. Along the walls were the students' paintings expressing their interpretations of African wildlife. Paintings ranged from the emerging talents of kindergarten children to the more sophisticated work of older primary school children. For the first time in our lives we became art judges and did our best to judge the works. Our role as art critics complete, we stood behind the lectern and spoke to the children.

Speaking to those small children sitting cross-legged on the floor before us was an entirely different experience to the multitude of talks we had given to adults elsewhere around the countryside. The sea of young faces peered eagerly up at us. They were so keen to hear of their television friend Safari and his experiences. They asked questions: 'Did he like to go to school?' 'Did he ever get into trouble?' 'What did he like about going to school?' The questions most children would ask.

I told them the story the way children would like to hear it. I told them how Safari's mother instilled in him the importance of being happy. We explained that when Safari arrived in Australia he was always happy. In spite of his afflictions, he would smile through those wrinkled-up brown eyes. He was happy.

After the talk Peter spoke to us. He said that he had a young student who was prone to mischievousness but always timid and withdrawn at the authority figures represented by the staff. Peter suggested to him that he could be like Safari and smile a little more. A later report revealed that this little fellow could be seen smiling more frequently, emulating Safari's happy way with life.

Saturday came, the day of the big event. A quick peep into Sue's kitchen early Saturday afternoon revealed trays of meat loaf and many cooked chickens along with hundreds of profiteroles, all in various stages of preparation for the evening meal.

We were very touched by the effort these hardworking country women had put in to make this event successful. Tiredness didn't seem to be an option. For them a great time for everyone and a good financial outcome was what mattered.

The evening started with a fashion parade from a local boutique. This part of the country was in a four-year drought but as I started to give our talk, down came the rain. Everyone hurried for shelter and new arrangements were quickly made.

A very tasty hot dinner for 150 was served. The evening culminated with an auction led by an hilarious country auctioneer egging on the bidders. It was a really memorable evening. This event realised something in the vicinity of $6500 which the committee directly banked into Safari's school's bank account.

We were overwhelmed by the generosity shown by the people of Trangie towards Safari and his school, and by the hospitality extended to us. It was a wonderful weekend, with new friendships forged and a promise to keep in touch. Again we have Safari to thank for the opportunity to meet wonderful people.

Along with the Safari story came opportunities for the doing of great good and the demonstration of great compassion. Royal Prince Alfred Hospital particularly was so very generous in its support for Safari.

But all that would never have been possible if Lesley Coverdale had not been touched in a profound way by what she saw beside the waterhole that day in Kasaala back in February 1999; by the plight of a small boy so terribly in need – need that she resolved that night to address in some way.

Lesley and Cliff's personal fundraising efforts through their church community, running trivia nights and trash and treasure drives and donations, resulted in their raising around $23 000. On the afternoon of Safari's arrival Lesley rang us and suggested that we take $100 a week plus petrol expenses from her fund to cover some of our costs throughout the year. This we did and are very grateful to her. But mostly we are grateful to her for bringing Safari into our lives.

Chapter 20

Sometime in 2003 we dropped in to the Royal Prince Alfred Hospital in Sydney to catch up with the staff on the Plastics Ward. They had been so kind and loving towards Safari through his trials and tribulations.

Michael Murtough-Coombes, the Nursing Unit Manager, remarked that the ward had received a letter, probably a card, addressed to Safari, all the way from England.

We opened the envelope which was addressed simply 'Safari, RPA, Australia' and were astonished to see that it was from a lady in Liverpool who had seen him on TV. We thought before opening it that it was probably from someone in England who had been told about Safari by a friend in Australia. But no, the lady said that she had been watching Safari on a satellite TV channel called Reality TV! She was touched by his courage and charismatic personality and felt she had to send a card wishing him well. We were very surprised by the idea of the *RPA* program going to air to audiences half a world away.

When we got home that evening Frank looked up Reality TV on that font of all knowledge, the Internet, and discovered that a company in London, Zone Vision, was broadcasting to audiences worldwide. One of their channels was Reality TV. When he looked at their TV guide sure enough *RPA* was there amongst other reality programs like *911*, *Police Camera Action*, *Blue Cross Animal Hospital* and others. Zone Vision, we discovered, broadcasts by satellite to 84.5 million homes in over 125 countries on five continents.

Since that day we have received many emails from across the globe, from Europe and Scandinavia, from Africa, from South America and from the Middle East. Not the flood that we saw when Nine broadcast *RPA* in Australia because Frank's email address is a little difficult to find on the Internet, but enough to show us that Safari and his story had captured the hearts of many people from all regions of the world. All the writers spoke as if with one voice, a voice we had heard from so many people throughout Australia as they saw Safari wrestle weekly with adversity but with a wonderful attitude and with the true joy of life. Often, the email correspondents wrote gratefully of the help and inspiration Safari had been to them in their own unspoken adversities.

Frank and I discussed how we in a developed country see the world in which we live. We take for granted intercontinental live television and all that it affords. We seldom stop to think that our affluence and technology are available to us purely through the luck of our place of birth. In Safari's case he came from a tiny rural village in a corner of the same world that has absolutely none of these trappings which we casually enjoy. But he was able to display totally, naturally and unconsciously his special qualities on a world stage, to inspire and appeal to the humanity in us all via a satellite, a tiny technological 'star'. All this from a young bush boy who thought, when he first arrived in Australia, that there were two suns – one for Kenya and one for Australia.

His mother couldn't offer her scarred child physical help for his afflictions. However, she gave him something of real value; the constant encouragement to, 'Be happy, always be happy.' He is blithely ignorant on one level of his impact on others in every corner of the global village we all inhabit. It seems to us that he has shown that regardless of our stations in life, our common humanity rises above our differences and each of us has the potential to shine. Safari is certainly a bright star.

As the writing of this book drew to a close in mid-2004, we went to the movies to clear our minds; to the local Avoca Beach Theatre. We had taken Safari to Avoca a couple of days after he first arrived so that he could experience the vast Pacific Ocean. Avoca was also the place where we learnt of his aversion to cold foods and something we thought all kids loved, icy cold paddle pops, and the place where we took Silas Nthaka after the Adelaide snakebite course, so he could share one of Safari's first Australian experiences.

Our trip to the movies started with a coffee in the theatre's garden lounge. As we sat reminiscing a woman and her husband entered. She saw us and quizzically said, as we have heard many times before, 'I know you from somewhere.' We soon learnt that we had met her before in late 2001. At that time she had phoned and said that she was terribly worried about an upcoming operation she was to have for a brain tumour. She felt that meeting Safari would give her the strength to carry her through this most difficult episode in her life. She felt that she needed in some way to draw strength from his strength; she met him and drew the strength she needed.

At the theatre she told us that the operation had been very successful and that she had so much to thank Safari for. She asked after him and was glad to hear of his life now.

What is the legacy that Safari has left us with? Certainly he has shown the value of courage and the insistence to be positive and happy, no matter what challenges life presents. He has become an inspiration to many people through his unconscious behaviour. Or perhaps at some deeper level he has some knowledge of his inspiration; we do not know.

Through his story he has acted as a catalyst. His village and his family have benefited in many ways from the generosity of Australians who have fallen under his spell. His schoolfriends in Nairobi – once residents of the overflowing slums and with little hope of a better life – have benefited. His school, with a noble vision of the intrinsic worth within all children and a determination to see it develop to full potency, has benefited. And Frank and I, through our journey with this little boy from the Kenyan bush, have been enriched extraordinarily, in ways too numerous to list.

We have enormous respect for Safari's mother Ngayau who with boundless wisdom taught and encouraged him to be the person he is today. My one regret is that through events beyond our control I was unable to know this extraordinary woman for more than a few hours.

When I look back at all that has happened I think Frank and I have been truly blessed with Amin and Safari coming into our lives. Ngayau's words, 'I just want him to have a chance in life,' are never far from our thoughts and we will continue to help our boys and their school. That day under the tree when she again expressed her thanks for caring for Safari she said, 'He is your son too.' I have pondered these words. Did she have some inner knowing that her own life would not be a long one? We wonder.

We have spoken to countless people in the 'Safari' talks we give. Many come forward later, each telling their own special story of how Safari helped them. They say they drew courage from him and strength when they needed it most. From him they learnt to 'live in the moment', to be happy. One grandmother told her grandchildren, 'Be like Safari and go *lala*' (sleep) as they had learnt from the *RPA* series.

Here is a small boy teaching many adults to be compassionate, to be brave, to be courageous in times of adversity and never give up hope. We are reminded of his confident determination in the village: 'One day I'm going to be fixed.' We wonder where his journey through life will take him.

After the lady left us in the coffee lounge at Avoca that day we sat and talked. We remembered this little boy who never complained, never said 'it hurts'. A little boy who loved everyone and who truly loved life. I recalled the day when I had a sore knee and Safari said, 'Come on, Mumma, lean on me, I'll help you.' Safari never realised just how many people did lean on him.

Epilogue

It has been difficult to decide where to end this story of Safari's odyssey within our lives. Forks in the road continually appear for us to explore and with them come new friends, new experiences and new challenges that enrich our lives and in some ways test our endurance.

In August 2004 we returned to Kenya for a short visit, mainly to see Safari and Amin. We had a very emotional meeting. The boys ran up, their arms outstretched; Safari couldn't speak, he just wiped the tears from his eyes. I think we were all teary that day.

Those couple of weeks with the boys went so quickly. We wanted to savour our time with them, knowing that once we were home only memories would remain, until the next time. I felt an overwhelming sense of love when Amin one day put his hand in mine and in his strongly clipped English said quietly 'I'm going to call you Mother.' Another meaningful bond had been forged.

We were shocked and saddened to see Safari's father and

uncles. They were so gaunt. Kasaala and the Ukambani region had endured a drought for the past year and a half, bringing famine to the subsistence farmers. The villagers had resorted to cutting charcoal, itself an assault on the environment, to simply eke out an existence. It brought home to us again the wealth that we are so lucky to enjoy and so often take for granted.

This has strengthened our resolve to continue to do as much as we can for Safari, his family, and those less fortunate than ourselves. On that trip, we also caught up with the doctors who attended the Adelaide Toxinology Congress and found them working under very difficult circumstances. Despite this, Dr Anisa Omar had 'uplifted' the government hospital in Malindi (in the words of her local Rotary friends) and we found it to be a tribute to her guidance as Administrator. But when she showed us the two spotlessly clean operating theatres we were amazed at the absence of any technology – no patient monitoring equipment and an anesthetic machine in need of repair. We have great respect for Anisa, and Dr David Musyoka at his hospital in Kitui, and the work they are able to do under such conditions. We see so much more help is needed in their hospitals and clinics, but there is only so much we can do ourselves.

We will continue our role as guardians of the boys' education and we will also keep up our talks, when requested, to those organisations still interested in Safari and Amin's progress and in their part of Africa.

As a result of one of our talks in the Hunter Valley more than a year ago, we have formed a friendship with

Rotarian Alan Morrison who has enlisted Rotary's help in a snakebite project. Rotary, with support from the corporate world, have already sent over 2000 elasticised crepe bandages to Dr David Musyoka's hospital in Kitui. These will form the basis of a snakebite prevention kit to be distributed throughout government health clinics like the one in Kasaala. David and Anisa's hospitals oversee many such clinics which are the first line in the delivery of health services to rural communities where snakebite risk is greatest.

Alan is also selling this book through Rotary Clubs, and the full margin will be devoted to a fund to address the other vital component of a snakebite treatment kit – antivenom. Along with the help of James and Sanda Ashe of Watamu Bio Ken snake farm, the hope is to establish a foundation to source antivenom at affordable prices and administer it via a flexible co-payment system to patients in need. The first step has been taken; since the doctors returned from the Adelaide Congress the knowledge of the proper treatment and management of snakebite patients is spreading. Dr David Musyoka has already trained more than 50 health workers in his area alone.

Our journey with Safari has been a transforming experience – an incredible chain of events that all began in that one terrible moment when a bare flame licked at a child's sarong. Safari has changed many, many people's lives, and will continue to do so for a long time to come. Along this journey we have felt witnesses to an unfolding and as yet unfinished play in the theatre of life.

SATHYA SAI SCHOOL
UTHIRU
21/JULY/04

To mama and papa,

Get greetings from me here I m fine and Learning well. I go to school in sathya sai school uthitu in Nairobi. I learn many subjects mathematics science Religious Education social studies English and swahili. my best is Education in human values, it has stories and songs that are interesting and teach me how to be a good boy. my friends are Amin Jeremiah ALLan shisundi Dominic otidha Linus onyango Eric Ababu and many others we play read and wash together. I Like playing foot ball and running about with friends. I also like Listening and reading stories

I am happy for every school day for I get to Listening to a new story during E.H.V Lesson and sing a song with my classmates at times with all Sathya Sai pupils

I am Looking forward to see ing you soon

with Love from
Safari

Acknowledgements

There are many, many people who have offered help and inspiration to me and Frank, both in our personal lives and in our journeys with Safari; we marvel at all that has taken place. Some of these inspirational people have already been mentioned in the book. Some are acknowledged below; sometimes their names appear in both places. Others have not been named individually but their contributions are equally appreciated. Our words of thanks here seem inadequate for the contributions so many have made.

First and foremost to our immediate families who are always in our hearts; we thank you for your love, support, encouragement and understanding.

To all the staff and management at Sydney's RPA Hospital whose generosity and love are beyond acclaim; the nurses whose unstinting devotion was pivotal in those dark days – thank you.

To the people of the Central Coast and to the people of Australia and globally who wrapped Safari in their hearts we say thank you for your kind thoughts, messages and ongoing support. And to the media who are continually generous, the *RPA* TV team who first communicated the story of hope and inspiration to an Australian and world audience – thank you.

Those business houses, churches, service clubs and communities which continue so willingly to support the Safari Appeal – our heartfelt thanks. To the many, many people who support and work for the Safari Appeal – we thank you for your tireless efforts. A special thanks in particular to Margaret Bushby for her devotion to the appeal.

To the Australian Kenyan and East African community along with the staff at the Kenyan High Commissioner's Office in Canberra who so clearly demonstrate to us their love for Safari – we send great thanks (*asante sana*). Indeed these words extend to the many supportive people in Kenya that we have been privileged to meet.

Finally but by no means least we thank all our new friends at Random House. Without their encouragement and support this book would not have been written. Thank you particularly Jane Southward, Karen Ward, Heather Curdie and Jane Alexander. Also John Bull of The Book Design Company and photographer Vicki Leopold for their contributions to the cover.

Further Information

For more information about Safari and the Safari Appeal visit **www.safariappeal.com** or contact Janet Seath and Frank Scaysbrook by email: frankscaysbrook@tac.com.au or by mail to PO Box 1991, Gosford NSW 2250.